THE PLAYER

THE PLAYER

Boris Becker

with Robert Lübenoff and Helmut Sorge

BANTAM PRESS

LONDON • NEW YORK • TORONTO • SYDNEY • AUCKLAND

Translated from the German by Christian Gotsch and Mari Roberts

TRANSWORLD PUBLISHERS
61–63 Uxbridge Road, London W5 5SA
a division of The Random House Group Ltd

RANDOM HOUSE AUSTRALIA (PTY) LTD
20 Alfred Street, Milsons Point, Sydney,
New South Wales 2061, Australia

RANDOM HOUSE NEW ZEALAND LTD
18 Poland Road, Glenfield, Auckland 10, New Zealand

RANDOM HOUSE SOUTH AFRICA (PTY) LTD
Endulini, 5a Jubilee Road, Parktown 2193, South Africa

Published 2004 by Bantam Press
a division of Transworld Publishers

A catalogue record for this book is available from the British Library.
ISBN 0593 05344 3

Typeset in 12.5/16pt Granjon by
Falcon Oast Graphic Art Ltd.

Printed in Great Britain by
Clays Ltd, Bungay, Suffolk

1 3 5 7 9 10 8 6 4 2

Papers used by Transworld Publishers are natural, recyclable products made from wood grown
in sustainable forests. The manufacturing processes conform to the environmental regulations
of the country of origin.

In memory of Franz, my grandfather, and Karl-Heinz, my father.
I hope to carry on their legacy and protect my family as they did.

CONTENTS

PROLOGUE

IT'S DARK. I CAN HEAR THE LOW VOICE OF A TELEVISION
commentator coming from the kitchen, where Noah is watching
basketball. Elias is cuddled up in my right arm, his blond curly
head leaning against my shoulder, his big blue eyes wide open.
The heavy children's Bible is almost slipping from my hands but
Elias demands I read some more. '"And Moses raised his staff
and looked up to the sky. All at once a wind appeared that
became a storm, and the sea began to part."' The door opens and
Juey, our dog, comes in. Soundlessly the golden retriever lies
down on the bedspread and pushes his nose under my left knee.
'"To right and left, walls of water arose. Moses guided his people
slowly through the opening in the sea."' The door opens again. It
seems the basketball match has finished. Noah lies down on my
left, his head very close to mine, his brown curls tickling my ear,
and I carry on reading. '"The Egyptian army hesitates, but the
Pharaoh calls for the attack. And as the Egyptians reach the centre
of the sea, the storm ceases and the water swallows them up . . ."'

It is utterly silent in the room. I can't move an inch. I'm like Gulliver in Lilliput, except that my captors, Elias, Noah and Juey, are all asleep. I feel such sadness and happiness at the same time that I don't know whether to laugh or cry. They say that in the moment between life and death you see your life passing before you like a film. I have this feeling now. What's happening to me?

FOREWORD

I COMPLAINED ON THE TENNIS COURTS. I CRIED, SPAT, BLED AND winced in pain. I talked to myself, and millions heard me. I protested, and annoyed everyone, from my fellow competitors and my coaches to the spectators and my parents. I was an adolescent under constant scrutiny, trying to grow up under the unrelenting gaze of people who really wanted me to stay just the way I'd been when I first won Wimbledon. The boy from Leimen, forever seventeen, permanently frozen in the dreams of a tennis nation, brought back to life once a year for Wimbledon fortnight.

The pressure was often unbearable. 'Boris seems to be there for everyone,' wrote the German daily *Stuttgarter Zeitung* in 1986. 'Nearly everyone identifies with him, whether as the *enfant terrible* or the cool victor. How nice it is that this multi-talented player from Baden is beginning to fulfil the many and varied expectations people have of him.'[1] But I didn't know how to meet those expectations. I was only allowed to let go and be myself after it was announced, 'Game, set, match Becker.' Getting thrown out in the first round was not what I was supposed to do. Let that happen and the papers would declare at once: 'Boris is finished.'

I've written this book above all for my children: Noah, Elias and Anna. It's for them that I want to set down the truth – the seconds before the serve that made me the youngest Wimbledon winner of all time, as well as the minutes after being sentenced as a tax evader. I would like to explain to them about my personal losses, and take responsibility for my separation and subsequent divorce. And I would like to explain to Anna why she does not have the surname Becker.

I want to talk about the things that happened behind the baseline, both during and after my career. How it was when John McEnroe, a man I regard highly today, called me an arsehole during a change of sides, and why the end of my tennis life also meant the end of my marriage. How it is that rumours of affairs appear in the press, so inaccurate they can't even get the hair colour right, while my true passions remain largely undiscovered. And how someone like me, the small-town boy from Leimen, took to sleeping pills and, when this didn't work any more, to alcohol.

I have faced considerable challenges and heartache since 1999: the death of my father, my divorce, the tax proceedings, my illegitimate daughter. I am still trying to make sense of it all. The more I ask myself, the less I know.

This book describes *my* reality. It records the stress I had to endure and to overcome, my doubts and fears, but also my guilt, and the pain I caused to others. Quite a few will disagree with me. They'll be upset, and declare that sportspeople are supposed to run, sweat, suffer – and shut up. A few decades ago, in the time of our great footballer Uwe Seeler, for example, this may well have been the case: overhead kick, header, and then under the cold shower. Some chanting in the changing room and a word or two about the missed penalty, and that was it.

However, in the media age, anyone who wants to be a star, or is one already, has to learn to communicate, just as I had to. Top-level sport has become popular entertainment, and in Germany I was the pioneer. Eighty-nine per cent of West Germans knew my name after my first Wimbledon victory, according to a survey done at the time. Volkswagen was probably the only German product that was better known than I was. 'Becker', as the US television station CBS declared in their news programme *60 Minutes*, was 'the first German national hero since the defeat of the German army in the Second World War'.[2] Today, every German over the age of eighteen knows who I am.

I had become a 'living legend', wrote the Hamburg journalist Claus Jacobi back then – against my will and at 'twice the speed of sound'.[3] But I never saw myself as a legend. I never saw myself as a Michael Jordan or a Muhammad Ali or a Max Schmeling. I knew what legends went through, especially the film stars – I'd read the books. Marlene Dietrich alone in a small room on the avenue Montaigne in Paris; Marilyn Monroe, sensitive and addictive, possibly murdered, certainly abused as a 'femme fatale'; Marlon Brando, still alive but living under the over-whelming shadow cast by his own fame; James Dean, dead and buried before the film that made him a cult reached the cinemas.

I was supposed to be both wunderkind and fairy-tale prince. But it wasn't like that. Instead of joy there was frustration, the heavy pressure of high expectations, the headlines, revelations and inventions by the media, the experience of racism and the burden of fame. During my fifteen years as a professional player, there was light and shade every day, and later on there was a period of real darkness.

In December 1985, the Swiss-German newspaper *Neue Zürcher Zeitung* wrote about me: 'The media have branded him Superman, the showpiece of the nation. The fuss around him is like that before the Christmas presents are handed out, and it seems to swallow Becker up.'[4]

Well, I survived. Today it's neither money nor power that keeps me going, but the challenge as a divorced man to be a good father to my children.

Sportspeople often experience great emptiness at the end of their career. Overnight, it's finished. No more applause, ovations, fans who want to touch you. John McEnroe once told me that his emotions after his final wins at the US Open and Wimbledon were as strong as at the birth of his children. He survived, but many don't. Football players who drown them-selves in alcohol or try to escape reality with the help of drugs. Boxers who throw their wives from a balcony or shoot at them through a closed bathroom door. Sports celebrities who fill in their lottery tickets at the newsagent's round the corner instead of signing autographs.

I haven't shot anyone or used cocaine. But I was dizzy and directionless, tumbling towards the edge of the cliff. Yet when-ever things looked hopeless, my survival instinct kicked in. And here I am. Just thirty-five years old, at the end and the beginning at the same time. Back in the qualifying rounds, just as at Wimbledon in 1984. And the tournament is called Life.

THE MAN ON THE MOON

I'M SERVING FOR THE CHAMPIONSHIP. FIVE STEPS TO THE baseline. My arm is getting heavy, wobbly. I look at my feet and almost stumble. My body starts to shake violently. I feel I could lose all control. I'm standing at the same baseline from where I served to 1–0 in the first set. 5–4; the end is getting nearer. I have to find a way to get these four points home.

My opponent, Kevin Curren, piles on the pressure. 0–15. 15 all. 30–15. 40–15. I want, want, want victory. I look only at my feet, at my racket. I don't hear a thing. I'm trying to keep control. Breathe in. Serve. Like a parachute jump. Double fault. 40–30. How on earth can I place the ball in that shrinking box over there on the other side of the net? I focus on throwing the ball and then I hit it.

The serve was almost out of this world, or at least its results were. This victory was my own personal moon landing. 1969 Apollo 11, 1985 Wimbledon 1. Back then, Neil Armstrong jumped from the ladder of the space capsule *Eagle* into the moondust and transmitted his historic words to the people of the world: 'That's one small step for man, one great leap for mankind.' But I couldn't muster words to meet the occasion. I could only think, Boy oh boy, this can't be true.

The tension disappeared instantly and I felt slightly shaky. My heart was beating fast. I left crying to the others, though: my coach Günther Bosch, my father and my mother. 'With the passion of a Friedrich Nietzsche or Ludwig van Beethoven,' wrote *Time* in its next issue, 'this unseeded boy from Leimen turned the tennis establishment of Wimbledon on its head.'[1]

Although my Swedish colleague Björn Borg was only seventeen when he entered the Wimbledon arena, he didn't win until three years later. John McEnroe started at eighteen but didn't hold the trophy until he was twenty-two. Jimmy Connors was twenty-one; Rod Laver, one of the greatest of our time, twenty-two. I was just seventeen years and 227 days old; I couldn't legally drive in Germany. I cut my own hair, and my mother sent me toothpaste because she was worried about my teeth. 'Boy King,' lauded the British newspapers. 'King Boris the First.' Meanwhile, King Boris was in the bath enjoying a hot soak. Back then, a physiotherapist was beyond my means.

From that day on, nothing in my life remained the same. Boris from Leimen died at Wimbledon in 1985 and a new Boris emerged, who was taken at once into public ownership.

Goodbye, freedom. Hands reaching out to you, tearing the buttons from your jacket; fingernails raking over your skin as if they wanted a piece of your flesh. A photograph, a signature – no, two, three, more ... Love letters, begging letters, blackmail. Bodyguards on the golf course and on the terraces at Bayern Munich. Security cameras in the trees of our home, paparazzi underneath the table or in the toilets. Exclusive – see Becker peeing.

And everything I did had consequences. One word of protest would lead to a headline. An innocent kiss would appear on the front page. A defeat and *Bild* would cry for the nation. A victory and the black, red and gold of the German flag was everywhere. Our Boris.

The experts would write that it was my willpower and the 'boom boom' of my serve that got me through. But it isn't explained away so easily. On that day of my first victory at Wimbledon, forces were involved that went beyond mere willpower. Instinct made me do the right thing in the decisive moment, even if I didn't know I was going to do it. My heart was big, my spirit was strong, my instincts were sharp – only my flesh was sometimes weak. And no one can get out of their own skin.

In 1986 Ion Tiriac, my manager, arranged an audience with the Pope. Ion is a devout man, and when he asked me if I wanted to see the Pope, I thought, sure, why not? I took my racket with me to get it blessed. At the time this was treated as crass commercialism, some kind of PR campaign for Puma, my racket-maker. How innocent I was then. I was only on the lookout for a little luck. But in the end, neither the man on the moon nor the one on the holy chair brought me victory. It was the indescribable, the unexplainable, the unheard-of, that got hold of me and sent me into a different orbit.

And all I had to do was keep winning, again and again.

WHAT IS THE SENSE IN IT ALL?

ON THE EVE OF THE FINALS WE ARE EATING AT PONTE Vecchio, an Italian restaurant on the Old Brompton Road, a few hundred metres from the players' hotel, the Gloucester. The same ritual as always. Spaghetti for me; spaghetti for all of us. 'If they didn't know us,' said Ion, 'they'd think we were all gay.'

I wasn't nervous, but euphoric. The final on Centre Court, and me a protagonist on the world stage for the first time. I had a quiet night, though I dreamt about the final. The images flashed before me just like a television broadcast, right up to the awards ceremony. I was holding the trophy, and then – the alarm goes off. Half past nine. The reality.

It's a forty-five-minute drive from Kensington, where our hotel is, to Wimbledon. Sometimes I watch the street scenes as we pass. A lot of antiques shops on the New King's Road, pubs, low buildings from which the paint is peeling. In front of us a red double-decker bus, behind us black cabs. We are slowly making our way across the iron Wandsworth Bridge. Constant traffic jams. Ion Tiriac, who's driving our black Mercedes, is trying to calm me down with words he'll repeat to me on many occasions to come: 'You have a right to lose. If you always have to find a thousand excuses, then eventually you'll give up the right to lose. You'll make yourself mentally ill.' And: 'Be true to yourself. Play your game. You will succeed.'

Since I'd beaten Pat Cash 6–4, 6–4 in the Wimbledon warm-up tournament at Queens, Tiriac had been convinced that I could win. He was in Argentina with Guillermo Vilas while I was playing against Cash, but he returned quickly, warning my parents that they'd better come over. We were in the process of making tennis history, although I didn't know this yet.

Günther Bosch, who is sitting in the back, says a few words in Romanian to Tiriac. Are they talking about me? No. Bosch is only suggesting a short cut. That much Romanian I understand.

My thoughts are rushing ahead. Changing room, locker 7 as always, from which I hadn't even cleared the dirty clothes from the day before. If my mother only knew! Some reserve shirts and socks are in there too. When we get to Wandsworth, the houses become greyer, the betting shops and pubs more frequent. The area becomes hillier, the traffic is stop-start. Then we're there. I can see a street sign – Church Road. People are queuing, thousands of them, like a garland stretching out across the grass. These are the true fans – no tickets, just hoping to get in. Each fan hoping for a ticket-holder to vacate a place in the stands, even if it means waiting four hours, even if it means not getting in until six in the evening. And there's the gate for the players: my entry to the stage.

Later, my opponent Kevin Curren is in the changing room sitting on one of the benches. 'Hi,' I say to him, but not a word more; neither to him nor to any of my later finals opponents. Ivan Lendl was unbearable. He talked and talked in order to shake off his nervousness, and told jokes that only he found funny. But I am wearing blinkers and sitting there like a zombie. That is my way of coping with the pressure, of concentrating. Nothing else interests me. I have to get myself into this trance, this total isolation, as if I'm in a tunnel. I made one exception – for Michael Stich, my fellow countryman. We know the result. I was talking, and he won. Today, on this day in July 1985, Stich is sitting in front of the television back in Germany. He has yet to sit his *Abitur*, the German equivalent of A levels, and to decide whether to become a professional. My Wimbledon final will encourage him to emulate me. In a small Californian town, Pete Sampras, one of the big talents of the USA, is playing a youth tournament. He too is following the final on the television. My victory, he would later say, spurred him on.

I'm eyeing my opponent in the mirrors on the walls. Is he showing any sign of nerves? Two hours ago I was practising with Pavel Slozil. I look at the huge clock. The BBC is showing portraits of the two finalists, but I'm not watching. I know this Becker guy. The physiotherapist is taping my ankles, something that became necessary before every match after I tore a ligament in 1984. Another look at the clock. I can feel a few butterflies in my stomach. I nibble at a sandwich. The tingling is getting stronger.

Thank God, so far I haven't had much time to dwell on all this. Thanks to the rain on Friday, I had to finish the semi-final against Anders Järryd on Saturday. After that victory, I was both happy and shattered. What should have been a rest day for me therefore wasn't, and that's how I retained my concentration and energy. The locker-room steward, a stocky man in a white coat, takes my bag, which is almost bigger than him. It contains seven Puma rackets wrapped in plastic, string tension 29–27, 30–28; sweatbands, shirts, but no bananas. These would come in later tournaments. And no talisman either.

I wouldn't call myself superstitious, but I used to have my rituals, which I believed in and which gave me confidence. Before the start of a match, I practised certain breathing, stretching and yoga exercises, to build up my ability to focus once I was out on the court. Or take my shoes. So much has been made of my untied shoelaces. 'Becker demonstrating cool.' Actually, at that first match Becker simply forgot to tie his shoelaces. After that it developed into a ritual which certainly looked like a superstition, but for me it was a means to an end. I had to get a mental and physical sense of the court, the stands, the spectators – to become one with the atmosphere and to breathe in the space. And so I would go on to the court with untied shoes, so that by doing them up on the bench I won a few seconds to take it all in.

We are waiting beneath the royal box for the signal to start. To enter the court we will pass under a board on which is famously written a couple of lines from Rudyard Kipling's poem *If.* 'If you can meet with Triumph and Disaster and treat those two impostors just the same'.

The steward advises us that the royals are present, and

please not to forget to bow when entering the court. The first steps on to Centre Court can be decisive. On this day, I instinctively entered with self-confidence, though in later years I would have to remind myself: You have to be first on Centre Court, head held high, chest out.

I feel no fear. I feel like a racehorse at the starting gate. My mind is so occupied with the match that hasn't even begun yet that I don't look behind or in front of me. Just one glance towards the coach, whose presence I find soothing. There would come a time when I would receive a warning over getting coaching from my advisers during a match: it's a code violation. I have no idea why. The controversy about coaching is strange. Sure, there are attempts to make a sign here or there, but in the heat of the match how could any player pick them up? The spectators now disappear from my line of vision, although I can still feel the atmosphere. The names of the finalists are announced.

Who will the audience applaud most? That is an important barometer, especially for my self-confidence, like the first applause for an actor on stage. What the opening lines are to the actor, the initial serves are to us. Umpire David Howie notes in clear letters on the scorecard: 'Warm up: 2.04. Play: 2.09.' The sun shines over Centre Court, which was designed in such a way that during summer no shade reaches it before seven p.m. The temperature has risen to 28°C. I'm touching the line with my racket – one of my rituals.

Kevin Curren, the man on the other side, is twenty-seven, South African born. He has thrown John McEnroe and Jimmy Connors out of this tournament, seeds one and three. Curren seems to be more nervous than me. My serves are coming on well, my people on the stands are nodding contentedly. After thirty-five minutes, the score is 6–3 to me. It is the first of a possible five sets. The first stage to the Everest that is Wimbledon. In the tie-break of the second set I'm leading 4–2, but then Curren wins 7–4. A punch in the solar plexus. All of a sudden I become uncertain. The heat is bothering me. Curren is getting stronger. I have difficulties with my serve. Advantage Curren. I'm getting angry, starting to scream and throw the racket – exactly what I shouldn't be doing. I'm talking to myself, yelling abuse at myself. 'Why are you letting this happen, *Dummkopf*, you stupid idiot!' But it helps. The anger is releasing new energies.

BBC commentator John Barrett will report (today I sit next to him in the BBC's commentary box; in 2002 I commentated on the finals together with him) that Becker had a serve like thunder and lightning. I've got the third set: 7–6. For the first time, I'm feeling secure. The end is in sight. In the royal box sits a field marshal, along with Juan Antonio Samaranch, president of the International Olympic Committee. When the Duke and Duchess of Kent clap in the first row, others in the royal box follow their lead. Fred Perry is seated, as protocol demands, in the fifth row. He won Wimbledon for the first time in 1934, and in 1936 he beat Gottfried von Cramm in what was the shortest final in history: forty minutes. I see neither Perry nor duke or duchess. I'm in the last set and a short way from victory. Championship point Becker.

The 13,118 spectators emit a collective scream. The first championship point is lost. My father puts his little camera away again. My mother closes her eyes, just as she will do in front of the television at home during many of my future games. I can't hear anything any more. At least, I hear sounds, but not words, not even those voices shouting from above:

'Boris!' Serve. Practised ten thousand times. It's in. The serve that will change my world. 'End: 5.26,' writes Howie on his scorecard.

The summit has been reached. I'm like Edmund Hillary on Everest. 'He's incredibly talented,' says Curren of me to the reporters, disgruntled, 'but not nearly as good as McEnroe.' Hillary, in the last metres of the ascent of Everest in 1953, must have realized what a burden he was about to take on. In his autobiography, *View from the Summit*, he wrote, 'What is the sense in it all? A man was a fool to put up with this!'[1] I too was to experience what it meant to be at the top. But the initial problems, at least, were easy to bear.

At the champions' dinner that evening the winners would be required to do the dance of honour, which would of course be a waltz. Boris Becker to Martina Navratilova: 'May I have this dance?' Now that really made me nervous. The day before, my forward-looking mother had, with Ion's help, taught me a few waltz steps. Ion had lent me his dinner jacket. At that point I hadn't even completed my semi-final against Anders Järryd, number six in the world rankings, but they were optimists, my mother and Ion, and they were proved right.

I'd felt a protective hand over me several times during this Wimbledon tournament. I'd played on one of the outer courts against the American Tim Mayotte. A dense crowd. Noise. I twist over on my ankle – it hurts. I hesitate. Shall I give up, or risk further damage? I'm walking towards the net, prepared to stretch out my hand. Where's Mayotte? He's still ten metres away. A handshake between us would have been enough to finish the match. Winner Mayotte. Having reached the fourth round, I would still have been a success, but I wouldn't have become the youngest Wimbledon winner of all time. Ion Tiriac told me later how he urged Günther Bosch: 'Bosch, do something! Say something! He should take three minutes out. Ask for a doctor.' Bosch warns me in a low voice: 'Boris, Boris.' As if I could hear among five thousand spectators! So Tiriac jumps to his feet and yells: 'Boris! Three minutes! Three!' I turn my back on the net and ask the chair-umpire for the doctor. The doctor makes his way slowly through the crowds. Three minutes, then the umpire tells me, 'Time's up.' I protest. The doctor didn't reach me in time but surely I'm entitled to be treated. It's now the referee's decision. He decides in my favour. After treatment from the doctor, I carry on playing. Twenty minutes later the match is over. In the changing room, I tell Tiriac I'm grateful: 'You won this match for me.'

Or earlier on. In the third round, I play Joakim Nyström. He has three match points against me on his own serve. I take huge risks with each return. Tiriac yells in Bosch's ear: 'He's mad! How can he play like this? Taking such risks!' Nyström is standing at the net. Match point, like a penalty kick. He misses. Two points for Nyström and the Becker legend would probably never have happened. I turn the match around: 3–6, 7–6, 6–1, 4–6, 9–7. Tiriac is puzzled: 'There are times in your life when everything happens either in your favour or against you.' Eighteen years later, during his speech at my nomination to the International Tennis Hall of Fame as its second-youngest member (Borg was the youngest), Ion was to remind the audience of this phenomenon which he encountered again and again, particularly with me.

At such times you can only act from the gut, and I usually instinctively do the right thing. If Friday's thunderstorm had not led to the interruption of our match, Järryd would have swept me off the court. Just one day later, he was so nervous that my grandmother could have beaten him.

Anyway, the champions' dinner scared me more than the final. I plagued then Wimbledon boss Reginald 'Buzzer' Hadingham: 'When will I have to dance? Do I really have to?' The thought of it was enough to finish me off. But then came my reprieve. There wouldn't be a waltz with Martina. This 'dance of honour' had been eliminated years before. Back at the Gloucester, I watched television. On all channels the announcement: Becker, Becker, the German wunderkind. First I had to take on board that they meant me. 'Boris Becker', the *Daily Express* wrote, 'stood tall and straight as a Prussian guardsman, the gold All-England Challenge Cup balanced on his head like a glittering helmet. Kaiser Boris I, teenage King of Wimbledon, was being well and truly crowned . . . now everyone asks how long will he reign.'[2]

The morning after, Tiriac took charge. 'We can now add a zero to the figure on each sponsorship contract,' he rejoiced. I don't know how many photographers followed us to the airport: scores of them. *Bild* came to see me in Monte Carlo. Ghostwriters wrote a column in my name ('My Victories, My Dreams'), which I seldom read. Tiriac assured me they were paying a fortune for it. That was enough for me. I didn't protest. The branding of Becker had begun, but I didn't realize then what a marketing treadmill I was stepping on to. Perhaps he was 'too young to know' that he was too young to win Wimbledon, commented the *Washington Post*: 'The promise is there, but it's way too soon to keep . . . Even if you are going to be the new Mozart, you still have to play one note at a time.'[3]

THE WEEKS OF COLD SILENCE

I CAN ONLY BE REALLY GOOD WHEN I FEEL A CERTAIN excitement inside me, when I sense that a relationship is developing between the actor on stage and the people watching. I once described my contact with the audience as erotic, and I compared my appearance in New York in front of 20,000 spectators to love-making. They not only want to see you, they want to have you; but they can just as easily hate you as well. They want to feel your power and your lust. They want your body and your soul.

When I hit the ball well, I raise my fist or do a little dance. The audience reacts, they come with me, and I feel their response, whether it's disapproval or approval. The hotter the game gets, the more fine-tuned this feeling becomes. I don't reflect any more. I simply let myself go, right up to the dive roll to the net at the end. I don't hear the umpire. I don't even look at the scoreboard – I keep count of the score myself.

When I reach the climax of this trance-like stage, the 'zone', the only thing I'm aware of is the onlookers. I don't actually care if they're for me or against me. That's not something you can guarantee. The spark catches or it doesn't, but either way I need the contact with them. Playing on a lesser court, Court Four at Wimbledon, for example, is a tragedy for me. I need Centre Court as the stage for my fight, man to man like modern-day gladiators. 'The mountains of a tennis life', wrote journalist Doris Henkel, 'are far apart, and the path into the valley is often more difficult than the ridge to the summit. And you only realize much later on where those eight-thousand-metre peaks really were, and those were the days when everything from A to Z, from the serve to the dream volley, fell into place.'[1] This is well observed. I have seen many valleys, but none of them as deep as the one from which I climbed my personal Everest in 1985.

The pressure that built up after my first great triumph was inhuman. Only the game counted. Tiriac and Bosch seemed even more obsessed than me. They saw me as a machine. After my first success at Wimbledon, Ion became my shadow. I felt captive, monitored, and I played very badly. This came to a head shortly before Wimbledon 1986. The warm-up tournament at Queens was the fourth in a row where I lost in the quarter-finals, after Paris, Rome and Forest Hills. I couldn't explain this to myself, and Bosch and Tiriac couldn't understand it either. I was discouraged and exhausted. I announced that I was going to spend the weekend relaxing in Monaco, and that the Wimbledon preparation would have to wait. 'No way!' fumed Tiriac. 'Goodbye,' I replied. I needed distance. I wanted to concentrate on what had made me strong in the first place: myself.

I returned as promised on Monday morning. Tiriac and

Bosch were waiting for me on the practice courts. Nothing was said. I'd hardly slept the night before, and they tortured me mercilessly on the court. I put up with it, as I do, grinding my teeth. This went on for two or three days. A few words about the exercises I had to do, then silence. Eventually I lost my patience. 'This can't go on, Ion. I've had enough of this show. You can drive me to the court, and then that's it. And you, Günzi, you can pick up the balls, but otherwise you let me practise the way I want to.'

The atmosphere stayed frosty for the first week of Wimbledon. Ice-cold silence. Then, in the fourth round, I played a match against the Swede Mikael Pernfors, to whom I'd lost a few weeks earlier at the quarter-finals in the French Open. I finished him off in ninety minutes: 6–3, 7–6, 6–2. Tiriac found his tongue again. 'Great. Respect,' he said, and he even showed some emotion – he patted my shoulder. Perhaps this was the breakthrough in our relationship.

We were staying at the Londonderry Hotel, which had a few more stars than the players' hotel of the year before, the Gloucester. The night before the final we ate in the San Lorenzo, the Italian in Beauchamp Place – even today my favourite restaurant in London – table 29, hidden behind the stairs, screened from the fans. Bosch, Tiriac, my sister Sabine, my parents – the usual entourage, and the usual dishes: salad, spaghetti with tomato sauce, and lemon sorbet.

Before my first Wimbledon final I felt like a child in a toyshop; everything was possible and I had it all before me. Every round I survived had been a triumph. Since then everything had changed. The training was more concentrated and less relaxed, and felt more like a state of emergency than anything else. The endgame against Ivan Lendl would finally answer the questions everyone was asking. Was Becker 1985 a fluke, or is he really a mega talent? It felt like a matter of life or death. At this stage, I defined myself solely through tennis and any defeat meant the complete loss of my self-confidence. Only victory could rescue me. In 1985 I was happy when the match began. In 1986 I was happy when it was over. It was the most pressure I'd ever been under. The wunderkind had to prove himself. Even I couldn't be sure how good I really was.

Lendl had never won Wimbledon, and he'd almost lost the semi-final against my friend Bobo Zivojinovic. It was only because Bobo was undone by the umpire in the fifth set that Lendl won. I preferred to have Lendl as my opponent. I knew Bobo too well, because we often practised together, and he could break my serve, but I couldn't break his. Lendl was already sitting in the changing room, and we didn't speak a word. Not his usual jokes, not even a comment, just silence. He was number one in the world. I was number six. He was twenty-six and wanted to win Wimbledon at last. I was eighteen, and had to win at least one more time. I was convinced I'd win. It sounds strange, but the previous night I'd dreamt of victory, just like the year before. Lendl, on the other hand, seemed frightened, almost transfixed.

I take the first two sets 6–4, 6–3 – a stress-free hour. In the third set he leads 4–1, a small crisis for me. Soon he's leading 5–4, and I'm serving. I go down to love–40. My attitude is, OK, let him win the third set, but I'll come back in the fourth. Then three second serves, three reflex return volleys ... Somehow I turn it around and win the game. Five all. I realize he's falling. Lendl serves – I break to 6–5. I'm serving for my second Wimbledon success. It's 40–30. When the match ends I'm on the same side of the court as in 1985. Lendl is devastated. 'Well played,' he says. I'm up in the clouds, immensely relieved.

I felt I'd been transformed from a boy to an adult. I'd opened the gate to the future and now I could have faith in myself. The victory in 1986 was the most important of my career. In 1985 I'd hardly known what I'd done; one year later I knew all too well. The reaction in Germany was overwhelming, but it left me strangely cold. After all, only a month before they'd written me off.

SECURE AND STERILE

NEITHER CASTLE NOR MOUNTAIN TOWERS ABOVE MY hometown of Leimen, only the cement works. Weimar has Goethe, Bonn can boast Beethoven, yet we in Leimen have to content ourselves with nearby Heidelberg castle – tram to Bismarckplatz, then change to the bus to get to the funicular railway. The town hall of this place of 24,000 souls is picture-postcard pretty, and so too are the half-timbered houses, but foreign tourists rarely find their way into Leimen's inns.

Leimen is a small town, where the butcher calls his customers by name, and the baker went to the same school as the man behind the post-office counter, who is married to the sister of the painter and decorator, who plays football in the same team as the baker. On Sundays the congregation gathers for mass at the Church of the Sacred Heart. My father was born in Leimen. My grandfather, Franz, worked as a fitter on the trams, and was, in contrast to his no-nonsense wife Helene, someone I could confide in. After all, I bear his name: Boris Franz Becker. He died while I was playing at Wimbledon in 1985, and nobody told me. They didn't want me to lose concentration.

My birthplace is therefore German provincial: clean, smug, a little sterile, but also pretty secure. Silence and order after ten o'clock at night, like in any bourgeois little town anywhere. My parents were hard-working. I took the tram to the Helmholtz school, I rode on my bike to my practice sessions, and my sister Sabine prepared my Nutella sandwiches. We lived in a picturesque house a kilometre from the tennis courts. Had it been ten kilometres, who knows? Maybe I'd never have touched a tennis racket but have played football instead. My father earned a decent amount. The family car was a BMW, then later a Mercedes; we had summer and winter holidays – we were doing OK, though we weren't millionaires. Punctuality and discipline were essential to my upbringing, as was observing rules and regulations. Church on Sundays and altar-boy duties were as much a part of my life as walks in the woods with my parents and sport on the television with Harry Valérien.

As a child I was bullied by my classmates because of my red hair. When I ran to my mother and complained she said, 'Son, use your elbows.' I took her advice too literally. Letters began to arrive from school because of the fights I'd got involved in. I didn't hate school, but I didn't love it either. My Latin teacher is one who will remain in my memory. When I had to miss his classes because I was taking part in a tennis tournament, he would test me in front of everyone, so on car journeys to and from tournaments I used to try to learn Latin, because I didn't want to give the teacher the opportunity to expose me in front of my classmates as a brainless sporty type.

Anyway, I rather liked him; he had a dry sense of humour.

Nevertheless, my eyes stay dry when I think of Leimen now. I spent a few pleasant years there, and those years helped form me, but when I return today to visit my mother, or to stand by my father's grave, it's clear to me that it's only my parents who bring me back.

Leimen is not home for me. 'Home' is the people I trust: my children, my family and my friends. They tie me to Germany more than any passport could. I don't just ask myself the fundamental question that everyone asks: Who am I? I also ask what Germany and my origins mean to me. I had the luxury of a comfortable upbringing. Instead of the chaos of Uganda or Kosovo, I was born into a stable country. Instead of being poor, we were well off. Instead of being an orphan, I'm the child of extraordinary parents. Instead of being a slave, I'm a free man. I'm a German, but my concern went beyond national borders very early on. This might have something to do with the biographies of my nearest and dearest.

My mother, Elvira, comes from what used to be known as Sudetenland. Her hometown was Ostrau, today Ostrava and part of the Czech Republic. She was driven from her home together with millions of her fellow countryfolk. Her parents, who owned a big farm, lost all they owned, escaping on a horse and cart to a refugee camp in Heidelberg. My mother never forgot that time. 'We thanked God that we survived that,' she has often said to me. Along with twenty other families from the same village she was settled in Leimen, where she met my father. My ex-wife Barbara was born in Heidelberg. Her father came from California and was African-American. His ancestors had been abducted from Africa. Barbara's American grandmother had worked on the cottonfields of the southern States. My sons are Munich-born and now live with their mother in Miami. And my daughter has a Russian mother and lives in London.

I probably inherited my inner strength – occasionally referred to as stubbornness – from my mother: this drive to survive and to fight on, to overcome catastrophe and come out stronger than you went in. What often caused me trouble was my exaggerated sense of justice. Even as a child, injustice made me furious. Later in life, my anger on the courts was seldom directed at my opponents, but often at the umpires. I couldn't bear misjudgements. These people didn't want to acknowledge the perfection I was striving for.

I've picked up from somewhere the story of a Spanish mother who said to her son, 'Should you become a soldier, you'll be made a general. Should you become a monk, you'll end up as Pope.' The boy became a painter. His name was Pablo Picasso. My mother also had dreams for my future. I'd become an architect and build houses like my father, or an academic, or perhaps a gynaecologist or a lawyer. But a tennis player? My poor mother. She'd trade in my fame and fortune like a shot if she could. Nothing would please her more than to have me living next-door-but-one to her (with my sister Sabine and her family in between), with views over Leimen and Baden, and lunch at half past twelve on the dot.

Leimen is history to me, a symbol of my quiet childhood, but also a symbol of provincial self-righteousness and envy. Jealousy of the neighbour whose car is more expensive, or whose son made the headlines as a tennis player, who lived the life of a nomad and came home only because for a few days he wanted nothing more than to be a son.

ELVIRA BECKER: HE IS MY SON

My mother has never been a public person. It took a lot of persuading to get her to contribute to this book. Here she is: Elvira.

BORIS WAS AROUND FOURTEEN WHEN THE FIRST TENNIS agent started knocking at our door. My husband was half for it, half against it. I was totally against any plan for him to turn professional. I said to my husband, 'Karl-Heinz, you know your son is very sensitive. So far he has always won. He doesn't know what it's like to lose. He hasn't finished school yet, and he still has some growing up to do.'

Yes, if Boris had won Wimbledon at a later date, then he'd have had the chance to get his *Abitur* [A levels]. I'm still sorry that he couldn't do that. He could have gone to university, but he missed the chance. Anyway, at some point we agreed: let's go for this professional thing. If it doesn't work out after a year, he can go back to school. We talked to Ion Tiriac, who was described to us as a rather scary-looking, shifty

Romanian. I didn't see him this way, though. He was honest enough to say he couldn't guarantee anything. On 1 June 1984 we signed a contract in Monte Carlo with Tiriac: one A4 sheet of paper. Boris signed it too. It was difficult for me. Boris was so young and I felt sorry for him, I can't deny it. In 1984, when he tore his ligament, I thought for a few seconds: Thank God. That's the end of this professional nonsense. He won't be able to do it any more.

He was no longer a child, but he was still a young person who needed his home. Luckily, there was Günther Bosch, who cared for him more like a mother than a father. Boris was in very good hands with him. I advised my son to go and see Bosch if he had any problems. If anything worried him, he should open up to Günther. Bosch kept in daily touch with us by telephone, wherever in the world the two of them were. Because Boris has one weakness: he rarely calls home. Later his physiotherapist, Waldemar Kliesing, took over this job.

If we saw on the television that Boris had lost, we'd send him a fax: 'Don't be sad, that's just life.' I know him so well. When I saw him whining on the court, I knew it was over for him – not always, but mostly. Because of time differences, we sometimes sat in front of the television into the early hours or right through the night. When I saw Boris lose his self-control, I cried. How often had I told him that self-control was an essential part of life? But when he felt that things weren't going well, that defeat couldn't be avoided, he went berserk. And he wouldn't want to hear what I thought of it later. 'Don't talk about it!' he'd say. Sometimes I wasn't even sad when he lost. It gave him a chance to take a break.

I can't describe how it felt to watch him on Centre Court at Wimbledon in 1985. Oh God, such a young boy! I knew that if he didn't lose his nerve he'd make it. If he didn't work himself up into that frenzy of his, he'd be all right. During the final I hardly talked to my husband. I cried after he won, and not just from joy. I asked myself what he'd have to cope with now. I always saw the downside.

Our business was completely disrupted after that win. We got sackloads of post, presents, even yogurt and fruit juice by the crate. I sent those on to the kindergarten. The fans addressed their letters to 'Boris Becker, Leimen', or even just 'Boris Becker, Germany'. And they arrived. He's a good boy, my Boris. Some kids forget about their parents when they get older. Not him. He's loyal.

On many occasions I did without an evening meal because I had to wash or pack his things. All that travelling caused quite a muddle. One day, not long after Wimbledon, he couldn't find his passport. We searched high and low for it until three in the morning. 'Well,' he said, 'I'll just travel with my Monte Carlo papers; they'll let me in without a passport.' And so they did. Ion Tiriac, who was on holiday in Capri and had borrowed a bag from Boris, called us two days later. He'd found Boris's passport in the bag. Such things often happened. Once he left his Wimbledon cheque – I think it was from the victory in 1989 – in his tennis clothes and it ended up in the wash. After that it was of course pulp, and we had to ask them to reissue it.

I always imagined my Boris hanging around somewhere on his own – horrible. If he was really down he'd sometimes call. He did suffer. 'Now I'm on my own again!' Once, after he broke up with a girlfriend, Tiriac called me. 'Could you come over? He's not in good shape.' We found an excuse and drove to Monte Carlo.

He has certainly not become happier with the years. More self-confident, of course, no question of that. He was always a bit of a loner. And he's a cosmopolitan. He could live in Monte Carlo, London, New York. But in a way he has also remained a bit of a Leimener. He sees the things that tumble down and explode in this world, and he has experienced them for himself. From a young age, he led a tough life. It changed him and made him mature very early. He was old for his years. Occasional stubbornness is part of his personality. Even I find it hard to tell him the truth sometimes, and need to have several goes at it. But he is the way he is. He is my son.

JUST BECAUSE!

I STOOD THERE BESIDE HIM, BUT HE DIDN'T EXIST ANY MORE. my father. The man laid out in front of me. On this day in April 1999 he seemed like a stranger to me. The right leg of his suit had slipped up above his ankle and on his skin I could read the word 'Becker', written with a blue felt-tip pen.

I pulled his trouser leg down over his ankle and kissed his forehead. For the first time in my life I'd experienced the death of someone I loved completely. I wondered if there was an afterlife – not that that would have given me any comfort then. This was goodbye. I couldn't cry any more, or talk any more. My father had only been sixty-four. I'd never again be able to argue with him until my mother intervened as peace-maker: 'Karl-Heinz, leave the boy alone!'

I was three or four years old when I first hefted my father's tennis racket out of the boot of the car and started hitting balls against the wall of the tennis club or against the shutters of our house. My father would whisper to my mother, 'He's not quite clean,' which is a saying in our part of Germany that means, 'He's not quite right in the head.' He'd yank me by the collar and pull me off the court whenever I lost my nerve during the Leimen club championships. I think I was ten or eleven when he gave me a hiding because I teased him with a Hitler salute. My mother always defended my father by saying he was just a bit 'rustic'. He would show his affection for my wife Barbara by giving her a bear hug without so much as a by-your-leave, and one of the last things he said to me was, 'Look after your family.'

In our house there were no racist jokes about Jews or about black people. My father loved the music of Louis Armstrong and George Gershwin. He loved his wife, too; they were married for forty-two years. He was a faithful man, loyal to Leimen and his friends. For three decades he played doubles every Friday night. He rarely played tennis with me, though. Instead, I'd hit a few balls back and forth with my sister Sabine, who's four years older than me.

Ion Tiriac remained a hero to my father until the end, and my father was never let down by him. An hour before the funeral the doorbell rang – it was Ion. It was the natural thing for him to do; he was almost family. We'd come full circle. Fifteen years earlier, Ion had rung my parents' doorbell intending to sign up Boris Becker, the new tennis talent. Cosmopolitan Tiriac, who was at home everywhere and nowhere, had started a friendship with my father that was so much more than a means to an end. One a worldly collector of Ferraris, the other a small-town man who was involved in fifteen local societies, clubs and committees as chairman of honour, treasurer, president or vice-president. My father was one of the few people Tiriac felt he could confide in. They got together for many a crisis meeting because Tiriac and I, or Bosch and I, or all three of us had had a row.

My father was the source of all authority when I was a boy. I didn't share his conservative politics, but I regarded his liberal values highly. Whether I was playing in a junior tournament in London as a ten-year-old (by the way, my first trip abroad) or whether I was winning Wimbledon, my parents' attitude towards me never changed. Our lives always stayed the same. Lunch at half past twelve, dinner at half past six. Five minutes late and you didn't get fed. Discipline with a capital D. To get a rise in my pocket money from five to six marks was a tough deal to negotiate. Any discussions that my father didn't like, or where he ran out of arguments, were brought to an end with the words, 'Just because!' That felt like dictatorship to me. I made this view clear to him and occasionally he'd raise his hand to me. Not a very Christian gesture, but nevertheless on Sundays at half ten we still had to go to church. Many of my friends wore earrings then, just like McEnroe and Agassi today. I wanted one too, but my father wouldn't have it.

Over the years I had many arguments with my father. Often we wouldn't talk for months on end. He'd assume rights that in my view he wasn't entitled to, even as a father. He liked giving interviews and he often signed autographs, though my mother warned him that I didn't like it. After I won Wimbledon the first time he set up a victory reception in Leimen with the television people, even though I'd told him I didn't want him to, and then I had to go along with it so that he didn't lose face. After that I warned him, 'Well, Dad, it was all right this time, but please, never again, OK?' Being passed from pillar to post was the last thing I wanted after Wimbledon.

But my father was a tougher nut to crack than I thought. After my victory in 1986, he arranged another reception in Leimen. A huge argument ensued.

'Cancel it,' I demanded.

'Too late,' he said.

'How could you do such a thing?'

'You don't respect me.'

I'd gone back to Leimen because I wanted some peace and quiet, and I didn't want to have to explain to the press yet again what this victory meant to me. 'That's it. I'm not talking to you for at least six months.' He didn't take my word for it, but I stuck it out. I still took part in the celebrations, though. My mother pleaded with me: 'Son, please do it or we'll never be able to show our faces around here again.'

From time to time I'd confide in my mother, but she didn't repeat things to my father because she knew he liked to talk. He didn't mean any harm; he just got carried away out of pride in his son. As soon as he saw a camera he'd want to be in the picture. Perhaps I'll be the same with my own kids! In the end, after a few battles, he was able to give me the space I needed. He didn't come along to every tournament simply to control me. I hope I'll have the same courage with my own children as my father did with me. I'm not sure I'll be able to, though. If my children were in the same position that I was, I think I'd want to be more hands-on, because I know how hard, how brutal this life can be. The ball's either in or out. There are no grey areas, and there's no negotiation. The game's won or lost. That's an education in itself. But it also gives you a certain freedom, because you grow up earlier and you can decide which direction you want to go in without too much external influence.

I often didn't call home for months. I wanted to be in charge of my own life. My father never expected money from me, and any suggestion of it would have offended him, but at some point I was able to persuade him to change from a Mercedes 300 to a 500 model – a present from me. Just getting my mother to accept a new watch was hard work. When I invited them to tournaments they'd discuss it between themselves. Her: 'Let's fly economy.' Him: 'First class.' My father was as fascinated by the world out there as a child with a Nintendo game. My mother, a down-to-earth woman, was rather confused by it.

Today, when I think about the fact that I had the opportunity to speak to my father shortly before his death, it doesn't seem like chance – it seems more like destiny, as though a higher authority was interceding on my behalf. It all fits together. I was playing Agassi in a final in Hong Kong. It was raining, so we couldn't play on the Sunday, but had to go out on court on Monday morning instead. That made it impossible to play the next tournament, in Tokyo, because I'd have had to be there by the Tuesday. So I decided to go back to Germany. By Tuesday I was in Leimen.

My father was still responsive. An ambulance was due to come at two o'clock and pick him up. If it hadn't rained in Hong Kong, I'd have been in Japan. If I'd lost in Hong Kong at an earlier stage, I wouldn't have dropped Tokyo and I wouldn't have seen my father before he died.

I'd phoned home on the Sunday and told them when I'd arrive, and he'd been waiting. The three of us were in the room: my mother, my father and me. I talked about tennis and my trips, about friends, various projects, Noah, Barbara's second pregnancy. Anything, just talk. I had to fill the space. I knew the end was near. I believe he put off his death until my return.

We carried him on a chair from the bedroom to the dining table, where he wanted to sit one more time. My father looked at the silver-framed photographs on display in the dining room: Sabine and her husband Mathias, their son Vincent, Barbara, Noah, me. He could still take it all in but he'd already begun to shut down. I had the feeling he didn't want to go on any more.

We helped my father to the sofa in the living room. I sat opposite him. He looked at me but didn't talk any more. The ambulance arrived an hour later. It was the longest hour of my life.

It was clear to me as soon as the ambulance arrived that my dad was going away to die. The paramedics carried him to the vehicle. He lifted his arm one last time. My mother was composed. She'd known for the best part of a year that he was dying. The chemotherapy had postponed the end, but it couldn't defeat the cancer. 'He won't come back. You'd better be prepared,' she said, a brave woman, as always. I stayed one more day with her, then I went to play in Monte Carlo. After the first match, I called Leimen. The news wasn't good. 'Your father's really sick. You'd better come at once.' I cancelled my next match, but when I got home my father had died.

A lot of questions remained. I would be facing my last Wimbledon only two months after his death. Could I play there again? Was it OK for me to do that? Would it make any sense? Did I have the strength for it? I began to realize how often I'd misunderstood my father; even now I sometimes catch myself doing things he used to do. I'm strict about the upbringing of my own children, as he was with me. Having children myself, I now see the other side of the equation. After my father's death, I went walking through the woods with Barbara and we talked about the past and about the future. My priorities were now absolutely clear – my children and my family.

It seemed as if everyone who had ever had a five-minute chat with my father responded to his death: Richard von Weizsäcker, the former German president; Gerhard Schröder, the Chancellor, who sent me a handwritten note; Juan Antonio Samaranch, president of the International Olympic Committee; my French fellow player Guy Forget, from whom I hadn't heard in two years; and ex-girlfriends like Karen Schultz and Bénédicte Courtin – all very sympathetic. We didn't send invites for the funeral. They just came: Günther Bosch, Ion Tiriac, friends and foes, united by death. I was like a rabbit caught in the headlights, and just focused on getting through the day. Every hour I looked at my watch and prayed for evening. The following weekend I was booked for a tournament in Munich: an opportunity for three or four hours' distraction.

CONDEMNED TO FREEDOM

AT LAST, CHRISTMAS HOLIDAYS WITH THE CHILDREN. I SLEPT
through most of the flight from Frankfurt to Miami. The
evening before, I'd gone out on the town with friends to bid
farewell to 2002, an awful year. The lights at P1, Munich's top
club, had already gone out by the time we left. What a night
we had! 'Here's to freedom!' was our toast. 'Champagne and
vodka all round!'

I was still woozy from the hangover and didn't quite
understand what this immigration officer wanted from me.
I'd shown him my passport, and was looking forward to seeing my children, who were waiting in Arrivals with Barbara.
But the man signalled me to stand against the white wall next
to his table. Baffled, I followed his instructions. The first-class
passengers had already left; business class also went through;
now it was the turn of economy class and I was still standing
there at the wall like someone who'd been stood up. After
more than half an hour had passed, another man in uniform

came and demanded I follow him. What on earth is going on? I thought. What have I done now? I had no idea. 'I have to question you. Please take a seat,' the man said abruptly, offering me the wooden chair in his sparse office. 'I advise you to tell the truth. What's your name?' The last time I'd heard this question was in October, in a court in Munich; but now I was in Miami and my children were waiting beyond the door.

I've been in a few tricky situations in my life, which is why I've trained myself to stay calm under pressure. And anyone who's had any contact with the American immigration authorities knows not to behave emotionally. I answered mechanically. 'My name is Boris Becker. I live in Munich. I used to be a tennis player. Now I'm a businessman and I want to visit my children.' The whole procedure took another hour. I tried repeatedly to find out what was going on and why I was being treated like a criminal, but I only got more questions in reply.

At last the guy picked up the phone. A few minutes later his boss came in. He recognized me and said in a deep, friendly voice, 'Mr Becker, you have a problem. You don't have a visa.'

'A visa? But I've been coming to the States for the past ten years and I've never had a visa.'

'But now you have a conviction. That's why you need a visa.'

So that was it. They had my tax conviction in their computer. 'But a few weeks ago I came in without a visa and didn't have any problems.'

'That shouldn't have happened. Someone here made a mistake.' The atmosphere grew chilly again.

'What's going to happen now?'

'You'll have to go back to Germany on the next plane. You can't come in without a visa.'

'What? Are you serious?'

I used their telephone to call Barbara. The mobile wasn't allowed. She was flabbergasted. By now it was five in the afternoon and she'd been waiting outside for three hours. Even the officers were embarrassed. In the past you could have got a visa at the airport for a fee of 120 dollars, but post September 11 this was no longer possible, not even for me. They found me a seat on Air France – the flight was at midnight. Lufthansa were kind enough to forward my luggage to Barbara on Fisher Island, while I was taken to the deportation room as an illegal immigrant.

It was a stale, windowless room smelling of sweat. Venezuelans, Colombians and a couple of prostitutes from Bogotà were waiting to be deported – and one Mr Becker in among them. I stared at the floor or into the middle-distance, or looked at the scared faces of the people around me. Gradually I began to adjust to this new situation. My fate was bearable, but what was waiting for these people once they got back home? Prison, beatings, possibly torture?

I was dog-tired; my clothes were taking on the smell of the room. No paper, no television, just a single Coca-Cola to drink. I spent seven hours in the deportation room: under arrest, imprisoned, without a passport or any contact with the outside world, just like the dealer from Medellín opposite me, or the smuggler from Costa Rica over there in the dark corner.

Around ten p.m. a federal officer arrives and sits next to me. A bear of a man. He's a tennis fanatic. He knows my whole story. We talk. He's divorced too. Within an hour this stranger is my friend; we even exchange telephone numbers.

Being in this strange atmosphere cuts through social barriers.

From now on, time flies. At eleven-thirty, my new-found friend in uniform takes me to the Air France plane. He discreetly hands my passport to the captain. I'll only get it back once we are airborne, when it's clear that this unwanted intruder really has left the country. One last firm handshake, a friendly smile and the officer disappears into the half-darkness. The senior steward in first class gives me a welcoming smile. 'Mr Becker, would you like your champagne and caviar before take-off or once we're in the air?' Goodbye nightmare, and welcome to the reality of a Wimbledon winner.

'I'll take the champagne now, thank you, and the caviar later.'

Champagne and caviar? If certain people in Munich had had their way I'd be being served bread and water. After all, their job is putting people behind bars, and their plan for me had been three and a half years.

Things had started to escalate in the week before Christmas 1996. I'd recently won the Grand Slam Cup in Munich, and had cashed in two million dollars in prize money for the four victorious matches. The media calculated that I earned $19,578 a minute in the final win.[1] *Bild* rejoiced in 'Boris's Christmas bonus', and in every paper you could read that in the previous year alone I'd made $4,312,007 in prize money, and that my career winnings to date were $28,692,014.

Now, hand on heart, dear reader – wouldn't you have been a bit envious too? For each minute of my final against Croatian Goran Ivanisevic during the tournament in the Munich Olympiahalle I earned the equivalent of an executive car. Eighty-three cars on a single Sunday afternoon. No doubt these figures made an impression on the tax inspectors, who'd been checking on me since 1991, because as soon as I had left for my Christmas holiday, right after the tournament – a plan I had made public in the press conference afterwards – they raided my villa in the Bogenhausen district of Munich.

Four days before Christmas, I was enjoying the warm Miami sun and playing basketball with friends in the front yard of our place on Fisher Island when I got a phone call from my lawyer, Axel Meyer-Wölden. 'Boris, just stay calm – the tax inspectors are at your home. They need the code for your safe.' I was gobsmacked. I could tell from Axel's tone of voice how serious it was. A cleaning lady had let them in and now they wanted to get at my safe. I gave the number, but apparently it got taken down wrongly and they didn't manage to open the safe. Another phone call, and a threat to dismantle the safe if the combination wasn't right this time. Had they already brought the tools, I wondered. I repeated the code – and the metal door opened for them.

'Just enjoy your holidays. Celebrate Christmas with your family. We'll take care of all this in January.' That was easy for Axel to say. I felt as if they were out to finish me off. Envy and resentment are the biggest plagues of German society, and I'd been too successful. A beautiful wife, a healthy son, success in my career, fame and glory, society's respect, and then on top of that a cool two million just before Christmas – the final straw. In January, when I saw the extent of the raid, it became clear that they really were out to get me.

My inner peace was destroyed; my privacy gone. There had been contract investigations and discussions with the tax people right from the start of my collaboration with Ion Tiriac. Tiriac's lawyers and advisers had been in charge of those matters while I played winning tennis. By the time of the raid – 19 December 1996 – I'd won forty-nine tournaments. I'd won the Davis Cup twice for Germany, and together with Michael Stich had got gold in the doubles at the Olympics in Barcelona. After the raid I didn't win another singles tournament. The sinister threat and fear of the unknown ate up my soul and destroyed my self-confidence. To win match point in a final you need enormous amounts of self-confidence. When I first retired at Wimbledon in 1997, it was because I had to be true to myself. It didn't make sense to chase tennis titles while my real opponent was the German authorities.

I didn't know what they were really after. When they brought the charges against me and raided my villa, the inland revenue claimed to have been searching for essential documents for my tax records. Afterwards the story changed. It became that I had a residence in Munich but was officially registered in Monte Carlo. My advisers had the impression that they wanted to find something, no matter what.

One and a half years after the raid, I received another blow. On 28 July 1998 the investigators went after my acquaintances, my close friends, my parents – at one and the same time, nine a.m. on the dot. Almost fifty private and office addresses were investigated, sixty witnesses were questioned – some 150 officers must have been involved. This was a raid on a major scale. Not, as you might expect, against remaining elements of the Red Army Faction, or terrorists from the Middle East. No, against Boris Becker.

Why should my friends be subjected to interrogation? Karen, my ex, was questioned for two hours. Eric Jelen, my tennis-mate, was stopped by investigators on the motorway and forced to drive back to his flat to be questioned. Officers entered the house of my friend Carlo Thränhardt's parents in the Eifel, who thought they were being burgled. This wasn't about murder or child abduction. This was the pursuit of Citizen Becker, who until now had had a completely clean record.

I was embarrassed in front of my friends and I felt guilty about the state's gross intrusion into their private lives. Overnight the authorities had turned them into witnesses to a prosecution. Or were they about to be charged too?

'How often did he visit you in Hamburg?' the investigators asked Karen. 'Did he ever live in the flat he bought there?'

'He rarely came to Hamburg. He never lived in his flat,' Karen bravely, and truthfully, replied. What she must have gone through – what an ordeal for her.

They cleared every single book from my mother's shelves and they showed no consideration for my desperately ill father. He was in a bad way, but had to cancel an essential chemotherapy appointment because of the raid. He lay exhausted on the sofa, watching helplessly as they went through everything: the kitchen, the cellar, the car. My mother, who was still shaking the day after the raid, noticed that the investigators had forgotten to search the ash pan in the fireplace. She said to one of them, 'You shouldn't forget to search this. You never know what documents might be hidden here!'

For six years, it seemed to me that the investigator Walter F. had only one goal: to hunt down Becker, day in, day out – probably a unique event in the history of Germany's financial institutions. When they didn't get anywhere with Tiriac's contracts, F. decided to target the issue of my residency. At the end of 1984, Tiriac had encouraged me to move my official residency to Monte Carlo. In 1991 I met Barbara in Munich, and in January 1994 I decided to return there officially. I wanted to live in Germany; I wanted my children to be born here. While other sport and media celebrities had turned their backs on this country, I went home. What was to prove my undoing was a room in my sister's Munich flat, where I had occasionally spent the night before I moved my official residency back to Germany. The tax authorities declared that this room had been my residence, and as a consequence I should pay 3.3 million marks in back taxes for my earnings in the years 1992 and 1993, which I had previously declared as income earned abroad and therefore not subject to German taxes.

Well, I'd known the room was a risk, but it wasn't even a proper flat, let alone my official residence. Nevertheless, I took responsibility for having used this room and later made my confession in court. But I might have been spared all this had I been more resolute about a certain matter in 1996.

After Wimbledon in July 1996, Barbara and I decided to officially leave the country again. Life in Germany had become too confined. On a Friday morning I had gone to the local authorities, taken a number, queued up and 'deregistered'. Friends I'd talked the matter over with had advised me to do it, but when I told Axel what I'd done, he was furious. At this point he had cancer and was taking heavy medication. He didn't have much longer to live and I didn't want to hurt him. Axel Meyer-Wölden was very important to me, and I couldn't give him the impression that I was going to abandon him in the last difficult stage of his life. On Monday I went back to the authorities and registered our residency once again.

*

The night before the hearing in October 2002, I was having dinner in the appropriately named Banknote Room in the Käfer restaurant in Munich with my team: my two lawyers, criminal-law expert Professor Dr Klaus Volk and tax expert Dr Jörg Weigell, as well as my mother and Sabine, and my PR man Robert Lübenoff. I'd asked them to join me for a last supper – out of a macabre sense of humour – some way of relieving the tension. A tense lawyer is a bad lawyer. We drank a wonderful New Zealand Cloudy Bay, and had caviar with fluffy mashed potato and baby turbot. It could have been a family celebration. We joked and laughed. Then the vendor of Munich's evening paper came in, a man who often pressed a newspaper into my hand. When he spotted me, he was about to turn on his heels to stop me seeing the front page. 'Boris: Am I going to jail?'[2] read the headline, and below it was a photo-montage with my face behind bars. My blood froze. The evening was ruined.

That morning I'd familiarized myself with the courtroom, together with my lawyers and Robert. I'd walked the aisle, sat in the defendant's chair and touched the judge's bench. This is what I'd always done before a big tournament: tried to take in the atmosphere, absorb the surroundings, so that when I played the match I didn't become distracted by what was around me. I asked my lawyers about every little detail: who sat where, and who did what and when and where. The security staff who took us round were very nice. 'You'll be all right, Boris. You'll get through,' they encouraged me in thick Bavarian accents. However, when they showed me the cells where the criminals got locked up during the break, my view changed, and I got really scared.

In the weeks before the hearing I travelled all over the world. I beat John McEnroe at a tournament in New York, visited my children in Miami, played a charity golf tournament with Michael Jordan in the Bahamas and went on a ten-day business trip to China. I kept busy so I didn't have to think too much. Four more to go, three more to go . . . I ticked off the weeks like a prisoner in a cell. Fear had had me in its grip, but now, on this Wednesday morning, I was completely calm. I was ready for the match, ready for the fight, no matter what was going to happen. That's how it had always been with me. When the time finally came and I entered the courtroom, I was calm and the nerves had gone. I was ready.

In the end I managed to sleep for five hours that night. I had a quiet breakfast with my mother at the Hotel Palace. Doc Weigell and Robert picked me up in my silver M-class Merc. Doc was driving in his own inimitable style, and I was sitting alone in the back playing a CD by Anastacia: 'Paid my dues' – it seemed fitting. Scores of photographers and cameramen were waiting behind the cordon at the entrance to the courtroom on the first floor. It was a quarter past nine when we took the lift from the underground car park. I had arranged with security that they'd let me in through the witness room so I'd have to endure only two metres of flashlights. A second battalion of photographers would be waiting in the courtroom. They were allowed to take pictures until half nine, when the judge would enter the room, so we went in at nine twenty-eight. I wanted to be in charge for as long as possible, but what I experienced here was new, even to someone as used to media intrusion as I was. I stood in front of the brown wooden table and orange seats because I didn't want any photos of myself on the defendant's chair. The photographers fired at me from above and below, some from no more than five centimetres away. They circled me as if I was a wild animal. Five minutes later, the judge finally brought this to a halt.

'I'm calling the case against Boris Becker.' With this, she started the match. After my personal details were confirmed, the prosecuting lawyer read out the charge. He's standing six metres away from me on the opposite side of the room – not such a disagreeable guy. 'Boris Becker rented a flat in the Gaußstraße through his parents as a cover-up. There in 1991 he spent fifty-nine days, in 1992 eighty days, in 1993 ninety-five days. He failed to declare his foreign income to the authorities in Germany, thereby depriving the inland revenue of 3.08 million marks of income tax – and a further 480,000 marks of wealth tax.' That was the charge.

For twenty minutes the judge, a firm but fair 55-year-old, had me talk about my life, from Leimen to Wimbledon and Miami. And then she made a statement that caused the temperature in the room to drop below zero. The prosecution and defence had failed to come to any agreement about the general terms of my sentencing in their preliminary talks. Their ideas about what my sentence should be had been too far apart. For several weeks the media had reported the case as being sewn up, saying that the court hearing was only a show, a publicity stunt, while a deal had been made behind closed doors. That was far from the truth. Now anyone could see that it was serious. This was about whether I could leave as a free man or would have to go to jail. A murmur went through the court. When the judge asked who would represent me, I replied that I was going to do it myself.

I felt all eyes upon me as I read my statement:

The proceedings against me have been going on for six years. And the tax inspectors have been investigating for ten years. Not much has come of this. I have been accused of renting a flat in Munich, as a result of which I had not paid enough tax in 1992 and 1993. That's all.

I have not been accused of, and it would be impossible to accuse me of, covering up income, hiding away money, having illegal earnings, or committing any crime of that kind.

All the amounts that have been discussed here have been accounted for. A German living abroad has only limited tax liability. Some incomes have to be taxed; others don't. I have declared that I live abroad and that the amounts concerned are earnings from other countries that are not subject to German tax.

If I had had a flat in Munich, I would have been completely liable for German tax and any money that I had earned anywhere in the world would have had to be taxed in Germany. That is what is at issue here, and nothing else.

The question is, therefore, whether the room where I stayed during my visits to Munich in autumn 1991 and autumn 1993 is a flat or residence or not. That is a matter of interpretation.

This was not a flat as I imagine a proper flat. It was furnished in such a way that you could just about sleep there. It had a bed, a bench, but not even a wardrobe or a fridge.

But the German inland revenue takes a different, and narrower, view.

I admit that some people had warned me about this. I disregarded their advice and decided to play it by ear. That was wrong, and that's why I'm standing here today.

The only point in the charge that is at issue is whether I had a flat. I don't want to argue about this, and I declare once again that I had known all too well that it could be seen this way, and that I had taken this into consideration.

You must believe me that these proceedings have taken their toll on me. Since their beginnings six years ago, I haven't won a single great tournament, and in the end it finished my career as a tennis player.

I take responsibility for a mistake that I made ten years ago and I know that I have to be punished for it.

I'd had my problems with this admission. After all the years of investigations and the press reports, I knew I would have to pay twenty or perhaps even fifty million marks in taxes. The essential question was simply whether a room could be a flat. A compromise or out-of-court settlement had become impossible by now. Only my confession could put the jurisdiction in a gentler mood. At any rate, I'd already paid the tax debts the inland revenue had demanded – 3,021,759 Euros for the years 1991 to 1995 – before the start of the hearing. That point had got completely lost among all the allegations. While other celebrities were enjoying fame and low tax abroad, I had paid the German state 45 million marks since my return from Monte Carlo.

During the break for lunch I walked past the cells again. The security guards had offered me their room to wait in. We'd ordered trays of canapés from the Käfer, which came in through a side entrance, and we bought Coke from the guards' vending machine. My lawyers were happy with the progress. Robert phoned a few journalists to see how they judged the situation, and to cheer us up he told us about the stories that were to appear in *Bild* the next day: how hairdressers would reveal the secrets of my new hairstyle, and how psychologists would explain why I'd been wearing a dark-grey suit and white shirt with a silver-grey tie. None of us found it very funny.

My lawyer the professor had caught up with the judge in the canteen. She put it to him that this time I should enter the courtroom through the main entrance, because the journalists and photographers had been annoyed by my use of a back route in the morning. I wanted to do as she suggested. We re-entered the court by the main entrance.

And how did the media react? 'Even in court, Becker enjoys putting on a show.'

Countless pages were read out loud from numerous ring-binders. Then the prosecuting lawyer had his moment. Having summarized the matter from his point of view, he then came out with this, for me, incredible statement: 'I call for a prison sentence of three years and six months.' He justified this by the high amount of the tax I had withheld and said, 'This is just as bad as if someone was carrying wads of undeclared cash around the tennis court in a plastic bag.' This was a reference to the case of Peter Graf. Steffi's father was sentenced to three years and nine months in 1997, because he allegedly evaded payment of fifteen million marks in taxes.

I felt anger rising and my instincts reawakening. I would have loved to jump across the table and grab the lawyer, and ask him if he was in his right mind. Three and a half years – that would mean no chance of bail. I tried to calm down. The man was just doing his job. My head was burning, though my face was pale. Now it was my team's turn. First Doc, who once again looked into the taxation regulations and the methods used by the tax investigators. Then the professor, who rounded things up with a strong emotional statement. The hearing was adjourned, to start again at nine-thirty the next day.

Back at the hotel, my mother had heard on the radio about the prosecutor's demand and was in tears. The news was on all channels. Even CNN had the headline: 'Becker on trial. The prosecutor is asking for three and a half years.' And on its website, *Bild* was putting together its headline for the next day's edition: 'Prosecutor demanding three and a half years in prison! Boris in shock.' And I was. How often had I been told that prison was not a possibility? Boris Becker behind bars? No way!

What would happen if the judge had a bad night tonight? If she had an argument with her husband, or got bad news from her family, or something? The game was over and I was in her hands. No second serve. It was her match point. How does the saying go? 'At court and on the high seas you are in God's hands.' I gathered all the crucifixes I could find in my hotel suite, held rosary beads in my hand and started to pray. 'Please help me. One more time. I will make it up to you, I promise.' But again and again those images flashed through my head. I saw the cells, I saw the guards, I saw myself as a convict in striped pyjamas. I ran through the worst-case scenario. Meanwhile, my beloved FC Bayern were playing a champions' league match in Milan; it was flickering on my screen. Oliver Kahn, Bayern's goalkeeper, was injured and had to leave the pitch. 'Oh, Oliver, how I would love to swap with you now. I'd put up with any injury if only I could leave the court as a free man tomorrow.'

A bleak and feeble moon hung over Munich's Angel of Peace as Robert, Doc and I headed to court the next morning. The professor was waiting in the underground car park. He nodded encouragingly. 'I have a good feeling.' What on earth did that mean? What did he know that I didn't? But there was no time for questions or answers, as one of the paparazzi was trying to get into the lift with us.

I made my way in a trance through the media pack to my chair. At nine thirty-one the judge read out the verdict, 'In Namen des Volkes', in the name of the people, in courtroom A101. It went on for ever, with thousands of different arguments. At least that's how it seemed to me.

I'm not really listening, just waiting for one of the lawyers to my right or left to give me a joyful push. Nothing happens. At one stage there's applause from the public gallery. I look right, I look left: Doc and the professor are concentrating on the judge's words. Then we are asked to sit. 'Was it all right, what she said?' I ask cautiously. 'Yes, it was all right,' answers Doc. But what does 'all right' mean? Acquittal? Probation? 'Two years' probation and a 300,000-Euro fine,' says the professor, 'but you may leave the court as a free man.'

I shake everyone's hand: the judge's, the jurors', even the prosecutor's. He'd done his best. In tennis, you congratulate your losing opponent for a good match. While Robert and the lawyers talk to the press outside the courtroom, I steal away through the back, once again past those cells I had eluded, into the car and away. I'm playing Tupac full blast: 'Me Against the World'. Tears are running down my face. These are tears of freedom. I call my friend and adviser Hans-Dieter Cleven, who has followed the process strategically over the months. 'Free! I'm free!' Seconds later, reality hits. The pursuing paparazzi don't get to see my tears, though. They get a wide smile. I've had to show my weaknesses and roll with the punches for long enough now. It's Becker's serve again.

Back at the hotel, I hug my mother and my sister. They've been waiting for me with a glass of Prosecco, but I'm in no mood to celebrate. I call my friend Joe. 'Listen, get the rackets, let's play tennis!' On my way out of the hotel, complete strangers clap me on the shoulder. 'We just heard the news. Congratulations! We're happy for you.' For an hour and a half we slam balls across the net. Sweat flushes the tension out of my body. But my match with the public is not yet over. I still want to convey my standpoint to as many people as possible: why it went this far and what it all meant to me.

The private plane is already waiting at the airport. Before my departure I give an interview to *Bild*'s Rolf Hauschild, whose headline the next day will read: 'Boris tells *Bild*: This was my biggest victory, bigger than Wimbledon.'[3] After that it's off to Hamburg, to Reinhold Beckmann. He usually broadcasts only on Mondays, but my story is big enough for the German broadcasting company ARD to put on a Wednesday-night special. The deal: sixty minutes, and they will broadcast what I have to say. No editing, no soundbites. After all, the whole issue was too important for me. I wanted a face-to-face with a journalist who, despite being a friend, could also ask penetrating questions. We'd done a few of those before and it had always been a challenge, but worth it. Becker uncut.

Twelve hours after the verdict, the Beckmann thing is done. The waiter at the restaurant of the Hotel Atlantic brings me half a lobster followed by fried Dover sole. I'm having a Chablis premier cru with it. One last interview with the celebrity magazine *Bunte*'s Paul Sahner, and one last answer: 'For the first time in ten years I feel free, really free.'

THE MAN WHO WAS MY MOTHER

When one person serves another in a way that is selfless and true, when he has dedicated his life to him and renounced his own wishes, sorrows and joys, then you can say of him that he has almost become an 'Eckermann'. The name of this man who was Goethe's helper for almost a decade . . . has become a byword for selflessness, for constancy in service, for simple, human loyalty.'[1]

I WRECKED SEVEN RACKETS IN THE MATCH WITH THE Australian Wally Masur, and it wasn't just Ion Tiriac who told me after my defeat that I'd acted like an idiot. Destroying my tools was nothing new. When I was young I'd often break things when I wasn't happy with my game. I think I set my own record in Barcelona in 1984, when I reduced eight rackets to kindling sticks because I lost in the first round against a Canadian by the name of Martin Wostenholme.

It wasn't this lunatic behaviour that got me into the headlines in Melbourne, however. It was the fact that 21 January 1987 was the day when I lost confidence in Günther Bosch. He remembers the story differently, of course, which is how it goes with controversy and divorce. Some German football fans are still convinced that England's third goal in 1966 was not a goal, and that the Soviet linesman betrayed them . . .

In my match against Masur, I almost got banned from the court. My behaviour on the court was mirroring my life off it. I was unhappy about the defeat, but most of all I was unhappy with Günther Bosch. I had to decide how – indeed whether – I wanted to work with him from here on. For three years he'd been like a parent to me, and had sacrificed a lot for me. As my own father said, 'The last thing he saw when he closed his eyes at night was Günther, and when he opened them in the morning, the first thing that met his eyes was Günther.' Bosch was 'Günzi', and I'd trusted him completely since boyhood. The German tennis association (DTB) had put him in charge of a group of four youngsters: Tore Meinecke, Udo Riglewski, Christian Schmidt and Boris Becker. I was the best of these talents and so eventually he travelled with me alone. In January 1984, I got the first ATP points in German satellite tournaments, and little by little I played my way to the top. Early in 1984, Bosch left the DTB and worked exclusively with me, because that was what my new manager Tiriac and my parents wanted.

After my five-set disaster in Melbourne against Masur, I told Tiriac, 'This can't go on. Günzi's getting on my nerves. He's no use to me any more. I don't need a babysitter, I need someone who challenges me.' Bosch had kept me on a long lead, and in my adolescence that was the right decision. He wanted me to be happy. He was convinced that as long as I was in good spirits I'd play well. He'd been very forgiving, and often calmed down the much more critical Tiriac. 'Leave the boy alone. Let him be.' Bosch was more psychologist than coach, more father-confessor than adviser. He had suffered with me and for me. When I tore my ligament in 1984 in my first professional tournament, he was beside himself. I was operated on in Munich and he sat at my bedside throughout my recovery. He was to me what Eckermann was to Goethe.

That day at the Regent Hotel in Melbourne, I spent two hours explaining to Tiriac why my collaboration with Bosch couldn't go on. Tiriac, however, pleaded with me to carry on with Bosch, and my father advised me from Leimen to think it over. Bosch was a man with no hard edges. He occasionally drank a small glass of wine, didn't smoke and was faithful to his wife Rodica. His wife, however, wanted Bosch to be Tiriac; she'd have loved to turn her husband into a great tennis manager. But Bosch wouldn't have been comfortable in that role. To me he had neither the substance nor the charisma. Rodica often accompanied her husband, because he could afford it, and I put up with it, but we rubbed each other up the wrong way. A sharp comment from her would be met by an equally sharp comment from me. After a while we stopped talking altogether.

Bosch lived for the sport and I was at the centre of his universe. We travelled together and ate together for months at a time, and the set-up didn't change even when a girlfriend of mine came on the scene. We'd still travel together and eat together, but there'd be three of us instead of two. I didn't want to leave Bosch on his own, but at the same time it was annoying having him playing gooseberry every evening.

To him I would always be the same Boris, who as number

two hundred in the world came through the first round in Melbourne at the end of 1984 and felt as if he'd invented the game of tennis. In the second round, I beat the American Tim Mayotte in four sets (6–4, 7–6, 2–6, 6–4) and made it to the quarter-finals. As a result I shot up the rankings to number fifty-four. Bosch and I toasted my breakthrough with mineral water. A few weeks earlier in South Africa, after my defeat in the qualifying rounds, I'd thought my dream of a professional career was over. In Melbourne in 1984 I could see light again. I knew I had it in me to play at the top. January 1985 saw me win in Birmingham against Stefan Edberg – considered invincible among the young players – in the Young Masters. My match against him was the first five-set match I ever played. I won 4–6, 6–3, 6–1, 4–6, 6–3.

Bosch continued to be considerate and forgiving, as he'd always been. I wound him up, misbehaved and embarrassed him. He never reacted as I wanted him to. He always let things pass. At some point he should have said, 'Enough is enough!' Instead he kept quiet and gradually I lost my respect for him. The young Becker had grown up, but Günther Bosch had failed to keep pace. He struck me as being a real dogsbody. He looked after the travel arrangements, the hotel bookings, my forehand, my practice partners, and he kept in touch with my parents. I could rely 100 per cent on my Eckermann. He sat on the coach's chair and it had become a reflex for me to look up at him, whether I'd hit a good ball or a bad ball. For years, from as long ago as my first Wimbledon, I'd been wondering if it would be a good idea to change coach. Even Tiriac wasn't always happy with Bosch's methods. They were chalk and cheese, those two. Before the final in Sydney against Ivan Lendl, Tiriac asked Bosch how I was playing.

'He knows which tactic to use,' answered Bosch. 'Dammit, you're supposed to tell him!' said Tiriac. 'You see,' I said to Tiriac. 'He doesn't tell me anything.'

On 21 January, Tiriac called Bosch in his hotel room and said, 'We have to talk – now. Boris is complaining about the teamwork and we can't go on like this.'

Bosch turned up, clearly surprised. 'I always meant well,' he said. 'I only want to help. Why haven't you said anything before?'

'A man thirty years my senior has to tell me what's going on,' I replied. 'I treat you very badly, and you just take it on the chin.'

Our argument got more heated, with Bosch loud one minute and whingeing the next. 'I realize this defeat hurts, but why are you telling me all this now?'

'This is nothing to do with the match. These are basic matters. This is about the relationship between coach and player. I can't carry on like this.'

Tiriac, the mediator, suggested we change the way we work together. Bosch should continue to come to the important tournaments, but the daily coaching would be dropped. Bosch, however, insisted that everything remain the same. He'd either coach me full-time, or not at all.

We agreed we'd think through the alternatives and get together again later, and in the meantime we might have found a solution. Tiriac warned Bosch, 'Whatever we decide, no press. No dirty laundry in public.' I was convinced, as was Tiriac, that Bosch would eventually accept the new way of doing things. How wrong we were.

Immediately after our talk, Bosch apparently told the ex-professional tennis player Hans-Jürgen Pohmann, who works as a television and occasionally print journalist, that he was going to quit working with Boris Becker. Back then Pohmann had always been very critical of me, and Bosch knew that – that's why he chose him. Next, still in Melbourne, he phoned his contact at *Bild* in Hamburg, for whom he was writing a column. At the time, of course, I had no idea this was going on.

Bosch stood firm by his decision: to leave. I was very surprised. Perhaps he'd had an inkling of what was coming and had prepared himself, so that at the right moment he could throw the contract in my face and feel he'd got one over on me, as well as earn the sympathy vote of the German public, who wanted to see this threesome go on for ever: Tiriac (Dracula), Boris (the virgin) and Bosch (the loving mother). I shook Bosch by the hand and left without a word. Tiriac and Bosch were to compose a press release – at Bosch's insistence. This is what it said:

> After careful consideration, it has become clear that the partnership with Boris is no longer possible because our opinions about preparation, tournament scheduling and everything that comes with them are no longer in line with each other. While I accept his struggle for independence as a person, and indeed have supported this struggle, I do not approve of his breaking free as a sportsman. I cannot accept his proposal that I become his part-time coach. He is still not perfect and has a great deal to learn as a player, and as a person too. Coaching on an on–off basis is not, in my view, feasible. This is why I have taken this step – because I do not want to stand in his way but want to give him the freedom to develop however he sees fit. I send him my warmest regards, and in my heart and mind I shall continue to be with him even when I'm thousands of kilometres away.[2]

That evening I went with a few friends to a Lionel Richie concert. I wanted to forget the whole thing by listening to what was my favourite song at the time: 'Dancing on the Ceiling'. I needed some distraction. There was a girl called Lisa who gave me some comfort. She went on to marry an American billionaire, so she did well. I couldn't believe my eyes when I left the concert: the press and television cameras were waiting for me outside the hotel and in front of the lift. It was about Bosch. It was like a thunderbolt. The German media hadn't published the news yet, so who could have informed the press here in Australia – who?

I thought I knew Bosch, but this took me by surprise. I was only nineteen, and I'd aimed for a fair solution to the problem of our disparate views and opinions. I knew, even in this awful moment, just how much I had to thank him for. Now, in front of the media pack, I couldn't believe that he'd been so false. I was angry with myself. Why couldn't I have sent him packing much earlier? Why had I been taken in by his tear-filled eyes and gentle ways? And what did I get for thanks? A kick in the backside. Tiriac once said, 'Becker never makes the same mistake twice.' I certainly wasn't going to let what had occurred with Bosch ever happen to me again.

Tiriac offered Bosch the chance to explain his reasons for the break-up at the following day's press conference at Kooyong Stadium. He declined, arguing that he'd already spoken to the journalists the night before, and they'd mis-quoted him. 'It's not easy for Günther,' Tiriac said at the press conference, 'or for Boris or me.'[3] Ion didn't want to take over from Bosch. The sort of close partnership Ion had had with Vilas didn't seem possible with me. In his eyes I was a man with a strong personality: 'That's why he is where he is today, and that's the way he'll be until the day he dies.'[4] He could easily write three books about my fantastic successes, he has said, but he could write several about my mistakes too.

Loyalty is tested at times of crisis – and Günther Bosch betrayed me. Flying out of Melbourne, he went straight to the TV show *Aktuelles Sportstudio* in Mainz in order to break our agreement and to sell his insights into our very private relationship. He went on to write newspaper columns which even years later included soundbites such as, 'He lives under the delusion that he's something very special. He's lost touch with reality.'[5] Or, 'It hurts me to see such a great player as Boris Becker lose in this way. It reminds me of many a great tennis player who didn't manage to quit with dignity.'[6] Quotes like these made me realize he no longer knew the man he was talking about.

In 1990, the German TV station SAT.1 bought the German broadcasting rights for tennis and Bosch re-entered my life. A decade after our split, he would still be talking about my day-to-day life and achievements as if he was an insider. I'm sure the viewers believed him – how would they know otherwise? That made me angry, so I restricted my collaboration with the station, not just because of Bosch but also because of the other presenters, who didn't know as much about tennis back then as they do now. I ignored Bosch. For over five years I didn't exchange a single word with him.

Günther Bosch had earned a nice living with me. Despite the unilateral nature of Bosch's resignation, Tiriac, who was still affiliated with the Munich-based lawyer Axel Meyer-Wölden, negotiated a pay-off with him. Bosch had been my coach for three Wimbledon years, and in two out of those three years I'd won the tournament. He had made his contribution, probably a significant one, and I was grateful for that. Whether I would have won without him by my side is impossible to say. The winning is what counts. After he quit, I became Wimbledon champion once again. Without him I moved to the top of the world rankings. I won the US Open and the Australian Open, and several other titles. I made good progress in my career, despite some setbacks. Coaches like Bosch dream of finding players they can care for and nurture, like a plant in their garden they can encourage to bloom. 'That's the best way,' he once said – but it is also the rarest. I found it weird that after his walk-out he didn't let go of Boris Becker. He got stuck in the past, obsessed with my life. He'd appear on any talk show. Where there was a microphone, there was Herr Bosch talking about BB.

Once, in spring 1993, I bumped into him on a flight from Nice to Madrid. Bosch was sitting a few rows in front of me, and I went up and sat by his side. That took him by surprise, as did the reason I gave for wanting to speak to him. It was his column in the German weekly *Welt am Sonntag*. Some of his stories were pure invention, which he composed either despite knowing better or out of ignorance. His response confirmed that he hadn't changed. Bosch didn't justify what he wrote; instead, he reassured me that I was the best, he only wanted the best for me, and he only wrote the best about me. I had put a very simple question to him and expected a straight answer, not false sentimentality. Since that encounter I've felt a bit sorry for him. Today Günther Bosch is a figure from the distant past. There's no pain and no anger – to me now it's all as far away as the moon. He was no Eckermann, after all.

THE BURDEN OF FAME

'BORIS HAS TO BE ALL THINGS AT ALL TIMES: WINNER, wunderkind, Prince Charming, heartbreaker. Boris has to be there for everyone: for his coach, his manager, his sponsors, his country. Boris is both emperor and sweet little boy, conquering the world with his tennis racket but staying loyal to his own country. Boris can never be ordinary citizen Becker, because Boris is a choreographed spectacle.'[1] That's how the *Frankfurter Allgemeine Zeitung* described in July 1986 the burden I had to carry. I didn't even have to complain about it myself. Others were already writing about the weight on my shoulders.

'A genius like Einstein', a 'shining light of global dimensions' was how I was seen at times of victory; 'the Rembrandt of tennis', with all the colours on his palette. But mind you, if I made half a dozen double faults, or if this 1.91-metre, 90-kilogram man slipped on clay, then the lights went out for the 'German God of Light',[2] as the Swiss weekly

Weltwoche called me. 'People from Yokohama to Patagonia adore this cheeky young man,'[3] wrote *Sports*. I had become a hero on the German stage – not just the actor, but the director, scene-shifter and manager all rolled into one – but others were selling the tickets.

Premier-league football matches had to be postponed when Boris Becker played. That left me speechless. Even famous writers like Martin Walser elevated the game of tennis to spiritual heights:

> Maybe you had to have as much to do with angels in your child-hood as I did to find Boris Becker so adorable. Fra Angelico painted angels like him. To make altarpieces of Boris and Steffi you'd have to be able to paint eyelashes, red ones or pure blond ones, the upper lashes almost enmeshed with the lower. Then to paint Boris you'd have to capture his look, which always contains so much all at once: innocence, impudence, reserve, passion, laughter, anger and sorrow. The rather oversized mouth deter-mines which of these will dominate. When Boris Becker wins, he looks the son of Kirk Douglas and Burt Lancaster. When he loses, he just looks himself. This fascination with the gods of tennis – there's nothing heavenly about them, they are com-pletely earthly, as banal as Frank Sinatra, Marilyn Monroe, VW, you and me. And just like us they are anything but eternal.[4]

A bit of a difficult character then, this Becker. What, I wonder today, did people expect of a seventeen/eighteen-year-old, about whom one of the most important German papers wrote: 'He's not far off from superhuman.'[5] I no longer understood the Germans – nor the whole world, in fact – and I didn't know how to escape from this suffocating embrace.

The German president wants to have a chat with me, the Pope gives me his blessing, babies are named after me. My father is beside himself with pride over his son. He is happy that Germany has got a hero once more – a new Max Schmeling, a man you can touch, like Fritz Walter or Franz Beckenbauer. My father liked those comparisons. My son, my countrymen, my country.

Max Schmeling, a name I'd heard before: a boxer who'd beaten the favourite, a black American called Joe Louis.

'When was that?' I asked my sport-obsessed father.

'1936.'

So that was during the time of Adolf Hitler, the same year that the Führer left the Berlin Olympiastadion in order to avoid the four-time-gold-medal-winner Jesse Owens, a black American. The year also when the German generals were probably making battle plans, and the Nazis were wondering which colour the star should be that the Jews were to wear on their clothing. Was it possible that Max Schmeling became a German hero because it was a black man he had knocked out in the twelfth round? But my dad was able to reassure me. Schmeling had refused to leave his Jewish manager Joe Jacobs, as the Nazis had demanded of him. Also, when in 1938 he lost to Louis, knocked out in the first round, he'd seemed relieved. A further victory would have made him 'an Aryan showpiece of the Third Reich', as he said later – something he didn't want to become. Unfortunately, we only met once, at a PR event. I was too young back then to ask any meaningful questions. A missed opportunity, which I regret today.

The name Fritz Walter, of course, rang a bell. Anyone who played football had heard of him. World champion in 1954, modest, decent, married to his Italia. No show, no scandals, just Fritz from the Palatinate. Franz Beckenbauer took over the mantle from Fritz Walter, though he was of a different generation and had a different attitude. Professional career in Germany with FC Bayern, in New York with Cosmos, divorced, world champion, European champion, children and more children. Success as a player, as coach, as a man. And to top that, he has managed to bring the 2006 world championships to Germany. What a man!

You never saw Franz unshaven or with uncombed hair, with his tie undone or with jacket and socks that didn't match. He always looked well groomed, and the same is true today. Franz could probably work out for ninety minutes in a sauna and emerge looking cool. That's the first impression you get of him. But it's an illusion, of course, as I was able to find out. Franz Beckenbauer bridges the past and the future. He is a thoughtful man, not nearly as superficial as he may appear. At his core he's a rebel. He tries to live up to his image, but he's not a conformist. He's always looking for the next move, and others follow. Franz is a leader, a border-straddling German: head of Bayern plc in Munich, home in Austria. Chief of the football world championship, vice-president of the German league. Certainly one of the most influential people in our society. And yet it is his own objectives that have priority for him. He won't be ruled by others.

Watching football requires patience, and scoring goals takes time. It was easier to cheer for me. Serve for Germany, boom, boom. No defeats scheduled. I had no idea about the desires the Germans projected on to me. I was no conformist, no shirker or coward – instead I went on to Centre Court seemingly fearless, raised my fist to the sky and screamed, 'Yeeeeeees!' It seemed as if people had been waiting for someone like me to arrive on the scene. But Wimbledon victories come without warning. Ion Tiriac said to me, 'Leimen doesn't exist any more. I'm going to explain to you now how you will change from being the boy from Leimen into one of the most famous people on earth, adored by your fans, pursued by photographers. Trust me.' The hysteria was greater than expected, and had I not had such a solid upbringing, and had my friends not stood by me, I would have sunk, and drowned.

I was lucky not to lose my footing altogether. I was often close to screaming, 'I can't go on any more!' What the boy from Leimen has to cope with, wrote the *Frankfurter Rundschau*, 'only Superman could manage without injury'.[6] I was no 007 either. Sean Connery had that job. In an interview I once remarked that in retrospect I'd rather have lost the match point against Kevin Curren in 1985. The interviewer asked me if I was serious. I really was.

I would have preferred more time: time to develop my game of tennis, and to develop my own character. Had I won Wimbledon at the age of twenty-three or twenty-five instead of seventeen, I would have become a better tennis player. When you play to win, you are forced to rely on the known, the proven. You can't afford to experiment. You live from victory to victory and there's no space to develop a new technique or improve your footwork. The question was only ever: will Becker win the next match? I remembered reading a play called *A Game* by Swiss author Max Frisch when I was at school, and I read it again. In it, a man is given an unexpected chance to start his life again from scratch. 'You have the opportunity to do it all over again but you can do it with the wisdom you now have.'[7] How I would have loved a chance like that!

I'd have liked to become a professional basketball player in America, a white Michael Jordan. Tennis is exhausting, not least because you are out there on your own, coping with stage fright all by yourself. In a team the players can celebrate or commiserate together, absorbing defeats collectively. To play in a team where, if you've reached the heights of a Michael Jordan, you can even choose your own team-mates, has got to be more fun than travelling the world alone and coping with the highs and lows by yourself.

Four weeks after Wimbledon 1985, I played the Davis Cup for Germany against the USA, on clay. We won in Hamburg for the first time in history: great celebrations, with Becker on top. Three days later I had to play in Kitzbühel. I was exhausted, but prepared to fight. Of course it didn't work. Wimbledon wunderkind lost in the first round to Diego Perez of Uruguay, 3–6, 1–6. The Austrians, who, in the era before the political turbulence around Jörg Haider, were known around the world for their hand-kissing charm, reacted like Sicilians. First they threw their seat cushions on to the court, and then the seats followed. Back then I didn't know what Günter Grass once said: 'Fame is something that people seem to like pissing on.' I was hurt and disturbed; what was going on here? Just a week ago I'd been the Mozart of tennis, and now I'd been demoted to a nobody and things were being thrown at me.

Whenever I lost, especially in the early rounds, I was seldom shown mercy. At the end of 1986, the *Observer* wrote, 'He needs extraordinary qualities of resilience and resolve to cope with the absurd expectations of his country.'[8] Günther Bosch once said that all the people who worked in the inner circle around Boris Becker felt as if they were in a spaceship, that it was like floating at zero gravity in space and looking for something to hold on to. How, then, must I have felt? I had become 'a prophet in my own country', wrote the French paper *L'Express*.[9] My private life had ended. It was like sitting on the lavatory with the whole world watching. When I got into a taxi after a defeat I'd often be asked by the driver, 'You don't want to do this any more then? Too many girls, too much money, or what?' I was booed in the street or insulted when I went shopping. The first threatening letters arrived at my parents', and blackmailers got in on the scene. Strangers followed me in their cars. Policemen had to protect me at football grounds, bodyguards accompanied me on shopping trips or a visit to the doctor. At home or in a hotel room I was still just plain Boris, but in those ten steps from the lift to the door I was transformed into the official Becker, the one everyone wanted a piece of.

Just to clarify: I happen to earn a lot of money for all of this. I was as keen to win as everyone else was keen for me to win, and I couldn't bear it when I lost. But the price I had to pay often seemed to be too high, and there were times when I would have liked the ground to swallow me up. Marlon Brando allegedly held a straw hat in front of his face when his plane landed, in the hope that no one would recognize him. In Munich I occasionally – mainly for fun – wore a black wig. I grew a beard to hide behind. I wore caps that I pulled right over my face – anonymous at last, or so I thought.

When I was successful professionally, my private life suffered. The endless training, the weeks of preparation for a Grand Slam – it was like being in prison. Killing time, coping with monotony, a thousand forehands, a thousand backhands, until you don't think any more but turn into a machine. Get those stupid feelings out of the way and move mechanically, over and over again. If you've got nothing else in your head except hitting balls then maybe this would be OK. But what if you want to find answers to questions that go beyond the base-line of a tennis court? There was nobody to talk to. The only thing Tiriac could think of to say when I felt low was that I had to realize there was another side to the coin; I had to take the bad with the good and be a man. Well, fuck them all.

I tried to find answers in biographies. Looking for people with similar experience, I devoured books by the stars of the post-war era. The poster for the James Dean film *Rebel Without a Cause* used to hang over my bed when I was rebelling against my father back in Leimen. I could under-stand how Elvis Presley and James Dean had lived their lives, but I never tried to copy their lifestyles with their uppers, downers, drugs and homosexuality. Had I been an actor I might have gone in this direction, but I was a professional sportsman, and my limits were clearly marked out.

Sure, I *am* a man. There were times when the women had a different name every night because I was trying to fill the lonely hours. It didn't really help improve my state of mind. In the end, I guess, it was the solid basis of my first fifteen years in Leimen that helped me; my engagement with my inner self and my interest in Eastern philosophy taught me a lot too.

'He who knows others is clever. He who knows himself is wise,' said the Chinese philosopher Laotse around three thousand years ago. 'He who defeats others has power. He who defeats himself has strength. He who makes his own way has willpower. He who is sufficient unto himself is rich. He who doesn't lose his place has persistence. He who doesn't perish in death, lives.'[10] Heather MacLachlan, who is today married to former US Senator Mitchell and who years ago worked for Tiriac, gave me this book. She knew that I, like so many young people, was searching for meaning, and that an improved forehand wasn't going to help me much in this respect. I couldn't find what I was looking for on the tennis court, even when I won Wimbledon or was ranked number one in the world. I was searching for the Boris I'd left behind at the age of fifteen, and the values I'd left behind with him. I didn't want to lose control over my life. It had become a life lived out of a suitcase. For forty-five weeks of the year I was a globe-trotting vagabond with three tennis bags, two suits, jeans, leather jacket, and a great pile of tennis shirts that often came back from the hotel laundry a size smaller than they'd gone in. Friendships were a rarity and time was always short.

Carl-Uwe (Charly) Steeb and Patrik Kühnen, also tennis professionals, were living a similar life and understood how I felt. I used to play tennis with them when the rackets were almost as big as we were. I could lean on these two and open my heart to them. But when were they around to help me? When the media were torturing me and Bosch was getting on my nerves, and Tiriac was still refusing to understand why I didn't want to do advertising for condoms, there was no one there but me. I felt particular distress after the defeat by Masur and Bosch's resignation. Germany was in turmoil over it. This cheeky Becker boy, they'd say, and once again I couldn't understand it. I asked Tiriac whether they'd all gone mad. In the ensuing weeks, I seriously considered disappearing off the face of the earth, changing my identity and starting all over again. What a stupid idea! Where could I have gone? And I didn't really want to run away from myself – I didn't find me all that bad. Reality, and my tennis life, would catch up with me anyway.

Every time I lost, I had to build up my morale all over again. When Bosch left I had to find a new coach, but Tiriac was against my choice, the Australian Bob Brett. 'Him? What's he got that you could possibly need? He's never even been in a Wimbledon final! How could you have any respect for him?' But Brett was tough – exactly what I wanted. He made it very clear what he expected from me: willingness, discipline, willpower, punctuality. Three hours' training in the morning, three hours in the afternoon. 'What you do after-wards doesn't interest me.' It was a pure business relationship.

Brett treated me like a grown-up, and during his time as my coach I had resounding success: in 1988 I won seven finals, and in the Masters I beat Ivan Lendl for the first time. The world of sport rejoiced at my resurrection. The next year, 1989, was to become the best of my career. I played twelve tournaments: I won Wimbledon, the US Open, the Davis Cup – and became number one in the ITF world ranking. For the Germans I was once again godlike – but after that I had to come back down to earth.

At the end of 1990 I was number two in the ATP world rankings, and Edberg was number one. At Paris Bercy I played him in the final and could have taken his place – the score was 3–3 in the first set, but then I tore a muscle. Only eight days later I was due to start playing the Masters in Frankfurt. My doctor, Hans-Wilhelm Müller-Wohlfahrt, gave me daily injections, calf-blood extracts and amino acids. For eight days I couldn't walk, let alone practise. Edberg only needed to reach the final in Frankfurt to stay number one. His departure before the semis would be to my advantage, assuming I got through myself. I beat Andres Gomez (4–6, 6–3, 6–3), who played in my group. Edberg lost his first set against Emilio Sanchez, but went on to win 6–7, 6–3, 6–1. I won my second match against Thomas Muster in two sets (7–5, 6–4). Edberg won again: this time against Andre Agassi in three sets (7–6, 4–6, 7–6). Damn it!

In the evenings I could barely crawl on all fours back to my hotel room. Edberg went on to win against Pete Sampras (7–5, 6–4), and played the semi-final against Lendl, before my match against Agassi. The Swede won 6–4, 6–2, reaching the final and holding on to the number-one spot, while I lost 2–6, 4–6 – and once again I was finished. I didn't even shower. For the first time in my life I missed a press conference. I was drained, exhausted. I passed my bag to my security adviser, Hans, and told him, 'I'm going on foot.' I walked the forty-five-minute route back to the hotel in darkness, still wearing shorts and a short-sleeved tennis shirt. It was November in Frankfurt and it was raining. I bought a Coke and some chocolate at a petrol station. Without my knowing it, Hans was following me in the car, always twenty or thirty metres behind me.

The next morning I told Brett, 'I have to get out of here. I can't cope with the storm that's going to hit the papers.' So I left for Australia. There was only one thing on my mind: to become number one in the ATP listing. For the entire year I'd been only one victory away from the top slot. Five years at the top but never quite at the very top. For the next seven weeks before the Australian Open I trained harder than I'd ever done in my life.

On 1 January I played a preparation tournament in Adelaide. I dropped out in the first round, 6–7 against Magnus Larsson, at 42°C in the shade on clay during the third set. That night me and my mates Charly, Patrik and Alexander Mronz drank the bar dry. The next day we played eighteen-hole golf in the blazing heat. At night, too much beer again. Then I told Brett, 'I'm flying home. I've had enough.' My return flight was booked for Saturday; I already had the ticket. In the morning I practised a bit, and in the afternoon I packed my bags. Then I stopped. Boris, I said to myself, where do you think you're going? You're staying put. What's home for you, anyway? Home's your suitcase. And Germany? Just imagine the cold. And then at the airport you'll have to face the reporters and all their questions again.

I called Brett. 'Let's go on training.'

In the third round of the Australian Open, I fought for five hours and forty minutes against the Italian Omar Camporese. The score in the fifth set was 14–12. We started at three p.m. on court number two, and when we finished at eight-forty p.m. it was still 40°C. During a match like this you forget where you are, whether it's Melbourne or Memphis, whether it's windy or still, dark or light. You find your rhythm and you have your routine: you go to the ball boy, you reach for your towel – always the same. You don't look at your opponent and you don't have any feelings. After five hours you're in a trance where nothing interests you apart from the next point. Two weeks earlier I had wanted to leave, but I knew I'd conquered my weak side. It's like the marathon runner who at some point reaches the 'wall' and either breaks down in front of it or gets over the top of it. I was hot and dazed and seeing stars, but in the end I got my reward: triumph in Australia against Lendl in the final, 1–6, 6–4, 6–4, 6–4.

I was hovering several feet above the ground. I forgot everything: the ceremony, the spectators, everything. I walked through one of the gates into the park in order to escape to my hotel and get some distance and quiet. One of the officials came running after me. 'You've got to go back. Everybody's waiting for you. You've got to accept the trophy.' He carefully took hold of my arm and walked me back into the stadium. I was, at last, number one.

I had to leave the Australian summer and return to the German winter for the Davis Cup match against Italy. Before that Müller-Wohlfahrt gave me more injections, otherwise I couldn't have borne the pain. The first night back in Dortmund I slept in two pairs of pyjamas, suffering from jet lag, tired and full of jabs. During practice on Tuesday afternoon, I was as stiff as if I hadn't played the game for years. Three days later I was up against Paolo Cane. I won in four sets (3–6, 6–1, 6–4, 6–4), and then in five sets against Camporese, once again (3–6, 4–6, 6–3, 6–4, 6–3). Physically I was done for, but our team won 3–2. We'd just made it, and I didn't have to flee in my car.

When I lost a match I'd listen to U2's fantastic song 'Where the Streets Have No Name' and floor the accelerator. This was how I tried to reclaim some privacy. In my car I could listen to music and scream, yell and cry unseen. The car was my refuge when everything outside was out of control.

I'd become a loner. Maybe I'd always been one in a way, and the decade-long pressure I'd been under had brought this side of me to the fore. The constantly changing nature of popular reaction made me lose trust in people. The lack of mercy, the intransigence and the intolerance I faced often shocked me, and the booing and the abuse got deep under my skin. I began to isolate myself, putting up a brick wall to hide behind. And that was how I survived.

AND EVERYTHING FINALLY DISSOLVES ITSELF IN SLEEP . . .

IT WAS A COLD OCTOBER NIGHT WHEN I ASKED MY WIFE TO shoot me. I stood almost naked on the terrace of my house in Munich, unable to bear the spinning inside my skull. That night I'd been to the Oktoberfest. I'd had a beer or two and a little schnapps, the way you do in Munich at this time of the year. As long as you are inside the tent amid the smoke, sweat and beer, you feel fine. Beware, though, what happens when you walk out of the tent and the fresh air hits you.

For the first time in my life I was totally knocked out and nothing, neither cold compresses nor aspirin nor mineral water, could bring me any longed-for relief. I'm not normally so delicate. I can take my drink. But that night I'd clearly crossed the line – and I admit it wasn't the first time that alcohol had given me problems. And that was in spite of the fact that I was a good boy really, who wasn't into drinking and smoking. My father had given me watered-down wine to try when I was a boy, and I'd experimented with smoking, of course – it almost ended in disaster in my parents' garage when I dropped an unextinguished match into the sawdust and set the place alight. The fire brigade had to come. Thankfully the car wasn't in the garage or my life would have been over at fourteen. My dad gave me a good hiding for that. Later on he also offered me a cigar, perhaps as further punishment. I was sick for days.

In principle, though, I was a clean-living young sportsman. None of my tennis mates smoked or drank, and peer pressure prevented me from falling for those temptations. Nowadays I like a glass of red and I've even built up a small wine cellar, but in the first few years of my career I didn't drink, not a drop. Neither did I go in for therapy. What could anyone have told me? I didn't take tranquillizers either, because a player has to be on edge, right on the very edge, in order to perform. You have to be acutely aware of your limits, physical and mental, in order to go beyond them. That is why any kind of help that's legal is quite welcome – that's how it was for me, anyway.

I would stand on the court, coughing because I was breathing too quickly or too slowly, gasping for air like a fish on dry land. People wondered whether this was an attitude, or whether I was actually ill. My problem was sleeping pills, and it was only in 1992 that Barbara finally threw the last packet out of the window.

Early in 1987 I couldn't stand the pressure any longer. Sleeping pills seemed harmless enough. Our Davis Cup team physician at the time, Dr Joseph Keul, asked us if we had trouble sleeping. This is quite a common problem among athletes. To be fit you need eight or nine hours' sleep a night, so we all ended up taking these new pills. They had a powerful effect on me: I slept like the dead. All the fear was taken away, and I got used to that. Indeed, most of us stuck with these pills. You wake up in the morning feeling pleasantly muzzy, all anxiety gone, nothing but a relaxed sensation in its place, and it takes some time before you're really awake and can think clearly again.

I used this stuff for several years. Eventually I started waking up in the middle of the night because the effect began to wear off after three or four hours, so then I doubled the dose. No one knew about these chemicals that were making me numb. Doctors advised me about the side effects, and the risks were clearly spelled out in the information leaflet. 'Taking this medication can lead to physical dependence. When ending the therapy, withdrawal symptoms may occur.' But I didn't want to know the truth. At times I couldn't sleep at all without the sleeping pills. Three or four tournaments a month, jet lag, stress, then one week off. The first night would always be spent tossing and turning: lying on my back, on my belly, on my left side, on my right side. About the only position I didn't try in my pursuit of elusive sleep was standing on my head. At the worst times, there was also whisky, which enhanced the effect of the pills.

I was absolutely determined to pull myself out of the slump that was 1987. I wanted to get back to the top, to win again. So I looked for a remedy for every little problem: two hours' training for the weak forehand; one hundred practice hits for the weak serve. Sleeping pills to fight the sleeplessness; painkillers to ease the pain. For loneliness there were women, whisky or both.

I had to reduce the number of tournaments I played because I needed more downtime in between to try to get away from the pills. Sometimes I didn't play for four weeks in an attempt to get back to normal. During the breaks I'd come off the pills, and the first two weeks of withdrawal would be hell. When you've got used to taking these pills over several weeks, the first days without them are a nightmare. I'd try to make myself tired, but end up lying awake until five or six in the morning feeling like death. I wondered how I could get out of this mess in one piece, but I didn't have an answer. Then I'd go back on the pills, but that wasn't much better: their side effect was to make me depressed.

I'd look blindly out of the hotel window, just feeling sad and numb. I'd often still be sleepy when I began playing a match, as I was in 1991 in Stockholm in the final against Edberg. I played the first set in my own private fog: 3–6. Then I won a great five-set victory. And afterwards? Instead of singing for joy, I felt deeply unhappy. Stockholm in autumn is dark and dreary – not the place for someone who's feeling out of sorts. Even the beautiful blondes with their blue eyes couldn't brighten up days as dark as these. At dawn, in spite of my triumphant victory against the former number one, I walked alone through the town in heavy rain, asking what on earth I'd got myself into – the chemicals were giving me a real attack of the blues.

Obviously I had to cut down the dosage before matches – at least I had to try. The result would be that I couldn't sleep at all. 'Everything finally dissolves itself in sleep, joy as well as pain,' mocked a verse of Goethe's *Prometheus* I'd learned at school. In my free time I managed to come right off the pills, but I was walking a tightrope. It was perfectly clear. If I overdid the pills, my career was in serious danger. But the longer you lean on a crutch, the more you come to rely on it. First one pill, then two. The impact tails off, so you up the dose.

I've had some bad nights, but I've always kept myself in one piece during the day – especially in public. I only went off the rails on my own in my room. My coaches never noticed anything. At ten p.m., after dinner, I'd start on the sleeping pills, followed by a couple of bottles of Heineken and then, to enhance the effect, a whisky. I'd read about the drugs they found in Elvis Presley's body after his death. His biographers talked about the game of 'Russian roulette' he played with drugs.[1] I never went that far, but during my worst period, from 1990 to 1991, I could wake up in the morning and not know where I was. On the day of my match against Miloslav Mečir in the 1990 Australian Open, I woke up from a deep sleep at ten in the morning – too early. I took another pill and dozed until three p.m. – fifteen hours of unbroken chemical fog. My match was scheduled for the evening, so I had a few hours left to pull myself together. Practice was scheduled for five. My head was clear, but my feet were still asleep – I could hardly lift them.

This carried on through the match. I lost the first sets 4–6, 6–7, still half asleep. I somehow managed to win the third. In the fourth I was all of a sudden wide-awake, and by eleven o'clock I'd taken it 6–1. By the fifth set I felt wonderful – again I won it 6–1. And that night? It might as well have been broad daylight. I finally fell asleep at eight o'clock in the morning. At twelve I went off again to practise. The pills were playing funny games with me, and we – the pills and I – lost the quarter-final to Mats Wilander, 4–6, 4–6, 2–6.

I almost overslept on the day of the Wimbledon final against Stefan Edberg that same year. I'd taken my pills the night before, but at four in the morning I was still awake. Practice was scheduled for eleven, so I had time for a chemical refill. At half ten I woke up dazed, as so often in the morning, but this time it was the morning of a Wimbledon final. I ran down into the front garden of the house I was staying in and jogged around. 'Free up your head, boy! Get those chemicals out of there!' I arrived too late for practice and began the game like a sleepwalker. 2–6, 2–6. Then at last, on the Centre Court at Wimbledon, I woke up. Good morning, Great Britain! I won the next two sets, but in the end I still lost everything, including any chance of sleep that night.

Bit by bit I swapped the chemicals for natural help. By the time my first son, Noah, was born, the nightmare was over. Because of him I had a wonderful reason to stay awake. I didn't want to escape into sleep any more. I didn't have to fight the loneliness that was tearing me apart. Noah set me free. Today I can sleep any time, anywhere: on a plane, during a red light – there's always time for a power nap. When I go to visit my family in Miami, I fall asleep when I board the plane in Frankfurt and wake up again in Miami. All I allow myself nowadays is a sip of Cloudy Bay, a wonderful wine from New Zealand, just for pure enjoyment – or to give a nice piece of fish something to swim in.

I've had to fight a few weird matches – those against myself. Nightmares, sleep disturbance, jet lag, weariness after long-haul flights – who hasn't experienced these things? In my case, the big blond who walked on to the courts, apparently ruler of all he surveyed, what bothered me most of all was claustrophobia. I couldn't bear the view from the window of an aeroplane on to clouds or snow-covered mountain peaks, so I always asked for the aisle seat. I hated feeling hemmed in.

I had to take a firm grip on myself not to lose it completely. It nearly happened once, after a concert by the three tenors Luciano Pavarotti, Plácido Domingo and José Carreras in the Munich Olympiahalle. Barbara and I met the singers back-stage after the event. We were going to a huge restaurant afterwards, where there'd be thousands of guests of honour. There were about ten of us in the stadium's lift: the conductor, the singers, wives and girlfriends. The lift got stuck. Not for a couple of minutes, but for half an hour. Thanks to my height I had space and air. Domingo, my wife and Pavarotti all held hands, hoping it would be over soon. Then Pavarotti began to hum 'Ave Maria'. I didn't say anything. I was just thinking of my own little unimportant life, and trying to hold myself together, though the thought of what would happen if no one rescued us soon almost drove me mad. The tenors sang one song after another, and everyone hummed along. Anxious arias – what a scene that was. Then there was a jolt – the rescue. The concert in the lift was over.

IN MONTE CARLO WITH TWO ROMANIANS

FROM THE BALCONY OF L'ESTORIL, TIRIAC'S HOME IN MONTE Carlo, you could spy on the young beach bunnies through the telescope he'd installed. Young women were very much to Tiriac's taste. Women over thirty had hit old age as far as he was concerned. Well, that was what he thought until he turned sixty, anyway.

It's a summer's afternoon. His sister serves us a pot of tea on a doily and leaves us alone. Tiriac wants to talk to me, as he often does when we're in Monte Carlo loosening off the tension of playing tournaments. A significant part of my life has taken place on this terrace – and it's not been the worst part, by any means. We talk about God, Germany and the whole world, Hitler, tennis mates and colleagues, caviar, children and – fascinating subject – his life in a communist country.

Ion is a child, and his father owns a little shop. Life in the Romanian town of Brasov, formerly Kronstadt, is bearable.

When the Soviet troops march in in 1944, his father is branded a capitalist because of the shop. He dies when Ion is just eleven and his sister is seven. Their nearly blind mother is 'incredibly strong'. Despite her limited education, she's a 'great reckoner', recounts Ion, and could do sums in her head 'faster than any machine'.

She must have passed on some of her characteristics to her son. And she was a strict woman. He sighs: 'God bless her. What a lady.' He says this in English; Tiriac and I mostly speak English to one another.

In the distance, a helicopter can be seen taking off from a luxury yacht. The pilot's probably being sent to Nice for caviar and champagne. Another yacht is heading for the harbour. The daily harbour fees for an eighty-metre yacht in Monaco during the summer season can be as much as a month's rent for a villa in Grünwald, a smart suburb of Munich. During the Formula 1 races, the prices double again. Ten years ago I chartered one of those yachts for fun. Just outside Monte Carlo we ran into a storm, and after four days the boat was a wreck. The sea was so rough that one of my friends ended up with a broken rib, another with a broken finger, and I spent the whole time hanging over the rails being sick. That was my last sea journey.

Ion is retreating into the past.

Inside the city walls of Kronstadt there are tennis courts. As soon as the temperature drops to −10 or −20°C, as often happens in winter, the children flood the tennis courts to create an ice rink. Sport is Ion's life, as it is for so many of his generation. The country is poor. In 1967, Nicolae Ceauşescu takes over leadership of the country and calls himself 'Conducator' – he's a megalo-maniac dictator. On 5 May 1955, four days before his sixteenth birthday, Ion picks up a tennis racket for the first time. Four years later he plays in the Davis Cup for Romania against New Zealand. Tennis lessons? Courses? All Tiriac does is to pick up the rich people's tennis balls in return for ten pennies a day and the occasional use of a racket.

'I was never a talent,' he says, 'but I trained hard, harder and harder still. I could have walked from Hamburg to Nice.'

He also plays table tennis, basketball, and skis in the nearby hills. Ion is selected for the Olympic ice-hockey team. Great. But he still has to work in the lorry factory where he's in charge of ball-bearings. As an untrained worker he earns around twenty-five marks a month.

Today he drives Ferraris, Mercedes and a Harley Davidson. He's got stacks of money, and I'm delighted for him.

In 1989, Ceauşescu was taken to a special military court and sentenced to death, then he and his wife Elena were shot. The scenes broadcast on television shocked me: the confused dictator, his distraught wife, 'due process' that was anything but, and an execution like in a bad Hollywood movie. Tiriac, who between 1980 and the uprising against the dictatorship had spent only four hours in his home country, returned to Bucharest. He bought up the third-largest bank, the second-largest insurance company and 19 per cent of the most popular television station, and now he's the official importer of Mercedes as well as 'Presidente' of the Comitetul Olimpic Român (the Romanian Olympic Committee). Ion has made it big since the end of our partnership. But it's not his ambition to go into politics. His friend Ilie Nastase, my former fellow competitor, stood in 1996 as a candidate for the Romanian parliament and for the office of mayor of Bucharest – and lost.

The trips to Sofia, Moscow and Leningrad as part of the ice-hockey team or to the French town of Vichy with the tennis team get Tiriac's commercial juices flowing. He leaves the country with five bottles of Cognac in his bags and returns with a camera. He exchanges this for ten pairs of tennis shoes, which he then swaps for thirty bottles of Cognac. Ion is particularly fascinated with America. His ice-hockey team is preparing for the Olympic Games on a frozen lake at a height of 2,000 metres above sea level, to which they have to walk on foot, but all their efforts are in vain. Bucharest cancels participation in the Games in the United States. This decision of his government's is the biggest tragedy of Tiriac's life.

One of the Tiriac family's neighbours in those years was one Günther Bosch, a tennis player, two years older than Tiriac and better off than him too, back then. Bosch was to become my coach, and my neighbour in Monte Carlo. Tiriac would get him to play chess with me every day as mental exercise, and to make sure I read a paper every day. Bosch had been working as a coach for the German tennis association and had pointed me out to Tiriac. When we talk about the past, Tiriac never tires of saying, 'I will always be grateful to Bosch for that.' And neither does Tiriac forget that Bosch encouraged my parents to enter into a contract with him.

Right out of a clear blue sky, as so often happened in Ion's experience under the communist regime, he's being called into the Davis Cup team against New Zealand. The factory worker wins the decisive point. Ion Tiriac becomes a national hero – at twenty.

At one point, however, Tiriac was banned for life by the state-ruled tennis association, because he didn't toe the line in the way the bureaucrats expected a member of the working class to. He never thought of fleeing the country, though. 'I was one of the privileged,' he said – at least in Romanian terms. At the university he was sent to, he was the first student able to afford a motorbike, and he followed this up with a red Skoda.

In 1964, Tiriac finally has his first encounter with America: his Romanian team loses to the Americans in the Winter Olympics in Innsbruck – 2–7. He will never touch an ice-hockey stick again. He's twenty-four years old, and wants to earn US dollars. In those days, a tennis player could earn a hundred dollars 'under the table' (as it was termed then) per tournament, if he was among the best.

In the 1968/9 season, Tiriac clocks up nineteen victories. After losing the final to the Australian Wimbledon champion Roy Emerson in Stuttgart, Ion buys his first Mercedes for $4,950 – a whole year's income. In Wimbledon he plays in the doubles on Centre Court, and as a singles player he once reaches the last sixteen.

'I tried everything, I gave of my very best,' he says. 'I just wasn't good enough.'

In 1968 he's still number eight in the world rankings, and together with Nastase, seven years his junior, one of the best doubles players in the world.

Even now, Tiriac regrets never having won the Davis Cup, despite having played forty-three matches for his country. 'I'd have liked to show the cup to my children and said, "Your father won this."'

Following a finals defeat in the Davis Cup against the USA, Ion Tiriac experiences one of the high points of his life: President Richard Nixon, enemy of communism, receives the Romanian team at the White House. Tiriac uses his own money to pay the tailor for the burgundy-coloured jackets the team wears, and pays his team's hotel bills from his own account. In the lobby of the White House, the US players are also waiting for the meeting with the president. Among them is the professional player Arthur Ashe, who won Wimbledon in 1975.

'Negrone,' says Nastase in jest ('Negrone' was the name Ilie always gave Arthur), 'what are you dressed like that for? Are you mad? They're going to chuck you out.' Ashe is wearing a sweatshirt and white tennis shorts. 'Richie is my friend,' says Ashe. Just then Nixon arrives and goes over to Ashe. 'Arthur, how's it going?' he says. 'Great, Richie, my man!' A strange land, this America. The Romanians, whose foreign minister has come over from a UN meeting in New York for this rare occasion, spend twenty minutes with the head of state, and ninety minutes with Nixon's adviser and keen sports fan Henry Kissinger, whom Ion meets again in 1998 at the football world cup in Paris.

In Tiriac's day, the professionals used to travel in groups: opponents on the court, but mates in the pizzeria. In the USA, team tennis is meant to attract the masses, and this is how Ion starts earning proper money. He plays with the Boston Lobsters. His fee for three months is $14,000.

This money had, according to Tiriac, been negotiated by his agent, the almighty Mark McCormack. Ion, however, wasn't content with his Lobster fee. He renegotiated a contract for himself and settled on $75,000. From this deal on, he knew he had a nose for business.

Tiriac is player, coach, manager and tournament organizer. For three years he plays doubles with Björn Borg, and he annoys the Americans, who have to play against him and Nastase in the Davis Cup in Bucharest. For US player Stan Smith, who took part in 1972, this was the first time he'd seen his opponents' family members on the court – as linesmen. The USA wins that year 3–2. Later on, Tiriac works with Nastase (who today lives in Bucharest), the Frenchman Henri Leconte and with Adriano Panatta, the sybaritic Italian. Ion splits up with Panatta after the French championships in Paris – because Panatta refuses to play during July and August, when he has holidays in Sardinia. 'You seem to have forgotten that Wimbledon is played in July and the US Open in August!' says Tiriac. 'No, no, I haven't. But life is for living,' says Panatta. 'Then off you go and live it,' says Tiriac, by way of goodbye.

Vilas, the Argentinian known as 'Gaucho' who stuck the cheques he won under his belt, was a different character. 'Never, ever,' said Tiriac, his dark eyes boring into me even more than usual, 'has there been a player prepared to work as hard as Vilas.' Tiriac had made it clear what he, as his coach and manager, expected from Vilas. 'You have to do what I say. And no answering back.' He also tried this with me, but he soon realized something: 'Becker listens and then he goes off and does what he likes.' But Vilas promised, 'If you tell me to dive into an empty swimming pool, I'll do it.' Before a US Open final against Connors, Tiriac had Vilas train for two and a half hours in the heat of New York. 'And then Vilas went on to wipe the floor with Connors,' Tiriac rejoiced. Together they founded a Dutch company, Tivi BV, who later signed me up. In 1985, Tiriac realized that Vilas was burned out, not least by the way he played. I remember the training I had with Vilas in Hamburg when Tiriac, before signing me up, wanted to see if I could stand the professional pace. I could.

After my first victory at Wimbledon, Tiriac and I spent four weeks in Monte Carlo doing hardly anything apart from talking out on his terrace. It was mostly about what I'd now have to face. Tiriac wanted to protect me, and that's what he did. If I'd been out for the night in Monte Carlo, the next day he'd know my every movement, even if I thought I'd been clever. My parents often spoke to him, since I was under his care, and that was a good thing. He also tried to talk me out of my interest in girls, but he knew me well enough to realize that if he banned me from doing something, I'd go ahead and do it anyway.

After we'd finished our talks on the terrace, Tiriac would show me the finer side of life: dover sole at the in-restaurant Rampoldi, with white burgundy to drink, candlelight, fine prints on the walls and diamonds in the décolletage of the women, who were both real ladies and the paid-for variety. Jimmy'z, the top disco, was three minutes away by car.

Dancing until dawn, drunk on rhythm rather than booze. Then to Tip Top for breakfast and to wind down again. I had to avoid bumping into Bosch in the lift, though – I could do without his reproachful looks.

I spent only a few months of the year in Monte Carlo. The rest of the time I was travelling. When I finally got a break it was usually in November and December, and these winter months can be long and dreary in the Mediterranean. The tourist season is over, the young people are gone, and then it can feel pretty lonely. At night I'd occasionally take my Porsche 959 or my Carrera Turbo out on the motorway. As a teenager I drove incredibly fast all over the place: not just on the motorway, but in town as well. I'm actually quite fearful by nature. Driving in Formula 1 would never be my kind of thing. I got my first driving licence in California when I was sixteen, and my second one in Nice, driving through those narrow streets and along the Promenade des Anglais parallel to the coast. The lessons and test were in French, but I passed first time. With my friend Patrik as passenger, I took the 959 on to the motorway to see how fast it would go. We managed 326 kilometres per hour. The road was three lanes wide but at this speed felt like a narrow woodland path. It was intoxicating.

It was at Jimmy'z, not far from the terrace where Tiriac delivered his strictures, that I saw Bénédicte for the first time. Tiriac was with me. I nudged him and said, 'Look at her. She's gorgeous!'

'She's not for you,' said Ion, without even turning round. He was always trying to keep women out of my life. 'She's already taken.'

Bosch, who was happily married, was also against my

having anything to do with women, but for different reasons. He wanted to be 'married' to me, and any woman who entered my life was a threat to him. Tiriac was convinced that a woman would get in the way of my tennis; Bosch was convinced that a woman would get in the way of him.

Of course I talked to Bénédicte, and danced with her too, but after that I was on my own again. And so I wandered, as I so often did, down to the group of rocks at the end of Monte Carlo's Larvotto beach. In those years after the first Wimbledon successes, I kept asking myself: What's the point of all this? Where is this taking me? Even then I dreamt of having a family – of having a house and a garden for my children. I saw all the affluence around me and knew it wasn't how I wanted to live. Monte Carlo was a stage set for a theatre play.

A few days after my first encounter with Bénédicte, I saw her again at the dentist. She was wearing sunglasses and her hair was done up differently, and she spoke to me. I was embarrassed because I hadn't recognized her at first. That was the start of a relationship that lasted two years. Bénédicte had been to school with Princess Stéphanie of Monaco. They were still friends and Bénédicte used to visit her at the palace. All the same, she was quite grounded. She showed me the Monte Carlo only the Monégasques knew. I'm still on good terms with her parents, who live not far from the palace. A steep staircase off a narrow street leads to their top-floor apartment. Their daughter married another man.

My relationship with Bénédicte wasn't a superficial celebrity affair. It was a real, happy partnership. Tiriac was convinced that we'd get married within two or three years. I won't get married before I'm twenty-five, I said. So we had a bet, the winner to get the car of his choice. I won. Tiriac tried to offer me one of his many Ferraris, but I chose a Mercedes Cabriolet, 1969 – and one year later, I married Barbara.

As long as I lived in Monte Carlo, I didn't have to justify to myself or anyone else the Porsche I drove at the age of eighteen, the latest watch, or the designer clothes and shoes I wore. The other youngsters in Monte Carlo all had the same things. The difference was that I'd earned the money to buy them myself, whereas they'd got theirs from their rich parents. But I didn't ask questions, and neither did they. And when I moved to Monte Carlo at sixteen it wasn't to save tax. When Tiriac suggested I move to the Mediterranean, Wimbledon was still just a dream. What I wanted from Monte Carlo was a little bit of independence, and the opportunity to focus on my training and to jog along the beach. Monte Carlo was my refuge. Before 1985, Boris Becker was a nobody. I lived in a small flat in the Château d'Azur. My mother had to sign the lease because I was under age. There was no sea view and no luxury fittings. I'd have a pizza at Le Baobab on the beach or a Coke at Norok, the bar that was run by Björn Borg's first wife Mariana, a Romanian former tennis player.

When I got my first advertising deals, I didn't care much for the millions. Only a year earlier I'd had to ask my mother for pocket money: five marks to go to see a film. Tiriac discussed these deals with my parents, who'd never seen so much money before. Figures are abstract things: the more money you earn, the more you lose a sense of its value. You get used to eating caviar, and at some point it begins to taste as ordinary as anything else. And I didn't need to show off, either. If there's one expensive thing that appeals to me, it's property.

I spent most of the time in my flat in Monte Carlo sleeping. The rest of my time was spent on Tiriac's terrace. But Monaco was not just for leisure. I had two Romanians breathing down my neck, who in their own youth had seen hard times and had experiences that made them chase me all the harder across the court. That's how it looked to me, anyway. Two or three hours in the morning, and again in the afternoon. Lunch at Tiriac's place or in the Monte Carlo Country Club. With each successful year I could afford a nicer place, further up, with a better view of the sea and sunsets. I moved five times: Casa Bianca, San Juan, Le Trocadéro.

The freedom that Monaco had to offer me then I still enjoy today. There's nothing wrong with driving a Porsche Cabriolet around here, or even – should I feel like buying one – an orange Lamborghini. Envy doesn't exist here. I don't have to worry about whether paparazzi might be able to get a shot of me at the roulette table in the casino. And no matter how much you lose, the croupiers stay as undemonstrative as coffin-bearers, and just as pale – I don't think they are allowed to have any contact with sunlight. They recognize me, say 'rien ne va plus' and remain silent. I'm not like Dostoevsky, who wrote in *The Gambler*, 'A real gentleman should not show excitement even if he loses his whole fortune.'[1] I only ever took small sums with me to the casino – five hundred francs – and if it was lost, well, never mind.

Not a word would appear in the press about my visits to the bar of the venerable Hôtel de Paris, nor about how many whisky sours I drank there. Boris Becker was just one of 26,000 foreigners who had a resident's permit for Monte Carlo. He didn't have a private income, but was a tennis player. And keeping company with local celebrities was easy enough. I didn't address Prince Albert as 'Your Excellency', I knew him from early on as Albert. Sometimes I hit a few balls with him after training. He's a good guy.

After each catastrophe, each disappointment with a woman, after the defeat at Wimbledon in the second round in 1987, or my hand injury in 1996, or whenever I just didn't want to be disturbed, I would disappear to Monte Carlo. After I met Karen Schultz at the International Championships at the Hamburg Rothenbaum, I invited her to Monte Carlo. But I couldn't prevent the press from doing their job: taking pictures of Becker kissing a woman, or of his naked torso.

In spite of such intrusions, I've had wonderful times in Monte Carlo. When I was with Bénédicte I lived at the top of the Rock at Number 3, Place du Palais. I had the top floor of a pink villa, right next door to the prince, with wooden windows and flower boxes and a view of the palace and the sea. This part of Monaco doesn't have modern buildings, only pink, yellow and sky-blue villas, cobbled streets and exotic gardens with cactuses, agave and palm trees – a beautiful spot.

The landlord of the Pinocchio would often set the table for me in front of the small fountain two steps away from his restaurant, where the walls were decorated with pictures of celebrities. He told me last time I was there that one of my portraits had been stolen. Whether the thief was an enemy or a fan I don't know. It's a village atmosphere: the policemen say hello, the paper-seller hands me the *Nice Matin* every morning. I drink my espresso 'avec un petit peu de lait, s'il-vous-plait'. Yes, I've improved my French dramatically! C'est vrai. In English I can tell jokes and read between the lines, but in French the language is still a barrier, which makes it difficult to socialize.

At the main entrance of the Monte Carlo Country Club, my name is engraved in grey stone with the date: 1984. So does this mean I did win on clay? Yes! But only at a youth tournament. In 1985 I was eliminated in the second round, and in 1987 and 1988 in the first round. In 1995 I led against Thomas Muster in the final, two sets to love, 6–4, 7–5, and had two match points in the fourth set. I lost. Heaven knows why in all my years as a professional player I never managed to win on clay. That defeat gave me physical pain: I was desperate. It was probably the toughest defeat of my career. I was a failure in my own eyes and in the eyes of my Monégasque friends. Perhaps it was a sign from above that I had my limits. A victory might have made me lose my humility completely.

In 1988, Bénédicte and I decided to break up. Things between us were no longer going well. Our last conversation in the flat was pragmatic. As I closed the door behind her, I heard Bryan Ferry's 'Slave to Love' on the radio. Was it a sign? Was this to be my fate?

It was after such unhappy events that I would sit with Ion Tiriac on his terrace and listen to his life story.

ION TIRIAC: A BITTER AFTERTASTE

Ion Tiriac played a decisive role in my life as a tennis professional. In his personal contribution to this book, he describes an extraordinary relationship.

HE'S A GERMAN, A 'KRAUT'. BORIS BECKER WILL BE GERMAN until the day he dies – and why not? I've lived in Monte Carlo for thirty years, and I'm still Romanian. Boris is a very sensitive man, and much more introverted than people realize. He's not shy, but he's quite touchy and unforgiving. I've made mistakes, quite a few. So has he. The difference is that he doesn't acknowledge them. Or maybe he does, but he won't let on.

Boris Becker had priority in my life. He was more important to me than my own family, even my own son. In 1984, when I signed him up, I didn't know if he'd ever earn a single penny. He was sixteen, and I was taking a risk. I wanted to build him up and guide him. We almost achieved our goal, but he didn't realize his full potential. He should have won three times as much as he did, he should have won more than Borg. The Swede was an idol for the young Boris. Borg had incredible footwork: he could run, he saw the ball early, and he was able to return it from any position. But that was it. He was the simplest of players. Boris can't be compared to Connors, either. Connors was like Michael Jordan, ready to bulldoze anyone who got in his way. On the court, neither of them saw father or mother, friend or foe. All they were looking for was success. Becker was more sentimental, more humane. He let his feelings run free.

McEnroe was more talented than Becker. He didn't have the same power, but he played like a chess master. McEnroe had the brain, Boris had the instinct. Mac programmed his moves and Boris played naturally. Sampras is also more technical than Boris, as Americans tend to be. Less emotional than Becker. Becker may have been born in Germany, his parents are Germans, but somehow his ancestors must have their roots in Italy, France or the Balkans. Where else could these emotions come from? We've had a great many arguments. Here's one.

Him: 'I'm only training for forty minutes.'

Me: 'You have to train for at least three hours.'

Him: 'Then I'll have no strength left tomorrow.'

Me: 'If you train now it will be easier during the match.'

He trained for forty minutes, played for five hours, and won.

Him: 'You see, I was right.'

Or the final against Connors in Queens. I advised him, 'Play serve and volley. Get to the net as often as you can.'

Him: 'I'm going to beat him from the baseline.'

This was one of Connors' strengths. Boris played from the baseline – and won.

Him: 'So, who was right then? From the baseline, Ion, from the baseline! Did you see it?'

Autumn 1984 in South Africa. I got there just in time for the last of the qualification rounds. Boris was in the third set, and lost. Why? Sunstroke. I said, 'You've been away from home for seven weeks now. Do you want to carry on to Australia?'

Him: 'I could stay away for seven years and still never win anything. Shit, shit, shit!'

Me: 'Bosch told me how hard you've been training, so there's no problem there. I'll stay another week and we can train here together.'

While I was training with Vilas, I could hear the cries from the other court. 'Shit, shit, shit!' Three hours of 'Shit!' Boris was carrying on training in spite of sunstroke, and so I made him an offer. 'If you like, I can put it in writing that with this kind of effort you'll be among the top fifteen in two years' time.' Bosch and Becker travelled to Australia and Becker reached the quarter-finals. I visited my friends Elvira and Karl-Heinz Becker in Leimen and announced to them, 'Your son is on the right track. He's made the breakthrough.'

I got Harry Hopman, one of the greatest coaches of our time, to advise me on how Boris's grass serve could be further improved, then I explained to Boris what the Australian had told me. His reply? 'I've got the best serve in the world. What do I want to change it for?' But he was always asking questions, wanting the answers to everything. He was curious, and dogged with it. Two hours later, Bosch came over saying, 'You won't believe it. Boris is on the court at the far end practising his serve.' And how many times did I advise him not to aim for the line at break point but to let his opponent play the ball? 'No,' he said. 'I like being close to the edge. I can handle it.'

In Portugal he once played exhibition. Since the Portuguese are not a big tennis nation, he had to play three sets against three different opponents. As early as the first set, he complained, 'I'm just wasting my time here. What kind of players are these?'

'Shut up and play!' I shouted at him. 'It's good practice and it's good money.'

And then he lost one of his sets. The next day he told me, 'I've got an injury.'

'Don't give me any of your fairy tales.'

'No, really, I can't play any more.'

I didn't believe a word of it, but I had to write my fee off. And of course it caused bad feeling between us. I felt as if he kept wanting to shock me and challenge me to see how far he could go. He wanted to wind the whole world up. He went by gut feeling. But when he caused trouble, he dealt with the fall-out. His father, whom he often nicknamed the Dictator, confided in me, 'The more I try to force him to do something, the more he rebels.'

If Becker was depressed, I reminded him, 'This is the other side of the coin. If you want to quit, then do it. You can tell yourself, "I've had four or five great years, I've made loads of money, and I won't have to work ever again. Now I'm doing something else." It's not too late. You can go back to Leimen and enrol in university. You're a grown-up and it's your decision.'

Sometimes he overdid the self-pity: 'My whole youth is gone. I've got no friends. I don't lead a normal life.'

'So,' I asked him, 'what is a normal life? Who lives it? For a normal person, the chance to lead your sort of life is non-existent.'

'Yes, but there are so many injustices in the world. Racism, for example – that's really awful.'

Becker did, at least during my time, donate a lot of money to charity: discreetly and anonymously. I told him back then, 'If you worry about the run-down suburbs of Hamburg, and you want to do some good in the world, then come to Bucharest with me. There are a million slums. I was born in one. You can't tell me anything.'

I challenged him and drove him on. I knew that if I didn't control him, he'd break out. At the Davis Cup final in Sweden in 1988 he told me, 'Ion, I've grown out of all of this. I want a normal life.' Steeb had just beaten Wilander 8–10, 1–6, 6–2, 6–4, 8–6, and Becker had beaten Edberg 6–3, 6–1, 6–4. Eric Jelen hit his racket against the wall in the shower, annoyed about a net call. I had to be both friend and therapist at times like this.

If there was something Becker didn't want to do, he simply said so. There were times when he wanted to play all in white and free of logos. I was always having to remind him that a professional sportsman earned no more than 15 or 20 per cent on the court; the rest came through commercial work, and sponsors wanted publicity in return for their money. At times Becker resisted and that led to arguments. 'If you don't want these contracts any more then we won't take on any more, but you still have to fulfil the existing ones.' Ford, for example, once complained to me because Boris, who had a contract with them, had been photographed in a Porsche. I talked to Becker about it, and he understood.

Boris was going to be known the world over, not just in Germany – that was my strategy. That's why he had to get into the *New York Times*, on Japanese television and on to the covers of Italian magazines. During a tournament on the east coast of America, I arranged for Boris to appear on Johnny Carson's talk show in Los Angeles. In the 1980s, Carson was *the* star and I wanted to develop Boris Becker into a global celebrity. The long flight to LA became the subject of another argument, so we flew in a private jet. The journey from east to west and back again was an added burden on him, but he still won the tournament, and on top of that the affection of the American people. For my sixtieth birthday Boris gave me a print: Bosch, him and me in that private jet.

Naturally, we also argued about women. I was against his relationship with Bénédicte, although she accepted his travelling and respected his work. I didn't want him to get distracted. He could still have fun with girls during his few days' break. Of course, Boris got his way – and he still won Wimbledon.

I will never forget those ten years with Boris Becker. They were an important part of my life. No one can take them away from me. I was probably one of the very few who wasn't dependent on Boris. I had an existence before Boris Becker came along, and I have an existence without him today. I stayed loyal even when Pete Sampras tried to lure me to America to become his manager. I wanted to continue working with Boris and not let him down. We were contractually bound. On a flight from Helsinki to Munich on his twenty-fourth birthday, he had signed the renewal of our contract. This must have slipped his mind when he announced our separation. Several months before the break-up we discussed the terms of an amicable 'divorce' in the presence of his father, but without any resolution.

Boris and I had started to drift apart. We often had differences of opinion, about commitment to sponsors or his training sessions. We argued more and more and saw each other less and less. It was obvious that Boris wanted his freedom, that he needed distance from me. He saw himself as strong enough to go his own way alone.

Maybe I'm an egotist, but I believe I did a good job with him. The way we broke up, though, will always leave me with a bitter aftertaste. I don't like it when people forget where they come from and who helped them, through belief and commitment, to get where they are. We'd met 'for a chat'. I hadn't a clue what was coming. Boris said to my face, 'Ion, everything that I have achieved is also thanks to you. I can't say that often enough. But the time has come for us to split up.'

The man I'd spent the last decade going round the world with wanted to put out a press release in the next thirty minutes. 'Here are the papers. Sign here.'

'Shouldn't we have a beer first and talk this over?' I suggested.

But no. 'The deal is done,' said Becker in English.

I think he put me in a taxi then. The lawyers did the rest, and we didn't see each other again until much later, at the funeral of his father, who'd been my friend. Nowadays we sometimes see each other in Vienna, Munich, London, and we're talking again. 'Do you remember the good old days . . .'

NEVER CHANGE A WINNING SHIRT

THE GUESTS HAD BEEN ASKED TO WEAR BLACK TIE. 'PRIVATE dinner with Boris Becker,' it said in blue lettering on white card. In the Salle Empire of the Hôtel de Paris in Monte Carlo, Giovanni Caberlotto, the president of Lotto, an Italian clothing empire and my new outfitters, said the hopeful words, 'As of now our turnover is three hundred million dollars. Our target is one billion.' He looked across to my table, where I was sitting with Barbara, and said almost pleadingly, 'And you, Boris, are going to help us, aren't you?'

'Of course,' I replied.

Lotto was a small company compared to Adidas, Reebok or Nike. Lotto had a contract with AC Milan, and now with me too.

The dinner was meant to mark the start of a prosperous venture. We toasted with a white Blason Timberlay 1990, and my new business partner served a Château Cap du Moulin 1985 to drink alongside the *risotto à l'italienne* and the *jambonette de volaille braisée à blanc.* Fine stuff, but I held back, because a little later that day – 18 April 1993 – I'd be playing my first match in the new outfit – on clay. The new Lotto shoes hadn't been worn in yet. My right foot is wider than the left, and my left foot bigger than the right, and while these differences are small, I do need shoes to fit perfectly. Paolo Pastrin, who was in charge of shoes at the company, had travelled to Monaco from the Lotto headquarters in Montebelluna to take my measurements.

After the match against Swiss Marc Rosset, I got Tiriac's voice on my answering machine. Lotto were concerned because I had allegedly made a complaint about my new Lotto shirt during the match, which had got picked up by the radio and television microphones. It was quite possible – someone, or something, had to be blamed for my defeat (6–7, 3–6). I kept playing in the Lotto outfit until my last Wimbledon, although I was no longer contractually obliged to. I could have made my dream come true and played for once all in white, but I wanted to demonstrate my loyalty to Lotto. To this day I still play in Lotto shoes. And superstition also had a part to play: Lotto was part of my tennis life, and you never change a winning shirt.

When I was just ten years old, I had a contract with the Italian company Ellesse – I didn't get paid but the clothing was free. I played with Adidas rackets, and whenever I destroyed a batch of them I'd tell my sponsor the materials had given way under the pressure of my forehand, which was not entirely untrue. The first logo that was stitched to my shirt had been negotiated by Tiriac even before my first Wimbledon, and that was for BASF, a German pharmaceutical and chemicals company. They paid thousands of marks – in return for which relatively small sum they got worldwide advertising, thanks to my 1985 Wimbledon victory. In my seven Wimbledon finals I used two brands of racket, Puma and Estusa, whose frames were almost identical.

If all I'd wanted was money then I could have quit tennis after my first Wimbledon victory in 1985. The fees from my advertising contracts would have lasted me for life, even though the sponsors then still had slight reservations: was that little Becker really world class, or a one-day wonder? McEnroe, Connors, Lendl, Edberg, Mecir and Noah were still around at Wimbledon in 1985, and Becker was not even seeded. I had to win for a second time to really get the money rolling.

Victory in 1985 opened the door; victory in 1986 opened the floodgates.

During my match against Pernfors I was fined a thousand dollars for being in breach of paragraph VD3a. The charge: 'During warm-up Mr Becker wore a tracksuit top on which an oversized logo could be seen. He played in two shirts displaying oversized logos (Coca-Cola).'

The more contracts I entered into – Mercedes, Deutsche Bank, Faber, Puma, Tag Heuer, Ebel, Coca-Cola, Philips, Fila, Diadora, Ford, Müllermilch, BASF, Ellesse, Seiko, Polaroid, Ferrero (Nutella) were all among my sponsors – the shorter my time off became. I got richer and more tired, more independent and less free all at the same time. Each sponsor expected five to ten days' commitment a year in return for their money: PR events; appearances, such as in 1998 at a Nürnberg department store for Lotto; adverts for Mercedes;

and, for AOL, either Becker with Formula 1 world champion Mika Häkkinen at the computer, or me on my own.

Nike made me an offer of $105 million plus share options for a seven-year contract. Altogether the deal would have been worth $300 million dollars, but I already had a contract with Fila, one of Nike's competitors. Tiriac tried to buy me out of the contract with the Italians, and failed, but they did increase the value of our contract. BMW wanted to name a convertible 'BB' after me. Their offer was below my market value, so the deal didn't come off. With hindsight, that was lucky, otherwise my partnership with Mercedes, designed to last beyond my career, would never have come about.

In 1987 my defeat in the second round of Wimbledon brought me some welcome relief from the endless round of high expectations and relentless money-making. Tiriac often lamented that I could have become a multi-multi-multi-millionaire, and to this day he doesn't understand why I didn't accept more contracts, like Björn Borg, who had about fifty contracts, or like Michael Schumacher does today. Ion is clearly right. I could have earned far more. And had I known back then how much life after tennis would cost me, perhaps I would have accepted a few more . . .

In a leading article in the magazine *Fortune* from June 1998, entitled 'The Jordan Effect',[1] I read about the influence Michael Jordan, the basketball phenomenon, has had on his nation's economy. The increase in spectator numbers for his then team, the Chicago Bulls, viewing figures, television rights, licence fees, sales of the Air Jordan shoes developed by Nike, adverts for McDonald's, Gatorade, Coke and Wheaties. The total: about ten billion dollars – all down to him. Admittedly, Jordan was an exception. His club paid him $34 million a year. This may seem excessive, even obscene, but what if you set it against a turnover of $10 billion?

Some smart-arses in Germany liked to ask how Boris Becker could justify the 2.6 million marks the German tennis association (the DTB) paid him for the five years up to the end of 1999. The question that should be asked is this: would the DTB still have earned 125 million marks for the television rights to the Davis Cup and the German tournaments if Steffi Graf and I hadn't given rise to Germany's tennis craze? A significant part of those payments was transferred to the regional associations, where some of my fiercest critics were. I gained my financial independence through tennis, not through speculation on the stock market or property deals. I had to run and fight for every dollar. Have I been paid by all those businessmen who profited from me – the manufacturers of tennis clothing, the magazines which increased their circulation thanks to my picture on the front cover, the people who built indoor tennis courts and made balls and rackets? During the first half of 1985, Puma, my racket-maker, sold 7,000 rackets; after my first Wimbledon victory this number increased to 63,000, and after my second win in 1986 the number reached around 300,000. In 1985, German television broadcast a mere ninety-five hours of tennis; in 1994 it was 2,150. When you look at it this way, I've only been given a fraction of what I was entitled to. But when you look back at the development of sport, and tennis in particular, I can only say that I was in the right place at the right time. The pioneers of our sport didn't see a penny, and the early professionals only got small change. In the current market, the screws seem to be being tightened again, and perhaps it's about time.

Wimbledon was and is the tennis Mecca, a place of worship

for a game that developed in the courtyards of castles and palaces and was first known as *jeu de paume*, because the rackets were roughly the shape of the palm of the hand. The British who wintered on the Côte d'Azur at the end of the nineteenth century and promenaded on the beach at Deauville took their sport to the continent. Men like Frenchmen Jean Borotra, Henri Crochet and René Lacoste, the Americans Bill Tilden and Donald Budge, the Briton Fred Perry, the German Gottfried von Cramm and his fellow countryman Henner Henkel dominated the tennis scene in the following decades, during which time the game slowly evolved and left its traditions behind. The introduction of the tie-break, which allowed the shortening of the sets, is one of the few basic reforms of the game that dates from this time.

Long tennis trousers and white shirts were part of the dress code at Wimbledon until 1933. Those were different, perhaps more elegant times. The gentlemen's final in 1925 between Lacoste and Borotra was moved to a Monday so the gentlemen could recover from their matches in the doubles and mixed doubles. In spite of the game's amateur status, quite a few players from that era managed to turn the public's fascination with their sport into money. Lacoste, nicknamed the Crocodile, ended up marketing tennis clothing which is still available today, its logo the animal he was named after. A laurel wreath still decorates the shirts of Fred Perry.

Between 1931 and 1963, a dozen Wimbledon winners turned their hobby into a profession, years before the international associations decided to admit professionals as well as amateurs to their tournaments, later designated 'open'. Amateurs like Australians John Newcombe, Ken Rosewall, Rod Laver, Lew Hoad and Tony Roche, the Spaniard Manuel

Santana, the Italian Panatta, Tiriac, Nastase and the German Wilhelm Bungert (who reached the final in 1967 and lost to Newcombe 6–3, 6–1, 6–1) got a few hundred dollars 'appearance money', which they often declared as expenses. The players travelled together from tournament to tournament, and in the years of amateur tennis three or four of them shared a room and occasionally their girlfriends too. They lived according to the philosophy let's-have-a-party-tonight-and-think-about-the-tournament-tomorrow.

Tiriac told me that on the eve of a match in London, he'd often go on a drinking tour with his next day's opponent. He was such a regular at the Ponte Vecchio that he seriously thought about buying the place. Now someone else has taken it over, and the Italian has gone. The walls were decorated with portraits of the players who had made tennis history. Alejandro Olmedo, for example, the Peruvian who won Wimbledon in 1959 – the Chief, they called him, because of his noble Indian bearing and his jet-black hair. He would move along the net like a panther and make headlong dives for balls that seemed unreachable. Today he's a tennis instructor at the Beverly Hills Hotel in Los Angeles, and keeps in his office a black and white photo of the Duchess of Kent handing him the cup. During my last Wimbledon tournament, he was guest of honour in the royal box.

My friend the music producer Berry Gordy keeps a photo on the piano in his living room that shows me in my tennis gear. I'm always touched, and also a little embarrassed, when I see the silver-framed picture. What have I done to deserve being exhibited so proudly? Berry's mad about tennis. He has a tennis court in the grounds of his villa, only a few kilometres away from where Olmedo teaches. I've practised there a few times, away from the fuss that accompanies a tournament. The gardeners switched off their lawnmowers, stood at the fence and silently watched me at work.

Tennis is no longer an elitist sport. People of all social classes, anywhere in the world, can enjoy and appreciate it. Even the Pope once told his fellow countryman Wojtek Fibak how much he'd like to practise for an hour with him – that was in the days when the Pope still went skiing. When John McEnroe bought a beach house in Malibu from Johnny Carson, the talk-show host asked for a premium on the selling price – three practice hours with McEnroe. Tennis also brought luck to Arnold Schwarzenegger. The Austrian-born actor met his wife Maria Shriver at a charity tournament. Nowadays he tends to play tennis on his private court in California's Pacific Palisades with Ralf Moeller, a former Mr Universe, like Schwarzenegger himself.

In August 1967, eight professionals played for the first time on Centre Court at Wimbledon, in a tournament financed by the BBC in celebration of the introduction of colour television. Herman David, chairman of the All England Lawn Tennis and Croquet Club, guardians of the traditions at Wimbledon, realized that the movement towards professional tennis could no longer be stopped. He called for professionals to be allowed to take part in the tournament, and for Wimbledon to become an open. Four months after the first colour-television broadcast, the British Lawn Tennis Association decided to keep up with the times. Then in March 1968 the International Lawn Tennis Federation stopped struggling against the tide, and for the first time professionals played officially at Wimbledon.

The amateurs, who weren't really amateurs any more, were

relieved. They no longer risked bans for illegal payments and were now allowed to organize themselves, for example, into the Association of Tennis Professionals – the ATP – whose early heads were Arthur Ashe, Stan Smith and the Yugoslav Niki Pilic. Thanks to Pilic – who later became my coach for a while and who also led the German Davis Cup team – the professionals and the International Lawn Tennis Federation almost came to blows only a few days before Wimbledon 1973. Pilic had refused to play for his country in the Davis Cup against New Zealand because, he said, of his professional commitments. The head of the Yugoslav association, an uncle of Pilic's wife, demanded his ban, which the international association duly imposed – at first for nine months, then reduced to four weeks. Pilic, according to the tennis writer Richard Evans, was 'far from being the most popular player on the tour. He exuded a superior air of self-confidence which rivalled that of Charles de Gaulle.'[2] But he gathered support from his fellow players: seventy-nine of them decided to boycott Wimbledon if the ban wasn't lifted. Their argument was that the ATP, not the national associations, represented the interests of the professionals. Niki was prepared to accept the ban and not play Wimbledon, but the ATP insisted on defending their position. It was a remarkable tournament that year. The Czech Jan Kodes, who before the boycott was seeded fifteen and after it moved up to number two, won the final against the Russian Alexander Metreveli, formerly number thirteen, subsequently number four.

After this boycott, everything changed. The ATP had shown the officials where their limits were. The players in white shorts became more powerful – and richer. In 1968, tennis's first officially professional year, thirty-one tournaments declared themselves 'open'. The Australian Tony Roche, who two decades later became Lendl's manager and friend, cashed in the most money that year: $63,504 – today's stars get that much for a single autograph event in a department store.

I didn't go into tennis for the big money. My parents, too, had other values. The most important question my mother would always ask was, 'Son, are you well?' Her most frequent observation was, 'You look so thin and pale! Is anything the matter?' That can't be said of all parents of future tennis stars. Some of them tolerate their children being tortured on a tennis court as if they were in boot camp. For many years the ILTF prevented players under sixteen from burning themselves out at professional tennis tournaments, but by 1974 the pressure from the International Management Group had become too great. Agents lured young players with fat contracts and negotiated directly with the parents.

The eighty-eight junior tournaments that were played in my first Wimbledon year had 3,772 participants – 3,772 talents and just as many hopes. The result wasn't friendship, but war. What the players are fighting for in the qualifying rounds before the Grand Slam tournaments, whether in Wimbledon or Paris, is a future. The golden years have to start here and now. They arrive with their backpacks, sports bags or suitcases they can't shut because the locks have long gone, broke but carefree and confident. Just like me in 1984, or McEnroe when he fought his way through the qualifying rounds into the semi-final in 1977. In 1984 I didn't, of course, travel by limousine. I took the underground to Barnes and then went by taxi to Roehampton. You mustn't think that the 'qualies' are played at Wimbledon itself – they take place on the grass courts of the sports club of the Bank of England, which during my time resembled football pitches, with humps and potholes, long grass here and short grass there. The lawn is not manicured and used for only two weeks a year, like that of Centre Court.

With me in the qualifying rounds in 1984 were Guy Forget, who went on to become the best player of his time in France, and Kenneth Flach, who was one of the best doubles players in the world in the 1990s. We were united by our dream to conquer the Everest of the tennis world: Wimbledon. For some young talents the qualifying round is the main event, whichever tournament it is. It's the first reach for glory and money, provided they have the nerve to withstand the pressure and the resilience to overcome defeat. How easy it all seems when you hear of million-dollar contracts, dinners in Monaco with sponsors like Lotto, trips in private jets, bowing before the queen. What comes before that is an incredible amount of hard work. 'Man isn't born with fortune,' wrote Dostoevsky, one of my favourite authors. 'Man earns his fortune through suffering.' And it's the same in life *after* professional tennis, too.

Four weeks after I hit the ball on Centre Court at Wimbledon for the last time, I announced that together with the business-man Hans-Dieter Cleven I had founded Völkl Tennis GmbH. 'Becker's turned businessman' was the tenor of the media response. That made me laugh – what had I been for the past fifteen years if not a businessman? Some kind of pure sports entity who was only after glory? The sport had always been in the foreground, but nevertheless I'd been in com-merce since I was sixteen. While my contemporaries went on to do an apprenticeship at the bank or the post office, I was thrown into big business. Professional sports players are entrepreneurs without the back-up of a going concern. Whether in a Formula 1 car, in the boxing ring, on the ski jump or on the tennis court, the sports player is determining the future of his business. Of course, you have advisers and support staff, but once you're out there, you're on your own. Your performance defines the level of your fee and the value of your next advertising contract.

I absorbed discipline and professionalism from childhood. The matches on Centre Court at Wimbledon start at two p.m. and it won't do if you show up at three, and you can't go into a match without preparation. I had to train, I had to have a strategy, I had to have a goal, and I had to know what I wanted to achieve and have the strength, determination and self-belief to get it. Sport is like business. In the end it's the big points that count.

As a sports professional you have to learn to be decisive, to deal with pressure and to find quick solutions to problems. The payroll is long: manager, coach, physiotherapists, lawyers and – above all – tax consultants. The top people in sport, those who achieve extraordinary results, have minds of their own and are not other people's puppets. They are the centre around which everything else revolves. I believe that Michael Schumacher is critical to the Ferrari team, rather than the other way round. Michael Jordan and Tiger Woods are personalities who define their surroundings and impose their philosophy on others.

Sport is simple, clear, direct, honest. Win or lose, the result is there for everyone to see. Business, on other hand, is much more complex and influenced by many more factors. A deal can be perfect, it can be beneficial for everyone involved, but it still might not happen because people hinder it out of political or strategic interests.

During the last years of my tennis career there were already signs that I wanted to stand on my own two feet more. It started with the split from Tiriac. Ion was part of my past, which I needed to leave behind. My subsequent collaboration with Axel Meyer-Wölden was more like an equal partnership. I'd sit down with him and discuss things such as: Where will I go in the future? What are my strengths and weaknesses? What do I feel comfortable doing? What am I good at? When Axel died in the summer of 1997, I became the head of the Boris Becker enterprise. By the autumn I'd started making preparations for my own marketing company. In July 1998 BBM – Boris Becker Marketing – was established in Munich.

At that time I was still playing tennis, but in business I was already 'hands on', as you say in English. I didn't just want to take the big decisions; I wanted to be involved in the decision-making process all the way along the line. The 'Becker' brand continued to run smoothly through BBM, but we didn't have much success with our new projects. In Germany we say that it's a fish's head that stinks, so when I looked for somewhere to lay the blame it had to be on myself.

I was impatient, trying to transfer the mechanisms of sport to business. In my previous career, a single well-hit ball could get a result, but now a number of meetings, concepts and presentations were called for. For the first time I really depended on other people, and I didn't always back the right horse. In this respect I'm very un-German. I tend to believe what people tell me. You might say this is naïve. I put my faith in people who promised me the stars from the sky above, and they couldn't deliver. I was new to the business and didn't always understand how it worked behind the scenes, so I wasn't cautious enough when it came to selecting either people or projects.

And my personal situation added to these difficulties. At the height of my marriage problems, I often couldn't stand it at home and fled to the office, where I threw myself blindly into all kinds of activities: a business lunch here, an interesting presentation there – I wanted to do all of it, all at the same time. A website, an organic food company, a telephone business – all exciting ideas. By the time I finally realized that the people in key positions were more interested in being associated with the name Becker than in doing a good job, most of the projects had already sunk. At that point, the people responsible were happy to hide behind me and even throw the odd stone. 'Not interested, not punctual, not a team-worker, impervious to advice' were some of the descriptions of me that were fed to the media.

I was under the spotlight and was judged harshly. I thought it was unfair to compare my first tottering steps as an entrepreneur with my skill as a tennis player and my Wimbledon victories. I may not see the climax of my business life until I'm fifty. But I'm on my way. If you want to win Wimbledon, you have to get through the qualifying rounds first.

I'd also underestimated the degree to which those who'd earned money through me as a tennis star would now see me as an industry competitor. The big marketing agencies didn't like the fact that I had access to the players and sponsors. Even people at the DTB, the German tennis association, for whom BBM was handling the tricky issue of Davis Cup marketing, stabbed me in the back. A sensational deal with a German telecommunications firm fell at the last hurdle because certain gentlemen at the DTB, who'd made a nice living from the success of Steffi, Michael and me, sabotaged the contract. When the deal fell through it was easy to point the finger: at Becker. It's of little consolation to me that the DTB has since divorced itself from those people. But far more important to me at the time was making the acquaintance of Hans-Dieter Cleven.

It was an eventful week. I'd gone to Monte Carlo and was staying in the President's Suite of the Hôtel de Paris. I was filming a Monaco special for broadcaster RTL. The Formula 1 circus was taking over the city. The closer the Grand Prix race gets, the less comfortable it is in Monte Carlo. I was glad to be leaving that night, escaping the jet-set capital, the paparazzi and all those intrusive questions about my private life. By the time the Lear jet touched down in Stuttgart, I was in a different world. Apart from a photographer from a local paper, no one had got news of my arrival. Instead of a champagne-and-caviar reception in the hotel lobby, there were grey-haired men in business suits going through their papers over pretzels and mineral water. Welcome to the world of Hans-Dieter Cleven, I thought to myself.

This was a special day for him. In a few hours' time the Technical University of Stuttgart was going to present him with an honorary doctorate. And what was Dieter doing? Just before his own personal Wimbledon, he was talking me through the details of our future partnership. It was May 1999.

Our mutual friend Charly Steeb had brought us together, and Völkl Tennis GmbH was to be our first joint project.

During our early meetings I noticed that private matters were discussed rarely, if at all. Beer, coffee and cigars were not served. Now I know that Dieter doesn't drink alcohol or smoke, and he doesn't eat fish or shellfish either. He doesn't have time for music or books. The last book he read was the biography of Sam Walton, the founder and proprietor of the largest trading company in the world. I hope that this book will be his next.

His manner was honest and open, his bearing impressive. He had sharp eyes and a clear voice. My first thought was, hey, he's not like the rest. All the same, his voice trembled a little as he addressed his guests in the unadorned but venerable banqueting hall of the Technical University of Stuttgart, all people he'd met during the course of his life and had not forgotten. He was born in Würzburg and brought up in Essen, and has lived in Switzerland for the past twenty-seven years. He was born during the war, in 1943, and never knew his father, who died at the front when Dieter was one year old. His living conditions were 'modest', or what might be better described as impoverished. He experienced hunger, learned to be frugal, and realized that the only way to succeed was hard work. As part of an extended family, living in cramped conditions with grandparents and an uncle, he developed a sense of community and learned consideration for others. Instead of watching television and going to kindergarten, he played the card game *Skat* with his grandparents, and so at an early age he got the hang of mental arithmetic and bidding high.

Today, Hans-Dieter Cleven is one of the most successful businessmen in post-war Germany, with an annual turnover of around 50 billion Euros; and with almost 230,000 employees, Metro is the second-largest trading group in

Europe. It was Dieter who started Metro, together with Otto Beisheim and others. Until recently, he was head of their holding company. His aunt Hanna, a.k.a. Sister Ruth of the Order of St Dominic, had wanted Dieter to become a cardinal, but the eighteen-year-old preferred to start a career with a commercial enterprise in Mülheim. The admin chief was one Otto Beisheim. The two of them became an incredible success story. On this evening in Stuttgart, Otto Beisheim is the first person Dieter thanks.

'And you, Eveline, you know that you are the second lucky break of my life,' says Dieter to his wife. I feel a momentary pang as this extraordinarily successful man presents his wife with his honorary doctorate. I'm glad for them both that after this long, hard path they've trodden together they've still got plenty of love and respect for each other, and I'm sad that I haven't achieved the same with my own wife.

How shall I come to terms with this man who's so different from me? Sure, he used to be a striker in a football team, he loves tennis, and today at the age of sixty he already has a golf handicap of twenty-one (despite John D. Rockefeller's recommendation in his autobiography to retire early and then take up golf). I have a handicap of eight! Although we come from two different worlds, we're made of the same stuff. We give our all to achieve success, we don't give up, however hopeless it all looks, and we've learned to treat victory and defeat the same.

I'm proud to have Hans-Dieter Cleven as a friend and partner, and I see him as a father figure too. This is no coincidence. I lost my father at the beginning of 1999, and met Dieter shortly afterwards. I can open up to him in a way I can't to anyone else, whether it's about private or business affairs. Whatever I've told him, and whatever he's heard about me, has never shocked or surprised him. In his speech in Stuttgart he said, 'I don't equate success with power and money, but with quality of life.' That's when I knew we were soulmates.

First, though, comes business. Dieter moved to Switzerland to realize his business ambitions, and I've now followed him. I retired from tennis, but my celebrity status has only got bigger – extraordinary but true. I knew how to play tennis, but I also knew how to have a dialogue with the public, and I'm reaping the rewards for that now. Other brands have to invest millions just to get noticed, but I can easily get publicity and build up an image. Dieter's role, in which he has a track record, is setting up structures and developing and success-fully implementing business concepts. The brand BB is well known. The task for Dieter and me is to fit the product to the brand and place it in the right market.

EVERY MOTHER-IN-LAW'S DREAM

I WAS TWENTY-THREE YEARS OLD AND FEELING LOW AGAIN, fed up with this existence in which I did nothing but hit tennis balls. No social life, no friends – the tennis court was the focal point of my world. I could only define myself through tennis: every time I lost, my self-confidence was shot to pieces, and every time I won I was flying once more. This couldn't go on for ever.

I was in this state as I prepared for Wimbledon 1991, and this time I had competition from Germany: Michael Stich. I knew from him our Davis Cup team. It hadn't been easy for him there. We were a tight-knit group and rejected the new boy at first. He in turn appeared to me aloof and reserved, and the others turned their backs on him both during training and at dinner.

So we were already familiar with each other when we met at Wimbledon. We even practised together, and we spoke every day. This was not how I usually behaved, and in some ways it was dangerous. I need tunnel vision, quarantine.

In the semi-final, Stich defeated Stefan Edberg 4–6, 7–6, 7–6, 7–6. Thanks to Michael, I became world number one again. I'd already had the number-one position in January, but I'd been toppled. After Michael's semi-final I played mine, against David Wheaton, and against all expectations I managed to get into the final once more after beating him 6–4, 7–6, 7–5.

That evening I sat in my rented house in Wimbledon, on my own again, of course. I cried tears of relief: I was world number one, right at the top. I felt my nervousness disappear. The pressure was off. I decided that evening that if I beat Stich I would retire – at the top, as Wimbledon winner and world number one. The mountaineer Reinhold Messner once said that the most important thing to think about when you're on the summit is how you're going to get down again. I didn't want a fall, but a controlled descent into a different life. Fortunately, it turned out differently. Or should I say unfortunately?

I behaved badly in the match against Stich. I whinged, moaned and complained. Subconsciously I was probably asking myself what was going to happen next. Michael played well, but I was exhausted and drained. I had problems from game one. Stich had the first break point, which he won. He returned my first serves easily; it was as if my mind was somewhere else altogether. I talked to myself constantly, the usual Becker-on-Becker dialogue. In the second set I gave away a 3–1 lead when I lost my service game. If Michael didn't make any big mistakes, he'd have it in the bag. He wasn't under any great pressure.

I had no grudge against him – he was a mate from the

Davis Cup team. Was it this that held me back? Would it have been different if my opponent had been Edberg? Of course I wanted to win, but we didn't have our horns locked. It wasn't all-out war. I couldn't find my rhythm, and Stich won 6–4, 7–6, 6–4.

After that, I got into my car and drove off – anywhere, just away, across London, I don't know where. Fulham, Chelsea? North or south of the Thames? Crying again. I was later to cry at my son's birth and my father's grave. I can cry in the cinema, or when listening to a wedding speech. That night I made a plan: you have to change your priorities, you have to make your own private life. After a few hours of driving around, I felt like talking to someone. I was missing human company. So I returned to what we called the Deutsche Haus, to the winner's party for Michael Stich. That gave the press another reason to criticize me: I was a gatecrasher, come to steal the show, when in fact I was just glad to be among people after the upset I'd had.

My fellow countryman had won Wimbledon, the second German to do so in the history of the tournament. Von Cramm had reached the finals in 1935, 1936 and 1937, and Bungert in 1967 – the winners had been their British, American and Australian opponents. Michael is the exact opposite of me. Pilic once said, 'Boris is a world star, and Michael is a world-class player.'[1] The *Frankfurter Allgemeine Zeitung* wrote, 'Becker is admired, Stich respected.'[2] I can't see inside Michael Stich, but I'm not sure he ever wanted to be in the limelight. The journalists were persistent, and often cruel: 'The Germans love Boris because he is how they want to be. They don't like Stich because he is how they are,' wrote *The Times*.[3]

Stich was the kind of player who would return to the

changing room after two hours on Centre Court with no sweat on his forehead and no grass stains on his shorts, whereas I'd look like a miner at the end of his shift: blood on my knees, dirt on my elbows. On court I spat, coughed, talked to the line umpires, talked to myself and cursed God. And Stich? Upright and clean, considerate and friendly. Just like mothers want their sons-in-law to be. He wins, and gets modest applause and mild appreciation. I whinge and suffer, and the spectators stamp their feet and the teenage girls sob. Michael must have had more of a problem with the image of Boris Becker than with the man himself. In 1997 he said in *Bild*, 'My problem wasn't with Boris. My problem was that I only rarely got the recognition I deserved for my achievements. It was always Boris who, even in his worst moments, got the attention.'[4]

Michael was the unloved son in the extended tennis family. He never quite grasped the mechanisms of the media, who played us off against each other. 'Becker said . . .' – and Stich would hit back without first checking with me whether I'd actually said whatever it was. He was often ill advised, and more than once people drove a wedge between us because they couldn't accept that Stich and Becker were not the same kind of beast. I recorded in my diary a lunch with him in Monte Carlo in spring 1994. 'Michael,' I'd said to him, 'last year you basically won the Davis Cup on your own, like I did a few years before. We are at about the same level in the world ranking, so let's go to the DTB together and talk to them about a joint contract.'

He looked at me, completely baffled, and said, 'Are you serious?'

'Yes, fifty–fifty. I can give this to you in writing. Our

lawyers can settle the details. We'll be better off if we can negotiate jointly.'

A few weeks later I read in the paper, 'Stich signs up with the DTB.' His fee was 1.5 million marks per year. He had done it single-handedly. A pity, I thought; we've lost a lot of money there. After that Meyer-Wölden negotiated on my behalf and got me 2.6 million marks per year. Stich was pissed off. He renegotiated and got more money.

I'm sure that we would have come to an agreement if it hadn't been for some of his advisers. Michael is a good guy and much more guided by his emotions than he would ever admit. He tends to act spontaneously and in accordance with his mood; he doesn't think strategically. That makes him like-able, and when we were alone with each other we always got on well, such as in Barcelona at the Olympics.

Barcelona was one of the high points of my career. I'd been nominated for the games in Los Angeles and Seoul as well, and each time had had to back down because of injury. Before the games in Korea, a few members of the German team – very few, perhaps five out of five hundred – were stirring things up for me, this multi-millionaire who hadn't done his military service and who lived in luxury in Monaco. I read this rubbish in the papers at my parents' house before we went on holiday to Sardinia together. We watched the Olympic Games on television there. It was grim – my father was bitterly dis-appointed. He'd really wanted his son to play for Germany.

Barcelona was something else. I spent several nights with the team in the Olympic village and this in itself was a great experience. I had the feeling that our team-mates were puzzled to find how normal we tennis-players were, neither spoiled nor arrogant. They were understanding, even when we moved to a hotel immediately before our tournament for some much-needed calm and concentration. You couldn't get gold in such high-pressure circumstances unless you all got along really well. Michael and I made it: we got the medal. It was an incredibly tough tournament. That evening we were all going to celebrate and have a night out on the town – but a few hours after the ceremony Michael went back to Germany. I think his girlfriend was waiting for him. I tried to convince him to stay, but he stuck to his guns: 'Nah, I don't fancy it.' This at the end of two weeks of joint effort and struggle, in temperatures of up to 50°C in the shade!

We see each other more often nowadays. In August 2002 we played together in Berlin for the first time in five years. Centre Court at the tennis club Rot-Weiß was jam-packed and German television (ARD) broadcast it live. Michael was sceptical at first, and although it was I who won, this sunny day in Berlin marked the beginning of a partnership between us. Michael began to have faith in me and to feel that we could get on together. At the Davis Cup re-match against the McEnroe brothers in Hamburg in May 2003, the two of us produced an event the like of which had never been seen before: 22,000 spectators, Nena of '99 Red Balloons' fame as a supporting act, live television coverage and a fantastic atmosphere. Now we're planning more joint events.

Perhaps Michael had to go through the highs and lows of his private life before we could get close. He, too, had to cope with separation from his wife and the death of a parent: his mother. He also dropped into an emotional void at the end of his tennis career. Now that we are no longer rivals, we can talk. No more need for masks to hide behind. The player Stich has become my friend Michael.

GREETINGS FROM THE BEETLE

THEY WERE SHAKING THEIR HEADS AND MUTTERING — A
Wimbledon winner, a world-class player, and he's not even
pushing himself. The Masters was coming up in Frankfurt in
November 1992 and I was practising with a Serb called Jovan
Savic, a talented young man. He wasn't in the world's top
hundred, and I don't even know if he was registered as a
professional, but I liked him. He was good to practise with,
as cheerful as his serve was powerful. I still work with him
today, and he numbers the Williams sisters among his
clients.

My coach in those days, the Austrian Günther Bresnik,
didn't like my choice. Even my rather reserved physio-
therapist, Waldemar Kliesing, weighed in: Michael
Schumacher, he said, wouldn't crawl about the circuits of
Monza or Nürburgring in a VW Beetle for his training.
Becker, Waldemar was trying to tell me, was Formula 1, not
Formula Beetle. They were unhappy about my training

methods, but they jumped for joy at Frankfurt: I beat Jim Courier 6–4, 6–3, 7–5.

Bresnik and Kliesing embraced me. I just said, 'Greetings from the Beetle.'

As long as I was committed to my sport, I was always at the top of the world rankings. So how could it be true that I was lazy about training – was I so talented that I could get by without any practice at all? Of course not. Nor was I often late for practice because I spent too much time with my girlfriend. Tennis was always my priority, and my coaches have often profited from that. But the people who really did the ground-work never asked me for a single penny.

My sister Sabine, for example, who's now an architect – though to me she was more of a psychologist. During our practice sessions she knew exactly how to transform the self-hatred that followed my defeats into positive energy. And there was Boris Breskvar, who as the coach of our regional tennis association played a decisive part in my development. He turned me into one of the world's best junior players, and he also prepared young talents like Steffi Graf and Anke Huber for their professional careers. At the age of fourteen, when I was already winning adult tournaments, I was practising with Breskvar at Heidelberg's Schwarz-Gelb, a club I played for in the district league.

According to the tennis officials of the time, however, I was barely suitable even for this modest level. The so-called 'monitor reports' didn't rate me. Of the youngsters of my age group who were rated – often because they complied with the rules of the club – did any ever get anywhere near the world's top hundred? I never fitted in, but the negative reports only served to spur me on. I wanted to prove them wrong. When I won the regional men's championships, I was only fourteen. I played international junior championships in Miami, took an overnight flight back to Germany and then played in the national league for my club in Mannheim, Grün-Weiß.

Before Bosch was assigned to me, my father suggested that Breskvar accompany me through my possible future professional career. Breskvar turned this offer down because he didn't want to subordinate himself to an adolescent in the way coaches were expected to. This is also why world-class players, say Wimbledon winners, rarely make good coaches. John McEnroe is a possible exception to this rule. That man's a genius. In late summer 1993 he coached me. He had been through finals himself, of course; he knew the pressure. We had a fantastic time together. Unfortunately, my mind wasn't on the job and I was worn out. Had we got together earlier, Becker–McEnroe would have been a great team.

I never saw tennis practice as combat training. I found the mindless build-up training of the Tiriac type – forty-five minutes of running, an hour of crosses, an hour of long lines – really tough. Day-to-day life in tennis is incredibly boring. In his book *The Fight*, Norman Mailer describes the monotony of Muhammad Ali's training camp and the system that underpinned it. 'The boredom creates an impatience with one's life, and a violence to improve it.'[1] Frustration is transformed into energy. The walk to the ring, or on to Centre Court, becomes a kind of release.

The coach is supposed to come up with new gimmicks, but after six months or a year at the most repetition sets in. But my coaches were never an excuse for a failure of effort on my part or scapegoats for my defeats. I looked to them for answers and to have my mistakes corrected, but after a while they would run out of ideas and I had nobody else to rely on but myself. I squeezed everything out of my coaches as I tried to improve my play: from Günther Bosch to Ion Tiriac and Bob Brett, from Niki Pilic to Tomas Smid (both of whom were fillers rather than long-term coaches), from Günther Bresnik and Nick Bollettieri up to Mike de Palmer.

During tournaments, the routine was similar to that during training. If I had to play a final at two p.m. I got up at half past eight. First breakfast, usually alone in my room: muesli, fruit, toast with jam, an espresso, perhaps a look at the papers too. Around eleven, I'd start driving tennis balls and this would last for forty minutes. Some tactical discussion with the coach, a bit of preparation for that particular opponent. Lunch at half past twelve, usually spaghetti with tomato sauce, or a cheese sandwich. Finally a game of cards with Waldemar Kleising, my physio, and Uli Kühnel, my racket-stringer. Then taping my joints up. At quarter past one, I would start to prepare myself mentally for the match – my focusing phase.

Talking of rackets: Kühnel always packed half a dozen rackets in plastic sheaths. They had already been used twice in training to take off some of the hardness. Rackets are as important to me as Anne-Sophie Mutter's violin is to her. Each string is 0.8mm thick; if Kühnel gets them wrong I play out of tune. Eight out of ten rackets were returned to the factory as unsuitable for professional playing. My racket weights 367 grams and is strung at thirty kilograms – Sampras has two or three kilos more; the Spaniards six or seven less, which turns the racket into a kind of mini-trampoline. The tension on my racket uses up my strength, because I have to control the stroke with my hand and arm. I was one of the last professionals to use catgut strings, which tear about half a dozen times per match. Agassi, Sampras and I, professionals who could afford it, worked with our own racket experts. Mine followed me, together with his machinery, as far as Australia. This investment paid off. My near perfection was partly thanks to the materials I had access to.

Amateurs often blame a drop in performance on their old rackets. What would the professionals say? Borg's five Wimbledon wins were played with a single brand, Donnay. Connors played half a dozen finals on a Wilson. I'm very sensitive to the smallest inconsistencies in a racket. When I changed from Puma to the Taiwanese supplier Estusa, a number of changes had to be made to the newly developed model. My demands got my business partners so worked up that they flew in one of the top racket experts from the USA. They spray-painted both their Estusa and my old Puma black, and asked me to tell them which one was the Puma. It took me just two hits of a ball – so that settled that.

When our contract with Estusa ended, Tiriac bought the remaining rackets from all over the world. Once they were used up, I approached Head. The company was prepared to 'bake' a few hundred rackets to my specific requirements. I finally bought the racket machine from them to secure my supply. With the end of my active career came the solution to my racket problem, thanks to my 50 per cent share in the manufacturer Völkl Tennis. Now I can make my rackets myself.

After the break with Bosch, I was trained by Ion Tiriac – the hard way. According to him, it was during those months that I played my best tennis. I didn't care for his mindless repetitions, but I worked my way through his particular brand of torture out of respect for him. And praise where praise is due: he improved my volley grip by making it more open.

I discussed with Ion various candidates to replace Bosch with. I was for Bob Brett, the Australian who'd worked under the legendary Harry Hopman in Florida, but Ion was against him because Brett wasn't a veteran of great battles, like Tony Roche was, and even worse, he talked too much. He had a tendency to make an analysis before the match and still be analysing it two hours later, which could confuse even the calmest player. All the same, in March 1988 I had my first victory under Brett in the Indian Wells final against Emilio Sanchez (7–5, 6–4, 2–6, 6–4). And we made further progress. During the first months we trained with a group that included world doubles champion Robert Seguso and top South African player Johan Kriek. It was tough training, really hard work. But I was prepared to do it because I wanted to win Grand Slams again, and I did have successful years with Brett.

In 1991 I won the Australian Open, and for the first time in my career I was number one – in Bob's hometown, in front of his father and his friends. My victory over Lendl was for him, as coach, like receiving a decoration, but all of a sudden he didn't want to carry on. Our break-up was awful, un-necessarily so. He turned his back on me, thinking that it would work to his advantage. Brandishing his new honours, he was able to get himself new and better contracts. He took over other players, among them the Russian Andrei Medvedev and the Croatian Goran Ivanisevic. Bob Brett, I reckon, didn't want to end up as a tour-trainer, but to have his own camp where he could be boss and not have to travel much, which was why making money was so important to him. It was a job, not a passion or a vocation. 'Après moi, le déluge' was his attitude towards me. Our partnership deserved a better ending.

When I met Nicolas Kiefer he was a backbencher among world-ranking players. He stayed with me in our home, visited me in Miami Beach and was without doubt a great talent. He rocketed up to sixty-four in the rankings. Then in Stuttgart in 1997 he tore a ligament. I supported him throughout his medical treatment and his rehabilitation with Klaus Eder in Regensburg. By this time Kiefer had joined the Mercedes junior team; they paid his expenses, including travel, and he could keep any prize money he won. Then his manager demanded an individual contract just for him. The people at Mercedes refused, arguing that Kiefer advertisements wouldn't sell their cars. I urged Kiefer's management and his parents not to disrupt him at this point in his development and to let him carry on in the team as before. His mother rejected my advice – I was a bad influence, I exploited her son and I tried to get between them.

The truth is this: at the end of 1997, I was prepared even to turn my coach Mike de Palmer over to Kiefer and to handle his management myself. At the Australian Open in 1998 he reached the quarter-finals and, after fifteen months with the Mercedes junior team, moved up to number twenty-five in the world rankings. Then he resigned from the Mercedes team. Several weeks before, at a DTB training camp, he'd wanted to know what I thought of Bob Brett as a coach. I said that he was great.

A little later, in February 1998, they started working together. This was before a tournament in Dubai. I'd told

Brett a few things about Kiefer: his weaknesses as a player, and in particular his strong relationship with his mother. Kiefer's play got worse and worse. Success was thin on the ground. Because I took an interest in his development as a tennis player, I got in touch with his parents and said, 'I'm wondering whether Brett is really the right person for Nicolas.' This confidential remark did not, of course, remain confidential. Before long Brett knew about it, and some time later he complained to me: 'My work and what I do is none of your business.' Kiefer also kept his distance from me – I guess Brett prejudiced him against me.

Kiefer, with Brett behind him and his mother by his side, went on to form an opposition to the Davis Cup team, which was under my leadership – a heavy burden for all of us. If we said black, they said white. In May 1999, one week before the Grand Slam in Paris, Kiefer played at the World Team Cup in Düsseldorf. He played such a great game against the Swede Thomas Johanson – winning 6–3, 6–2 – that we asked him to take my place in the doubles, because I wasn't fit. At first Nicolas didn't say yes or no. 'I have to talk to Bob first.' Then he came back and declared, 'I can't. I'm ill.'

'What do you mean, ill?' we asked. 'Just a few minutes ago you were playing world-class tennis!'

But Kiefer refused to change his mind. Tommy Haas was going to take his sick team-mate's place instead, but Tommy wasn't well either. 'I can't play. I've got a huge blister on my foot.' I decided to scrub the doubles, but Tommy pulled himself together. 'Fuck it, I'll play,' he said, and together with David Prinosil he went on to win the match against the Swedes.

Brett and Kiefer were in the stands. Kiefer seemed relaxed

and didn't look in the least bit ill. I was annoyed and got on to Bob. 'Why are you causing trouble?'

'I don't want to talk about this in front of all these people,' he replied.

'Well, you have to.' I raised my voice: 'You're behaving like an idiot, Bob. Be honest with me.' Kiefer then told the press that everyone in our team was lying and that no one was telling the truth about him. What a song and dance. Davis Cup coach Charly Steeb tried to mediate and talked to all the people involved. 'It went very well,' he reported back. 'Everyone's going to play in the Davis Cup.'

Three days after the peace talks, while Charly and I were holidaying in his house in Majorca, we got a phone call from Kiefer. 'I'm not playing. These differences can't be resolved in a matter of only eight weeks.' Charly tried to talk to Brett again, who by now was back in Australia. The message was loud and clear. As long as Becker was involved in the Davis Cup, there would be problems.

In the end, Kiefer didn't play in the Davis Cup. Eventually he did take part, but to this day he hasn't been convincing in the German team, and as an individual player he has also started to decline. To me, he wasted his talents. And by the way, Bob Brett ceased to be his coach a long time ago.

Günther Bresnik, whom I'd employed as my coach after Bob's departure, was the opposite of Brett – he was someone who enjoyed life. The Austrian intended to experiment with me, to try out his theories on me. The diamond that was Becker was now placed under the microscope in order to be polished to perfection. When we started working together in autumn 1992, I already had several hundred tournaments under my belt, so I had a fair idea what I had to do to win. In short, we weren't on the same wavelength.

As a person Günther was fine, he was a good guy. We worked at it for nine months, then I decided to end it. He was hurt and passed a few stories to the media, but I was used to that by now. He then became Austria's Davis Cup coach and national coach, and set up the tennis centre Tennis Point in Vienna. Towards the end of our partnership I'd really got on his nerves with my constant stonewalling. He complained about my stubbornness, for example in the Austrian magazine *News*. 'If I suggested something, he'd reject it. And he'd say in his own defence: "This doesn't work for me. I'm different." So I'd wanted to know what was so different about him, to which he'd say: "You wouldn't understand anyway." '[2] Today we're back on good terms. In contrast to the separation from Nick Bollettieri that was to come, I'd call my 'divorce' from Bresnik relatively amicable.

Bollettieri, to me, is a complete non-starter. How on earth did he become my coach, then? As you say in English, 'Shit happens.' I knew who he was, of course: the self-confident coach and mentor of Agassi. My lawyer Axel Meyer-Wölden's children had practised with Bollettieri. The coaches who worked under him knew their stuff. But when Axel suggested I take Bollettieri on as coach, I looked at him in disbelief and then laughed. This man who looks like a walking commercial for suntan lotion, this toothpaste-advert poster boy? The man was bread and butter to divorce lawyers, too. I think he once counted his divorces for me: five. He's up to seven now. In spite of this busy private life, he managed to establish a training centre in Florida, the Nick Bollettieri Tennis Academy. It's now run by the sports-management group IMG, but Bollettieri remains the company's trademark.

I had a look at the academy in November 1993. With Bollettieri, each day had a fully structured timetable. Just the right thing for a sixteen-year-old talent, but fairly pointless for a professional like me. At that time, however, neither my physique nor my game was at its best. I had to reduce my life once again to tennis alone, and a rigid regime seemed to be the best therapy. And I met excellent players and teachers there – David ('Red') Ayme, for example, the red-haired coach who later went to work with Haas. Ayme was a warm-hearted person. He managed to motivate me, he worked hard, and on top of that he was loyal. A great guy, who loved pizza and football, a real Southerner. His colleague Mike de Palmer was a notch higher, though. He was a coach who had learned discipline with the US Navy SEALs. Early in 1995, I told Bollettieri I wanted to work with de Palmer.

Bollettieri would fly into tournaments on the morning of the first match, dazzle with his smile and show off his shining Florida pelt. He'd earn a princely sum for this display, although not as much as Bosch and Brett. But I did experience one high point with Bollettieri: my semi-final against Agassi at Wimbledon in 1995. Andre had parted from Bollettieri on anything but friendly terms, informing him of his sacking by letter. I wasn't on good terms with Andre back then either. He'd made some disrespectful remarks about me. Now the day had come: high noon on Centre Court. It started disastrously. Soon I was losing 2–6, 1–4. He was wiping the floor with me and it was utterly embarrassing. Bollettieri and de Palmer shrank in their seats. Finally I won my serve: 2–4. In a show of gallows humour, I lifted my arms in mock triumph. It was then that the atmosphere changed – the audience was now behind me. I went on to defeat Agassi in four sets: 2–6, 7–6, 6–4, 7–6. Bollettieri was overjoyed, but this wasn't to last. Shortly afterwards, I wooed Mike de Palmer away from him.

I wanted to get away from Bollettieri the showman, who'd always been more concerned with his own branding than anything else. I'd offered Mike a three-year contract several months before Wimbledon, but he'd turned it down. His father still works for the tennis academy, and Mike didn't want to be disloyal to Bollettieri, to whom he was also contractually bound. Axel Meyer-Wölden was given the job of telling Bollettieri in Florida that I was no longer interested in continuing our collaboration. He was shocked, hurt, angry and disappointed, as he later wrote in a book – a book in which he also published a number of insults I could happily have strangled him for.

So Mike did become my coach, and he could be brutal. All the same, I stayed with him for five years, longer than I stayed with any other coach. We managed to strike a balance between the relationship we had as friends and that we had as employer–employee. We handled victories as well as we did defeats, like adults should. The Masters final in Hanover in 1996, which I lost to Pete Sampras after four hours – 6–3, 6–7, 6–7, 7–6, 4–6 – was among the best games I ever played. With Mike de Palmer, I reached the level of obsession a player needs to set all his energy free. You have to go as far as the border of madness without crossing over the line. That I leave to others.

HAS EVERYONE HERE GONE MAD?

I HAD AN IDEA WHAT IT WOULD BE LIKE — SPOTLIGHTS ON the ceiling would throw their beams at the floor, just like at any game in New York's Madison Square Garden. That sort of thing made it hard to hit the ball when you served. And all the trappings: popcorn and cola, beer in paper cups, T-shirts, noise. Our driver steers the black limousine to a side entrance.

The guards at the door give off that rough New Yorker charm: 'Move on!' 'Come on — tickets.' 'Lady, where's your badge?' 'That's Boris — let him through.' Bare walls, with guards everywhere whose muscles swelled beneath black uniforms — though perhaps some of those bulges were guns. Finally we reach the door of the dressing room. More uniforms. They let us in. 'Hello, darling,' says a man in make-up. It's Elton John.

On this day in October 1999, he's the one playing here, not me. Twenty thousand people will cheer my friend. We were drinking tea in his suite at the St Regis that afternoon. He'd sat there in a tracksuit amid a sea of bouquets. He loves flowers. They've got to be as beautiful as possible, and they must be fresh every day. He's basically a shy man, he told me, and he drew strength from the flowers' magnificence. We talked about ordinary things, and about current affairs, for example Jörg Haider, the right-wing Austrian politician. Elton follows the news regularly, and so he knew that I'd retired from Wimbledon.

'Darling,' he said, 'I'll miss you.'

Tonight he'll play for the forty-eighth time at Madison Square Garden and, as always, the concert is sold out. Two more performances and he'll have equalled the Grateful Dead's record. Elton has to go on stage, and we have to go to our seats. I'm walking across this floor for the first time in ten years, for the first time since I lost the Masters final here to Edberg 6–4, 6–7, 3–6, 1–6. The atmosphere then had been rough, unrefined, cold. You walked in and felt like an ant in an aircraft hangar. I seemed to lose my spatial awareness in this cavernous place. I could hardly gauge length and height any more – especially since we'd had so little time to practise on-site.

The day before the match, they would have been playing ice-hockey or basketball in there. The audience was merciless to begin with, or else uninterested. People come here to eat popcorn and hotdogs; they don't care much for the players at first. They want to be entertained, and anyone who fails to do that gets booed or whistled at. I did what I enjoyed and did well: I played with passion. This went down well with the New Yorkers.

I look around the packed house, then up at those bloody spotlights on the ceiling. I hear the fans start to stamp their feet – for Elton, not for Boris. He's there on his own at the black Yamaha piano and they applaud even before he starts his first hit – 'Your Song'. One massive hit after another, for three hours. One hundred and eighty minutes solo, as long as an average match in the Garden.

Barbara gets to her feet as Elton ups the tempo. The atmosphere is somewhere between a carnival and a kindergarten. Outside in the car park, even the cars begin to rock to the rhythm. The audience dances in the aisles, us included. This is New York live.

Around midnight, Joe, an Italian immigrant, steers our limousine across the Avenue of the Americas. Back in Rome his father has disinherited him, he tells us, because he's in love with a girl from Cuba, much to the old man's disgust. And so Joe has to earn his living as a driver, and he's OK with that. 'The future is now,' he preaches. 'Here and now.' The radio plays Frank Sinatra, 'New York, New York.' People are rushing, always hurrying somewhere, never slowing down. When I drive into town from the airport, my first thought is always this: Has everyone here gone mad? Such endless rushing. You can get anything you like at any time of day or night here. And after three or four days you start running too, just like everyone else.

The city throbs. If you let her, she'll carry you away with her. The wind howls through the canyons between the skyscrapers as powerfully as anywhere. The city is ice-cold in winter and suffocatingly hot in summer. The galleries and shops in SoHo stimulate the tastebuds – and the credit card. All around you are people dressed as though they're on their way to a fancy-dress party. Everyone plays his own role, either looking for an identity or just born to be a New Yorker.

New York could have been my city, not least because this place swallows its people up and gives them anonymity – provided you avoid SoHo or Bloomingdales and Barneys, Fifth Avenue and Central Park: in other words, the whole of Manhattan. That's because wherever you go now, European tourists are already there. They know who I am, but no one else recognizes me. There were times when I've walked for three or four hours through SoHo without being recognized by a soul, free as the breeze. Even during my worst periods, this was possible in New York. Ten thousand superstars live here. Who cares about Boris Becker? I'd struggled with my celebrity status for a long time and New York was a breath of fresh air. As far as sport is concerned, however, I couldn't concentrate here, perhaps because I was enjoying my freedom too much. I could chat with girls and do whatever I liked and it wouldn't appear in the following day's papers, which was fantastic.

Once I went to a salsa club, the Copacabana on 57th West. Hundreds of people were queuing outside, most of them Latinos who wanted to dance to live music, and none of them asked me for an autograph. The women were made up, their breasts swelling out of low-cut dresses. The men wore tight-fitting suits and kipper ties. I wondered what they did in the daytime. Were the women doctors, tailors, maids? And the men – which one was the drug-dealer, which the lawyer? Or even both at the same time? Who cares? 'Fun' was the key word: instant gratification. I still had to smoke my Monte Cristo outside, as demanded by law, though carrying a pistol would have been legal.

There's probably no other city in the world written about as much as New York. I've read a lot of those books. Anything can happen to you here. On the avenues you can see people who might have jumped out of Woody Allen's *Manhattan*, as if this were a gigantic film-casting suite. And characters from *The Great Gatsby*, *Breakfast at Tiffany's* or *The Bonfire of the Vanities* sit next to you in the snack bar, talking to themselves or hefting the *New York Times* Sunday edition, which weighs about five pounds. 'All of everything is concentrated' in New York, John Steinbeck wrote, 'population, theater, art, writing, publishing, importing, business, murder, mugging, luxury, poverty. It's all of everything. It goes all night. It is tireless and its air is charged with energy.'[1] I was blown away when I arrived in New York the first time. Madison Avenue in place of High Street, Heidelberg – I was enraptured, even by the city's darker side. McEnroe once said to me that in New York he'd be relieved if on his way from the airport to his flat no more than six people called him an arsehole or a wanker. There's no safety net, and at no time can you retract your elbows, relax and think, 'Someone will look after me.' There's no one to look after you.

My first appearance in New York was in December 1982 at the international Rolex Youth Tournament, which was preparation for the world championships: the Orange Bowl in Florida. I lost in the second round, 6–3, 6–3, to Edberg. He seemed invincible then. Together with Patrick McEnroe, John's brother, I also played doubles, and this time didn't lose until the final.

We stayed in a kind of youth hostel at Glen Cove on Long Island, and took the subway to the city for the obligatory sightseeing: Empire State Building, Manhattan Circle Line cruise – the real tourist number. Back then, I only knew the States from television series like *The Streets of San Francisco* with Michael Douglas and Karl Malden. I was nervous, even a little frightened, for the first few days. I was only fifteen. Everything here was a hundred times bigger and louder than in Europe. It was like peering into a huge termites' nest and seeing them all rushing around. Somehow this heaving mass functions, though nobody understands quite how. During a later visit, I went to some of the dodgier parts of town with Charly and Patrik: a peepshow, and a striptease joint on Times Square. My mates always sent me in to buy the tickets because I was the tallest and looked older than them.

In later years, I'd stroll down Fifth Avenue on match-free days. The city still held me in its grip: the endless stretch limousines that could have held entire school classes, and the caravans of yellow cabs rumbling over the potholes. But I'd also seen the dark corners of the glistening city. No one wandering off the main streets can avoid the homeless. They live in the side streets in cardboard boxes. This is where the American dream turns into a nightmare. These images always shocked me, but, strange as it may sound, they energized me too. I knew that wasn't how I wanted to end up, and it made me fight that bit harder on the court. I will beat my next opponent. His mother can cry over his defeat tonight, not mine. This is how the society works, whether you like it or not.

It was always my aim to get under the skin of those cities where I was a privileged guest, and New York was certainly an education. At eighteen I made friends with a drug-addict and persuaded him to show me the seamier sides of town. He took me to East Village and all the places where you could get the stuff. He's clean now, after two brushes with death.

There's one New York experience I'll never forget. After

my unexpected defeat at the hands of Swede Joakim Nyström
in the fourth round of the US Open in 1985 ('Germany's
quieter than a graveyard,' Tiriac told me), I did what I had
become in the habit of doing after losing: I cruised around in
a car, my place of choice for peace and calm. A friend had lent
me his blue Mercedes 500 and I drove off aimlessly, one mile
north, two miles west, left, right, anywhere, with no plan. I
found myself in a situation like that of Wall Street broker
Sherman McCoy in Tom Wolfe's *Bonfire of the Vanities*. He
loses his way in a black and Latino quarter. Two figures
emerge out of the gloom and stand by McCoy's Mercedes.
Robbers? His lover, Maria, accelerates and there's a soft
impact as they flee the Bronx into the luxury of Manhattan.
The police find McCoy and charge him with hit-and-run
driving, and then, as the boy hit by his car dies, with
unlawful killing. McCoy faces divorce, bankruptcy and
impoverishment.

On the edge of Spanish Harlem, I was moving towards the
traffic lights. At the junction I noticed a bar, and standing in
front of it a group of men. Six or seven of them, armed with
baseball bats, made for my car. They were just a few steps
away, the lights were still on red, but I floored the accelerator.
None of them tried to get in my way as I sped off. What
would have happened if I'd run one of them over?
That would have been the end of King Boris. My defeat by
Nyström was forgotten. Once again, I'd escaped.

New York is a special case where tennis is concerned, too:
the jets that drone overhead at the Louis Armstrong Stadium,
usually when you're in the middle of an argument with a line
umpire; the restlessness of the audience; the ketchup-soaked
papers from abandoned hotdog boxes that blow across the

baseline. In comparison with this, Wimbledon, with its traditions and the discipline and calm of its spectators, was another world. Flushing Meadow, the US Open, forms a particularly stark contrast to every other tournament. Almost anywhere else, the spectators are more or less calm and generally stay in their seats. No one in the audience would, say, play saxophone. In New York, however, everyone does whatever they like. It's basically impossible to play here. It took me a long time to find my bearings in this atmosphere. I couldn't get on with the American way of playing. I got angry with everything – the planes, the fans, just everything – and I let it distract me. The spectators were merciless. Either they booed at me from beginning to end, or they supported me just as uncompromisingly.

Before the US Open in 1985, McEnroe declared that my victory in Wimbledon had been a fluke, and that I was really still just a nobody. He'd chosen his words carefully and he'd meant to fire up the audience. They were to get their showdown in the quarter-finals: defending champion McEnroe against Wimbledon sensation Becker. But I'd already lost one round earlier, to Nyström, and the media had me down as someone who couldn't stand the pressure and who'd spoiled the show for everyone else.

In January 1986, in the Masters in Madison Square Garden, I faced Ivan Lendl in the final – my first American high point, even though I lost in three sets. In 1988 I finally managed to win the Masters – after playing the final against Lendl again. It was a great match: fifth set, tie-break, 6–5, Becker to serve. I muffed my first serve, but the second went in. Two, four, ten, twenty strokes in a trance. After the thirtieth it became a reflex response. Altogether we hit the ball back and forth seventy-two times. Finally my ball struck the top of the net. The audience screamed. I'd already turned away, assuming the ball was going to land on my side. But no. It rolled along and plopped on the ground immediately behind the net on Lendl's side. Victory after five hours. One fan wrapped the German flag around me before I could even shake hands with Lendl. He took my hand without saying a word. We'd had a few encounters on the court but had never said much to each other in private, so why should he be chatty now? I was totally wiped out. The longest rally of my life was over, and the New York fans had taken me under their wing.

At the end of his show, Elton John remembers John Lennon. In the 1970s Elton had jumped on to this very stage to embrace his fellow countryman. Lighters and matches illuminate the gloom of Madison Square Garden like stars in the night sky. Elton's song sounds as sad as if it was only yesterday that Lennon was shot in front of the Dakota Building in Central Park. But of course it was 1980 when Lennon was murdered, one of 1,812 people killed that year. They're all buried and forgotten – only Lennon lives on.

NO STREET BATTLES IN BED

WHEN I WAS A TEENAGER I WENT SKIING WITH MY PARENTS IN Val d'Isère, Wolkenstein, Santa Cristina and Verbier. I wasn't a bad skier, though unfortunately not as good as Alberto Tomba. But when I'm faced with memories of my romances, I'm forced to slalom more wildly than Alberto ever did . . .

It was quite a wild time, and some of the stories in the gossip columns were true. Women who appeared with me in the headlines and the photos have now settled for lives without me. They might be married – a teacher somewhere in an East German town, the wife of an Austrian aristocrat, the mother of many children. My separation in 1990 from Karen, whom I'd met in Hamburg, wasn't a very happy time – how could it have been, after such an intense relationship? For a long time she'd subordinated her life to mine, and never complained about it in public. The papers had their own ways of writing about our relationship. Ms Schultz, 'red Karen', seduces 'our Boris', was the charge made by the right-wing press. I was in great danger: wasn't Hamburg-Eppendorf the very place where communist Ernst Thälmann had incited his comrades during the years before the Second World War, when this part of town was populated by the working classes who were fighting the Nazis in the streets? Karen had settled in Eppendorf – though it had been gentrified since then. And when Boris visited her for a couple of days or dropped his tennis kit off in her flat, she was feeding him with lefty literature, brainwashing him between the sheets. Or she'd lead me to the squatters in Hafenstraße, pulling me by the laces in my tennis shoes, in order to show me how big money oppressed mankind. They'd have us debating Che Guevara while the steamers blew their horns on the river. What rubbish.

At home I'd talk politics with my father often enough, who would denounce me as a dreamer or a fool when I made a stand for better wealth distribution, or against racism, or for aid in developing countries. He was close to the CDU, Germany's conservative party – I wasn't.

It is definitely not the case that love had turned me into a lefty. There were no street battles in our bed, and Karen was not my tutor. Her views were more social democratic, even Green: muesli, Birkenstocks (which I also wore then), parka and Arafat scarf – these were all part of her style. But as always happens, with time the scarf and the Birkenstocks disappeared.

Years after we broke up, the tax investigators went to question Karen over the tax affair 'Becker, Boris'. She told them the truth: that I'd only spent a few days in Hamburg. She could have lied, perhaps to pay me back for our failed relationship, but she was as straight then as she'd always been.

We'd never fought. We'd just realized at some point that we weren't made for each other, and that our way of life and our convictions were too far apart.

The media spun the weirdest stories about me and women. Bénédicte, for example, had been 'called in' to prepare me for the higher echelons of society, to act as my chaperone and to make sure I behaved appropriately in Monaco's social circles. It made nice reading: a fairy tale – like much of what appears in the gossip columns and the gutter press. 'Boris, gentlemen don't drink red wine from their toothbrush mug!' 'Don't lick your knife!' This is how they imagined me being groomed for high society. The little boy from Leimen discovers the great wide world.

Even before I moved to Monaco, I knew about the difference between men and women. I had plenty of kisses in sixth grade. The girl's name was Bettina and she was the doctor's daughter. It was from her that I first began to discover the secrets of intimacy. Back then, Boris was still Boris. It was Wimbledon that took away my innocence. I was a teenager, and I had to relearn everything I thought I knew. To paraphrase Erich Kästner, 'Every girl wants his autograph, or at least his child.' How could I be sure that this woman, who was being so nice to me, wasn't just eyeing up my celebrity status, angling for her own bit of the glory? This is not a new phenomenon, but I was still very young then. Today I know that I come as a package: the public Boris and the private Becker are inseparable.

Only one woman who kept me company at night exploited me back then – or, rather, exploited herself. I met her in a nightclub in Frankfurt. *Playboy* offered her some money and made the most of our love affair when it was over. Under the headline 'Match report', she talked about our two 'wonderful nights' and our tête-à-tête in a 'pub hidden away around the corner'.[1] But that was all.

It can be difficult for a self-confident woman to enter my stage and act a supporting role. I had the leading part in this play. Tennis was my profession. My schedule, my matches, had priority. Some women cope well with this, because they know that they get to play the lead when the tournament's over. And of course it isn't easy when a Becker relationship finishes, especially for the woman. The lights have gone out, and she's relegated to being an 'ex'. This isn't about me being a great guy – it's just that the woman by my side enjoys the best of attention: the best table in the restaurant, first-class tickets, front-row seats. And then all of a sudden it's over. Life goes dark and envy turns to pity or even schadenfreude. From headline to oblivion.

I've always tried to maintain a reasonable relationship with my ex-partners, so that every now and then we can enjoy a glass of champagne together without being at each other's throat. I even managed to achieve this with Angela Ermakova, Anna's mother. I've visited her a few times and we've sat together like grown-ups and talked about Anna, her life, her worries, her future.

I can't imagine life without a relationship. I've never been on my own, at least not for long. A woman fills up my life in every possible way. I need a partnership in which I can exchange ideas, feel understood, where my opinion counts, and where intimacy grows out of trust. My partner has to be strong enough to criticize me and to stand up to me. She also has to be independent, financially and intellectually. That's what gets the hunter in me going.

Of course, she could easily be fair-haired and pale-skinned. I can't really listen to that stuff any more: Becker and his typical prey – exotic, dark-skinned, dark-haired. I've had as many blonde as dark-haired girlfriends. It's the person that counts. She has to be comfortable in her role as a woman. My experience tells me that most women are looking for someone to protect them – a man who has strength, who radiates strength. This is also important when it comes to sex. It might be exciting if the woman takes the role of initiator for one or two nights, but I believe that the prospects for the relationship are better if it's the other way round. Her age isn't important to me. Sexiness isn't dependent on youth or a cute rear, but on a woman's confidence and her ability to let go.

As a young tennis player I had to defend my private life, especially from Tiriac, who, if I was to be with a model, would rather it was on an advertisement shoot than in bed. I was meant to abstain; he wanted to cash in. After Ion and I went our separate ways, he had two children with a beautiful woman called Sophie. She was a friend of Barbara's; it was she who got us together.

When I was involved in a romance, at least Bosch and Tiriac were tactful about it. In his long-winded way, however, Bosch made it clear what he thought of women in the life of a professional sportsman – not very much. But he couldn't stop me. He knew how unbearable I could be if someone got in my way. Tiriac's basic question was this: does sex reduce an athlete's powers? Before Wimbledon or before a football match, it's the same issue. Should managers isolate their players into forced celibacy? Does abstinence improve the kick, or the serve? In my opinion this kind of prison-like regime does nothing but drive a player mad, especially those who are used to living with a woman. When I prepared for Wimbledon, my current partner was always with me. During the tournament we slept at the same hotel, but in different rooms. Her presence meant stability, security, comfort, all of which had little to do with sex. We now live in the twenty-first century and professional players won't let coaches rule their sex lives any longer; and if they try, the players will find a way round it.

The press have put a lot of women in bed with me: bankers' daughters, It girls, TV stars. In post-match press conferences, was I supposed to talk about my love life or my serve? People already knew my score on the court, so I guess it was more interesting to find out how I scored with women instead. And how the German soul longed for that woman to be Steffi from Brühl!

I can say with certainty that I have lost more tennis matches as a result of the pressure of expectations than as a result of my love life. I played worse when I *didn't* have a relationship, because then I'd be out looking for some kind of consolation. After one such raid on the Paris night, *Bild* came up with this headline: 'Disco-Boris caught. No more dancing in Paris.'[2] Out in the first round. I was twenty-three and her name was Eva.

Now I know what to do if I want to go out with a woman without being photographed. I arrive on my own and I leave on my own. The woman leaves the place through the emergency exit or the kitchen, and I disappear into the darkness. Once, however, when Karen and I had retreated to the Royal Palm Hotel on Mauritius, my plans went wrong. We went diving in the kind of suit you can walk around the seabed in, and said hello to the fishes. Our diving instructor took souvenir photos of us with his underwater camera. A few weeks later I discovered pictures of us in the German magazines – how had the paparazzi managed that? The explanation was easy: the diving instructor had made a few extra prints and sold them on.

I had to learn to go around with my 'look out – camera!' antennae out. But I never dreamt that this would get even worse when my tennis career was over.

WELCOME, HERR HARTEL

SHE ALREADY HAD THE CURLERS IN – THE NEXT DAY SHE WAS travelling by train to the catwalk in Salzburg. But her friend Sophie persuaded her to get dressed again because she didn't want to turn up at the Café Reitschule in Schwabing, Munich on her own. It just so happens I'm there too. I watch her. She eats and doesn't say a word. At the first opportunity I sit next to her. Without asking, I take a sip of her beer, look her in the eye and say, 'There's nothing more to be said. It's all clear.' And she replies that she's never heard such a stupid chat-up line before. It's 1 October 1991.

She is beautiful and black: Barbara Feltus. The others are leaving but we want to carry on. 'Your place or mine?' I say. I'd prefer hers as I'm staying at the Hotel Raphael. 'Another stupid line,' she says. But I have no ulterior motive. I just want to avoid ending up on the gossip pages. I'm not even thinking about a relationship, although I am looking for some kind of a private life. She wants to go to Schumann's bar – neutral territory, as she calls it. I have an orange juice and she drinks whisky. Her train is at six, my flight to Tokyo a few hours later. We see some people who are on the early shift.

I steer my green Ferrari through the Theatinerstraße. It's a pedestrian zone, but I didn't know that. The policemen who stop me don't believe me. They're not fans of tennis, or at least not fans of Becker. The breath test is negative. Perhaps it's not working. Try it again. Still negative. The early hours of the morning and not drunk? How can that be? They check the papers and the car. The Salzburg train won't wait, so now I have to drive over the speed limit. At Barbara's door I say, 'I'll come up with you and help you pack.'

'I know what kind of help you've got in mind.'

I ask her for her phone number. She has to write it down twice because I don't want to lose it. On the flight to Tokyo, my physio Waldemar Kliesing sits next to me. 'Waldemar,' I say, 'I fear I've just met the woman who's going to be my wife.'

'You're kidding.'

What I didn't know was that I'd already met Barbara before, as a child. A friend of my father's, a graphic designer, was friends with a photographer called Ross Feltus – Barbara's father. And at parties, three or four times a year, Barbara and I had played together.

I called her every night from Tokyo and told her tall stories about women I'd been to nightclubs with. Completely insane. I was just sitting in front of the television and dreaming of her. 'You can save your stories and save your phone bill too,' I heard over the line.

To stand a chance, people have to be able to argue with me and point out where I'm going wrong, or just say no, like

Barbara did. She wasn't frightened of me or of my life. She was right for me, and I acted on gut feelings, as always. I know this tendency of mine to follow my instincts can get me into trouble, but I've had few reasons to regret decisions I made on this basis.

I saw Barbara again in Munich, between tournaments in Tokyo and Stockholm. On our second date she was a full ninety minutes late. I waited. She was the woman I wanted. But there was no physical contact between us then. I won in Stockholm and was desperate for her. Barbara was in Munich and I was on my own in this misty city, alone on the waterside in the rain. Over the next few days she had to go to Frankfurt for another fashion show, so I paid my parents a quick visit in Leimen, telling them I had to shoot off urgently somewhere else. Well, it was true, but I didn't mention Barbara.

She was staying in a small pension, sharing a room with another model. Not a suitable place for getting closer to each other. We decided to drive to Wiesbaden, where there was another fashion show the next day. On the motorway I lost my patience. I stopped on the hard shoulder and kissed her for the first time. It was November, and the radio was playing 'Black Cat' by Janet Jackson. Barbara, who's a singer herself, remembers the tune to this day.

At the Penta-Hotel in Wiesbaden, Barbara gets out of the car, goes to reception and books a double room for Harry Hartel and his wife Sabine – or was it Susi? We check in. I'm hiding my racket under my coat – I could never leave the tool of my trade behind in the car. I'm wearing sunglasses, a cap pulled down over my face. 'How would you like to pay?' the receptionist asks Barbara. I'm standing behind her and without thinking I pull out my credit card and hand it over. Of course it bears the name Boris Becker. The receptionist looks up briefly and, without missing a beat, says, 'Welcome, Herr Hartel, we hope you enjoy your stay with us.' His wishes were fulfilled. That was my first night with Barbara. And I would like to thank the gentleman on reception for his discretion.

Another goodbye, another separation. At the Masters in Frankfurt in November my first match is against Agassi. I lose: 3–6, 5–7. I call Barbara and ask her to come. It's late and there are no more flights or train connections that day. 'Take a taxi,' I tell her. The bill is enormous but the cab driver is happy. Barbara has brought Sophie with her. What am I going to do with her? The hotel is fully booked. And so Waldemar has to share his room with Sophie. He's an honourable man from Aachen, married and faithful to his wife. His wife trusts him, and rightly so. The telephone rings and Sophie answers because she's expecting Barbara to call. Frau Kliesing is on the other end. Her husband Waldemar dies a thousand deaths. I go on to win my next matches – against Stich (7–6, 6–3) and Sampras (6–4, 6–7, 6–1), and Waldemar's marriage pulls through.

In the weeks before Christmas, I'm now absolutely sure. Barbara is the woman for me. I first propose to her in a McDonald's in Hohenzollernstraße in Munich – she tells me I must be going mad. A few days later, she has an emergency appendectomy – then I really am going mad. I'm about to leave for my tour of Australia, which means ten weeks without her. The thought of leaving her on her own after the operation is unbearable. She battles against the doctors and her mother, insisting on accompanying me. She gets her way. Her health didn't suffer, but I had a feeling she might suffer in other ways as we officially 'outed' ourselves in Perth on

New Year's Eve. I'd talked to her about it in Germany, and during the flight I also tried to prepare her for the flashlight bulbs in the face she'd have to endure. *Bild* reproduced an old modelling publicity photo of hers. 'Babsie-Strapsie, Boris Becker's new girl.' 'Cappuccino-coloured.' And *Bild* went even further than that – either we agreed to an exclusive interview, or they'd print revelations of Barbara's love life. They had a very particular work ethos.

Those were tough days for Barbara, and not just because of *Bild*. Before Melbourne she'd never experienced what I was like during a tournament: the sheer graft and the tunnel vision. Instinctively she did the right thing. She was quiet and reserved. I hadn't expected anything else from her. In the third round I lost to John McEnroe: 4–6, 3–6, 5–7. Once again I escaped in my car, but this time Barbara was next to me. Driving had never felt so good.

So I had a week on my hands before the Davis Cup match against Brazil. I got a map, put it on the table in front of Barbara and said, 'Where to? Bora Bora? Tahiti?'

We had a fabulous time. Motorboats bobbed up and down in the water next to the runway, palms waved their fronds at the terminal building, and through the glass floor of our bungalow we watched colourful fishes swim over white sand and around coral. Our paradise for five days. Next came the Davis Cup. We arrived in Rio two days before the team, but Barbara's presence annoyed both team-members and coach. She was the only woman in the group, and a stranger to them. In the end she went back to Germany on her own and hid out in her father's house in Düsseldorf, away from the hysteria of the press.

Like millions of other Germans, my parents heard about

our relationship from *Bild*. In November 1992 in Bercy I beat Guy Forget 7–6, 6–3, 3–6, 6–3. I was happy – I'd won a tournament with Barbara, and in spite of Barbara. We had champagne in the players' lounge, and then I talked to my mother for the first time about Barbara and me. I wanted to talk about the children we would have – I was already looking forward to becoming a father – and she warned me, 'Just imagine what a hard time they'll have in a German school.' Barbara heard this, and said nothing.

In the spring of 1993 I reserved a table at our favourite restaurant in Munich, the Bogenhauser Hof, and asked the pianist to play – when I gave the sign – 'Summertime' from Gershwin's *Porgy and Bess*, Barbara's favourite song. When she went to the ladies', the moment had come. I hid a diamond ring in her whisky soda. This time it was going to be a real old-fashioned proposal. She took a sip of her whisky – where was the ring? It was wedged beneath the ice. The pianist extended 'Summertime' by several minutes while the ice melted. It was wonderful and moving. The next day I called my parents. 'I've got news. We're engaged.' Nothing was said – was it shock or silent joy?

Some people wanted to take my decision to marry Barbara as a political message, but it was love, just love, with no thought about the colour of her skin. I made our engagement public in April 1993 by shooting a provocative front cover for the German magazine *Stern* together with Barbara. We were both almost naked, my hands covering her breasts. My mother reacted in the same way that many other people did: 'Is this quite necessary?' It was.

In February we thought Barbara was pregnant. My usual thoughts during training sessions – slice, topspin, stop – gave way to a preoccupation with nappies, bottles and baby tears. What was life going to be like from now on? Could I cope with this? What would touring be like in a threesome? For four long days I mulled over these questions. Then suddenly I had the answer; I knew how it would be – it would be great, fantastic, a child! But it turned out to be a false alarm. I had to wait a bit longer.

The tournament in Rome in May 1993 turned into a special event. Not because of the final, which I lost to Andrei Tchesnokov 2–6, 6–3, 6–7, but because Barbara had gone to the chemist's. I was waiting for her in our suite in the Excelsior. Instead of shopping bags from the smart stores of the Via Condotti, she held a piece of paper – the result of her pregnancy test, in Italian. Except for 'al dente' and 'domani', I didn't know any Italian. And Barbara wasn't quite sure if she'd understood it either, but the test seemed to be positive. A gynaecologist in Munich confirmed our translation: we were going to become a family.

I was Catholic, unmarried, and Barbara wasn't ready for marriage. Her parents are divorced; mine celebrated their thirty-sixth wedding anniversary that year. A few days before the start of Wimbledon 1993, I took my parents out for a meal and told them. My mother, who had seemed so unmoved before, couldn't help but be moved now, and my father seemed almost relieved: 'At last, I'm going to be a granddad!' I reached the semi-final and lost to Sampras 6–7, 4–6, 4–6, while Barbara's belly began to swell. In New York, at the US Open, I told the press the good news during a breakfast conference at the Peninsula on 5th Avenue. Our child was going to be born in January 1994. On the sports front, however, not much was happening for me. For the first time I didn't qualify for the Masters in Frankfurt. A bitter blow. In the Grand Slam Cup in early December, I lost in the first round to Wayne Ferreira. Barbara was eight months pregnant, and my thoughts had somehow moved away from the tennis court.

What a year – the split with Tiriac, Barbara's pregnancy, and still no wedding. Barbara wasn't worried, but I wanted to get married, and I wanted to do it before the birth. I didn't want to have to adopt my own child afterwards, as I would have to do in German law. Axel Meyer-Wölden recommended a venue for our wedding: the Austrian ski-resort Kitzbühel, a romantic setting with snow-covered mountains. We liked the idea. The wedding should take place at a weekend. Our plan remained secret for just one day. Then the press announced: 'Becker – wedding in Kitzbühel this Friday'. We had to abandon the dream of snowy mountains and steaming horses pulling our sled, Barbara wrapped in furs to protect her and the child from the cold. We booked the Schlosshotel Bühlerhöhe from Friday to Sunday, with only close friends and family invited: in total no more than twenty guests.

That Thursday it snowed in Munich. We planned our escape to Leimen, and from there to the hotel an hour away, near Baden-Baden. Our booking in Kitzbühel hadn't been cancelled, and the television crews moved into position. Barbara and I drove into the Sheraton in Munich. We were followed by a few dozen press cars, as well as paparazzi on motorbikes. I parked the car. We went into the hotel and took the lift to the underground car park, where Carlo Thränhardt was waiting with our escape car. We flattened ourselves on the back seat and left the car park at sixty miles an hour.

Because of the snowfall we didn't reach my parents' house

until two in the morning. I called them from the car to tell them we'd arrived. They didn't know about our change of plan and had, like our other guests, packed for the journey to Kitzbühel. My parents knew me well enough not to be too surprised, but when I said to my father at around four in the morning, 'On Friday at four p.m., twelve hours from now, I want to get married in Leimen's town hall,' he swallowed hard.

'How are you going to manage that? You can't do that at such short notice.'

I appealed to his pride. 'Who else could pull this off apart from you?'

And he did it. The mayor himself married us. Of course, the press couldn't be fooled for long and the photographers and reporters duly appeared on time in Leimen. But at least they couldn't break through the walls of our hotel.

I wanted to marry Barbara after three months. After we'd been together six months, I wanted to have a child with her. I made the right decision. In my relationship with Barbara I rediscovered myself. During the last years of my career I was a long way from being number one in the world, but that didn't bother me any more. My family had become my passion. Tennis was just another thing to do. My sons' love keeps me going even today. They don't know about the money or the fame. When Noah was just a few months old, he'd start to laugh when he saw me and he'd hug and kiss me. It was profoundly moving – pure love. Now he's bigger; he tells me if he doesn't like something. He allows his moods to rule him. 'When I've finished my food, you'll read me a story. You promised.' One of his favourites was a story about Sams, a creature who makes people's wishes come true, full of characters with funny names. Noah loved it, and I enjoyed reading it to him.

The love of my children has given my life real meaning. When on 15 December 2000, two days before our seventh wedding anniversary, I filed for divorce at the family court in Munich, it was the greatest defeat of my life.

WHY?

THERE WAS AN EERIE SILENCE, JUST THE WIND WHISTLING
around our house. The long alabaster dining table looked as if
it had been abandoned. It was usually decorated with candles
and flowers, but that evening there was just the tablecloth,
like a shroud. The children were in bed, the staff had the
evening off and the bodyguards weren't around. Barbara had
made some sandwiches. I was sitting at the head of the table
with a small wheat beer in front of me. She was sitting on my
left with a glass of champagne. She loves champagne. It was
shortly after ten, a Saturday night in November 2000.

I had spent the day in my office. Some people had come
from Paris to fit me for a mask for a Mercedes advert with
Mika Häkkinen. In the advert we were to play an aged Boris
and an aged Mika who, decades later, still love their Mercedes.
I got a shock when I looked in the mirror. Was this what I'd
look like one day? Oh God! Barbara was also at the office, but
instead of making fun of my new looks, she seemed strangely

anxious. She sensed what was coming. I decided there and then that at dinner that night I was going to tell her.

'Barbara, we can't go on like this. We'll have to separate.' She was very calm. She didn't yell or cry, and she wasn't surprised. At that point she didn't even ask why. Like two grown-ups, we started to talk about the practicalities of the split. 'It's late November. There's no point in you packing your things and leaving the house now. The best thing is to stay here with the children. Next week, I'm away in Cannes shooting a commercial, then I have to go to New York, and I've got AOL commitments. When I get back to Munich in between, I'll move into the hotel, but I'll be around for dinner and spend time with the children or pick them up in the morning.'

She nodded. 'OK. If you think this is the right thing to do . . .'

I kissed her goodnight and we went to bed. She slept in the guest room and I slept in our bed.

There was no mention of divorce that night. We had reached this point a dozen times before and I had already moved to the hotel for one or two nights on a couple of occasions. This time it was serious. I wanted to draw a line and make it clear to her that we couldn't go on like this, or at least that I couldn't. We'd talk again around Christmas time and see whether we had a future or not. I wanted the separation in order to rescue our marriage.

It was a short night. After three and a half hours' sleep, I was wide awake at five o'clock. While I tossed and turned, my thoughts were doing somersaults in my head. I was sure it was the right decision. We needed to be apart to see our feelings for each other for what they really were. We needed the distance in order to restore our closeness. I couldn't stand it in the house any longer. Within minutes I'd packed two suit-cases. The previous night's wind had brought a cold, drizzly rain. I felt very low as in the early-morning darkness I left my house and my family.

'Mum, get breakfast ready, I'm coming.' It was eight o'clock and I was an hour away from Leimen. I was flying over the motorway in my M-class Mercedes, hardly touching the road surface. My tension was slowly dissolving.

'Has something happened?' she asked.

'Yes. I'll tell you when I get there.'

Breakfast was already on the table when I arrived and I could smell the coffee. My mother hugged me without saying a word.

'I've left Barbara.' I looked at her, expecting her to pass judgement. But she only asked, 'What about the children?' My mother has seen a lot in her life. She's never been that much interested in 'why'; she's always been much more concerned about what you do next.

For me, however, the 'why' was clear. The separation from Barbara was not a spur-of-the-moment decision, nor was there another woman involved, and the baby in London had little to do with it either. The end of my tennis career was also the beginning of the end of my marriage. Today I can see that clearly. I'd basically finished back in 1997, when I bid my farewell to competitive tennis at the Wimbledon final against Pete Sampras. For the following two years I wound down, playing a bit here and a bit there, to slowly get away both physically and mentally from the world of professional tennis. What I had overlooked was that Barbara also needed to pre-pare for the future. When I finally closed the door on tennis at Wimbledon in 1999, she asked me, wide-eyed, 'That's all very well, but what am I going to do now?'

Barbara had a clearly defined role in the Becker Tennis System. She represented us to the public, she kept things going and she watched my back. She was as match-focused as I was. While I was fighting on the court with all the strength I could muster, she believed in the spiritual support she gave me, the supernatural strength she was able to mobilize. So I'd taken away her raison d'être. At the same time as making my farewell tour, I was also setting up my office and founding my marketing agency. Four weeks after my last match, against Patrick Rafter, I took over 50 per cent of Völkl Tennis. My life after tennis had started before the last match point; for Barbara, however, a yawning gap opened up. Before my departure from tennis, the Becker family and their entourage had one common goal: my success on the courts. This goal had now ceased to exist. The person who coped least well with this was Barbara. I should have prepared her, but when it happened in July 1999 it was a big blow to her. It was my mistake, and we would both pay the price.

The result was endless arguing. Our differences, which had formed the basis of our initial attraction, became unbearable. Her bad time-keeping began to grate. 'I don't know how I've coped with this all these years. When we agree to leave at ten, you're never ready before eleven. The kids are yelling, friends are waiting for us, and the show we wanted to see is over.' Today we laugh about it, but back then I reached a point where I couldn't take it any longer.

There are some ways in which I'm really Teutonic. I have my schedule and I adhere to it rigidly. If a match started at two p.m. I got up at eight-thirty, had breakfast, started practising at eleven, had lunch at twelve-thirty and so on. If you don't respect your partner's schedule, organization breaks down and daily life results in chaos. Simple plans for the family are ruined and you end up rushing around putting fires out instead. I had my new work, my business meetings. I also knew that the issue of tax evasion was becoming more serious and that the fact that I'd fathered a child in London was going to become public. I had a lot on my shoulders, and on top of all this I was supposed to organize daily life at home as well. It was too much. I didn't have enough energy or enough room in my head for it all.

And then there were all those people in our house. It was always packed. There was the family from Thailand – mother, daughter and sister, who acted as cook and nannies – and all the bodyguards. The threats we lived under and what we had to endure in terms of security were crazy. At times we had up to ten people at home, twenty-four hours a day. And, of course, there were also friends, relatives and acquaintances. In my working life I have to deal with a lot of people too, so I just wanted peace and quiet when I got home. I wanted to be able to walk naked through my own house, or just let myself go and chill. Instead I had to put on a performance, even at home. My batteries became more and more drained, and I had nowhere I could go to recharge them – at a time when I needed all the energy in the world.

We argued all the time. As a tennis nomad you move every week from one interesting city to the next. You meet interesting people. Before you have a chance to discover how dull they actually are, you've moved on. Now Barbara only had me to talk to most of the time, and I can be demanding. I disarm people and get straight to the point. This side of me could unnerve Barbara. On the other hand, I could be boring and bourgeois: sitting on the sofa, watching football, drinking beer and playing cards. A few days before we split up, I'd celebrated my thirty-third birthday. I'd gone with a few mates to the Olympic stadium in Munich and watched a grotty match where FC Bayern beat Lyons 1–nil in the Champions League. But for me that was a great way to celebrate my birthday – without any song and dance. Afterwards we all went to Schumann's, my favourite bar in Munich, where Barbara had put on a show that was over the top and not at all what I wanted.

We'd lost our intimacy. To the outside world we were the perfect couple, the darlings of the tabloids. Barbara in a pink silk dress and Boris in black tie next to producer Arthur Cohn at the Oscars in Los Angeles. Boris and Elton John playing tennis at the Beverly Hills Hotel; in the background, mother and sons playing in the pool. What a perfect picture. Barbara was the 'first lady' of Germany, and at a state reception at Schloss Bellevue she could bewitch French president Chirac as easily as German president Johannes Rau. The more we wanted to escape the darkness that was our private life, the more we sought the limelight. We fled on to the stage where millions could see us, because at home there was not enough space for the two of us, and like two actors we let the world believe all was well with us, when in fact it was in ruins.

'For some time we've been aware that our understanding of the priorities in our relationship was not mutual. We now know that we can't go on any longer. We are separating, but there's no talk of divorce.'[1] On Tuesday 5 December 2000 at 12.34, this press release was sent out by my PR agency lübMEDIA over the fax machine. What happened next has been described by my PR adviser Robert Lübenoff as follows: 'Nobody believed it. I had to resend dozens of this release with my signature on because most people thought it was a spoof.'

It was deadly serious, but the country didn't want to know. 'Babsi? Boris? Breaking up? This was about as likely as Edmund Stoiber and his CSU (Conservative Party) asking the Greens for political asylum,[2] was how *Stern* put it. Under the headline 'Is nothing sacred any more?' *Spiegel* wrote: 'Another great illusion shattered – the dream of romantic love, the perfect relationship and long-lasting happiness. The age-old and yet always new story of the short-lived nature of heaven on earth has shattered the beautiful image of the multicultural dream couple, and with it the image of another kind of Germany.'[3] And another magazine, *Bunte*, which a week before had celebrated me on their front cover as 'Germany's sexiest man' and over the years had built up our marriage into a national treasure, told its readers over fourteen pages: 'The dream marriage that wasn't.'[4]

Bild was already one step ahead. 'Is it over because of *her*?'[5] the paper asked. And twelve million readers believed that Sabrina Setlur, a German rap star, was the reason for our split. Later on, Sabrina and I really were a couple for a while, but at that point she was just a good friend – of Barbara's as well as mine. Parts of the international press even thought that there was a political dimension to the end of our relationship. 'Nazis wreck Becker's marriage!'[6] said the *Sun*. *The Times* asked itself: 'Is the failure of Boris Becker's marriage a signal for Germans that racially mixed marriages are burdened by too many cultural problems?'[7]

The official divorce rate in Germany then stood at 36 per

cent,[8] which meant 3.9 million divorcees. At that point Barbara and I, however, still belonged to the group of married people living apart, of whom there were 1.3 million. That we would go down in history forty-one days after our press release as the second-fastest divorce in post-war Germany, I would never have thought possible. But events were spiralling out of control.

On the Monday after I'd poured my heart out to my mother, and before the press release had gone out, I'd flown to Hamburg to celebrate my fifth anniversary with advertising partner AOL. No one – my friends, my business partners or the press – knew what was going on inside my head. A day later, I was back in Munich packing clothes for my forthcoming business trips when everything came to a head. Barbara was running around distraught. She wanted to go to America, to a hotel in New York. The phone lines had been red hot the previous weekend, and friends had come by the score to our villa in Bogenhausen. The result was that everything we had discussed just forty-eight hours before had gone out of the window. I began to think that America might not be such a bad idea. As soon as the press release went out the media would have a field day, and it might be better if the family were abroad. And we had to tell the media so there was no chance of rumours spreading like wildfire. 'OK then,' I said. 'But don't go to New York. Go to Miami, to Fisher Island. You'll be left alone there.' Nicknamed the VIP ghetto, Fisher Island in the sea off South Beach had for some years now been our private refuge, our island of peace and security.

That's when Barbara realized I was serious. Even her threat to take the children to the States hadn't made me change my mind. She was confused and uncertain. All of a sudden she said, 'Don't go. We'll manage. Please let's try.'

But I didn't want to go back on what we'd decided. 'No, Barbara. This is my decision. We desperately need this break.'

She pulled herself together and said, 'OK, then I'm going to Miami.'

On Friday morning she flew off with the children. The press release went out on Tuesday, and I also gave an interview to the German press agency DPA during my Mercedes commercial shoot in Cannes, as an act of damage limitation. I didn't want the media to tear us to shreds. 'We have fought long and hard for our marriage,' is how DPA editor Andreas Bellinger headlined the interview, and he quoted me: 'On one hand my wife was like the queen at my side. That is and was a wonderful role to play, but it was also restrictive, oppressive, perhaps in the end overwhelming. That's why I cannot accuse Barbara of anything. I have nothing but respect for my wife that she coped with this for so long. She handled it all extremely well, but time does not go by without leaving its mark. That's what we are paying the price for now.'[9]

Barbara had been away with the children for a week. We talked over the phone, still arguing. At one point I wasn't allowed to speak to the children any more. 'They don't want to talk to you,' she said. But Elias could hardly talk at all yet, and Noah and I had been bound heart and soul for the six years of his life and I knew he'd never say something like that. I began to worry. Barbara had her friend Kim with her, the wife of my tennis-mate Charly Steeb. I had never completely trusted Kim and felt she was a bad influence on Barbara. So I called Charly: 'Get your wife out of there. This is none of her or your business. Or else.'

On Sunday morning, nine days after Barbara had left, I was on my way to Miami.

The apartment was empty, abandoned. No Barbara, no Elias, no Noah. 'Where on earth are they, dammit?' Nobody knew a thing, or perhaps they didn't want to tell me. Hours passed, and a thunderstorm rolled in. I called all the people I knew in Miami, and I eventually found them with Tariq, an Arab friend of mine. 'Yes, Barbara and the children are here with me,' he said.

'Give me Barbara,' I demanded. When she came to the phone, I said, 'I want to see the children now. Bring them here or I'll come over there.'

I was trying to stay in control. She was cool, and sounded strange, and didn't want to speak to me for long. Tariq came back on the line. 'Tariq, I want to see my children right now. I'm coming over to get them.'

Tariq tried to calm me down. 'Listen to me, Boris. I'm your friend. You're both very emotional. You're not yourselves at the moment.'

But that just made me angrier. 'I've travelled all the way here from Munich and I've been sitting in this empty apartment for hours. I have every right to see my children!'

Tariq didn't give in. 'You're not setting foot on my property today. If you do, I'll call the police. I'm doing this for your own sake.'

I set off anyway. Tariq didn't live on Fisher Island but in Miami Beach, so I had to get to the ferry first. For security reasons Fisher Island can only be reached by ferry or helicopter. I didn't have a car, so I had to get to the ferry on foot. In the meantime, the thunderstorm had broken and it was raining heavily. I was soaked to the skin in minutes, but the drenching cleared my head. I walked back home and called Tariq. 'I'll come over tomorrow.'

The next day we hugged each other. 'Thank you, Tariq.' I had calmed down, although I'd had a bad night of it. 'Where are the children?'

My friend replied that Noah was in school.

'What do you mean, school? He goes to school in Munich. What are you talking about?' Elias was lying peacefully in a cot. His nanny looked up at me, concerned.

'Barbara's very angry. You'd better watch out, Boris.' There was a warning undertone to his voice.

'What should I watch out for?' I told Tariq my version of events, and he was taken aback. This was hard for Tariq – he loved us both.

Finally I got Barbara on the phone. 'I'll be there in an hour,' she said. More waiting. After three hours I left Tariq's house to go for lunch at my regular haunt, the Sports Café in South Beach. 'Please come and meet me there when you're ready,' I said to Barbara. As soon as I switched off the mobile, I noticed that a car was following mine. After all my years in the company of paparazzi I have a sixth sense for this kind of thing. 'Oh shit. What's happening now?'

I got out of my car. The man got out of his. He was a bit smaller than me; I could handle him, I thought. He asked me whether I was Boris Becker. I said yes, and he handed me a twelve-page document. 'Case No. 00-30252 IN RE: The Marriage of Barbara Becker, Wife, and Boris Becker, Husband . . .' I read, feeling sick. 'Would you please tell me what this is all about?' I asked.

'This is the first step in the divorce process on American soil,' he said, and got back into his car.

I stood there for a moment as if I'd been turned to stone, but then my ever-reliable instinct kicked in. Not in my worst nightmares had I dreamt that Barbara would serve American divorce papers on me. Six months before this she'd renewed her American passport, and now Noah had been enrolled at an American school in a matter of days. I was beginning to smell a rat. Perhaps while our arguments had been escalating over the past two years, Barbara had been formulating Plan B.

And back in Germany, on this very day, the news broke: 'Boris's love child. Is *this* the true reason for the break-up?'[10] Was there some kind of conspiracy between London and Miami? Did they all want to finish me off at once?

During our early years together, Barbara hadn't liked Miami at all. It was me who'd chosen Fisher Island for us. During the last few months, however, she'd been spending weeks at a time there. Later I heard a lot of rumours about networks that had been built, connections that had been set up and preparations that had been made. The fact was that only two weeks after we'd decided to separate, my wife was so well organized that Noah was already in an American school, and as early as 8 December her lawyers were ready to file a case at Miami-Dade Circuit Court in order to secure her exclusive custody of our children and appropriate alimony.[11]

With the serving of the papers outside the Sports Café, a procedure that would be unthinkable in Germany, I was forced to submit myself to American legal processes. It seemed that Barbara and her lawyers, in particular one Samuel Burstyn, were going to hang me out to dry. I was asked to produce all my bank statements, insurance policies, records of pension plans and other investments, credit-card statements, share documents, bonds, inventories of property and possessions, income-tax records of the last three years, my diaries of the last three years, video and audio tapes that had resulted from various investigations, and even the current status of my frequent-flyer accounts with all the airlines I'd used over the last few years. All of this had to be produced within forty-five days.

It was madness. I was stripped bare in public – because in the States almost all court documents and processes are public. Any paper in the world could print all the details from the files of the court case *Becker* v. *Becker*. Barbara's case was based on bold assertions: allegedly the Becker family, including myself, had lived on Fisher Island for five years. Allegedly Barbara didn't have her own bank account. Allegedly Barbara feared that I wanted to kidnap the children. All of this my wife solemnly affirmed.

I went into the Sports Café anyway and ate a lunch of mozzarella with tomatoes and spaghetti al pomodoro, just like I used to eat before my big matches. Barbara, of course, didn't show up, but in her place came Andrea, whom I'd hired as her secretary a few years before.

'Please have a word with Barbara. I don't want to do this through the lawyers. If it's about money, she should tell me what she needs. You've known me long enough to know that won't be a problem.'

On 16 September 1993 we had signed a pre-nuptial agreement at a solicitor's in Munich, in which the rules were laid out in the event of divorce. Since those documents were published in connection with the hearing in Miami, I'm not revealing anything new when I say that if we divorced Barbara was to get five million marks. So what was her point, what was she trying to achieve?

That afternoon I finally met up with her. She had left Tariq's house and returned, together with Noah and Elias, to the apartment on Fisher Island. On the balcony things came to a head in a bitter argument.

'Barbara, what the hell are you playing at?'

'I'm going to get the best lawyers in Miami.'

'OK, then I'll get the city's second-best lawyers. But this is going to be dirty, and neither of us will gain from it.'

I left the apartment and spent the night in a hotel on Fisher Island. The next morning we met again. Meanwhile I'd been in touch with my advisers and lawyers in Germany and got the name of a lawyer in Miami. This was a final attempt to prevent the affair from escalating, but it was the same as the day before: screaming and shouting.

'I have to go now. I have a meeting at three with the second-best lawyers of Miami. But in the end it will all be shit, because neither of us is going to win.'

The children were running around in between us. Barbara kept shouting and swearing at me. I tried to remain calm and pleaded, 'Please, not in front of the children.' She positioned herself in the doorway and shouted, 'You're not going!' I ran through the kitchen and out of the back door. I wanted to get out – for her sake as well as mine. An hour later I was sitting with my lawyers in Miami. The battle had begun.

'The Boris return came one week later: precise, and painful for the wife,' wrote *Stern*.[12] I had positioned my armies of lawyers. There were Baker & McKenzie, one of the biggest worldwide legal firms, who were based on the nineteenth floor of an office block on Brickel Avenue in downtown Miami. In Munich I'd put my trusted lawyer Georg Stock in charge. After the last encounter with Barbara I'd left Miami as quickly as possible and met up with him. I sympathized with Barbara, in principle, and could understand how she'd become so furious. It was me who had left her. It was also me who had betrayed her and made another woman pregnant. But I didn't want to let her destroy me and I didn't want to destroy the Becker family. As soon as I realized that over the last few months Barbara had prepared a plan in case our marriage failed, my instincts were reawakened. Becker developed his match plan, but this time I wasn't playing to win. I was hoping for a draw. This situation was new to me. The lawyers in Miami split their sides laughing when I said, 'I don't want to defeat my wife. All I want is a future for our children.'

On the evening of 14 December, I had a meeting with my lawyers in my house on Lamontstraße. The silence made me apprehensive. All the laughter had gone. We analysed the situation as soberly as investment planners. The result: the pre-nuptial agreement that Barbara and I had entered into in 1993 was only valid in Germany. It was therefore necessary to deny the American courts jurisdiction over our divorce. To achieve this we had to file for divorce on German territory in a German court. This was the only way to prevent a divorce war in the United States.

The next day, two days before our seventh wedding anniversary, we filed for divorce at the family court in Munich under the reference number 0220003302, on the grounds that the marriage had been failing for around two years and the two parties had lived separately within the common home. Several attempts at reconciliation on the part of the claimants had been unsuccessful, or had failed after only a few days.

Countless discussions, encounters of the most emotional kind and a lake of tears were reduced to legal jargon.

At the same time, my US lawyers filed an appeal against the case being heard in the States. After all, the Becker family were resident in Germany, Barbara and I had married in Leimen, and Noah had been going to school in Munich. On 19 December – by now I'd lost all contact with my children – we filed at the federal court in Karlsruhe for 'the return of the children Noah and Elias'. Our claim was not based on the grounds that Barbara had taken the children to Miami against my will, as was often falsely reported in the media, but on the Hague Convention, which since 1980 had regulated aspects of civil law in cases of international child kidnapping by parents of different nationalities. It is applicable even in those cases where children were taken abroad with the agree-ment of a custodian (and it was I who had advised Barbara to go to Miami for a while), but where the stay in the other country turns into a permanent one. In order to round off our counter-attack, on 20 December at Munich's family court we asked for an interim injunction, demanding the return of the children to Munich and giving me sole custody. The legal ship was in full sail – but I still wanted to enjoy Christmas with my children.

So I returned to Miami. On the morning of 24 December, as agreed with Barbara, I picked up Noah and Elias. At long last the three of us were together. Had my boys already changed? Had Barbara set them against me? Did they still love their daddy? I felt uncomfortable to start with. I watched every gesture and examined every remark they made. Soon my fears had gone. We went window-shopping in the mall, ate burgers, had fun. My mobile rang. One of my lawyers told me that Barbara's lawyers claimed I wanted to kidnap the children. Barbara was distraught, they said. I tried to reach her, but her mobile was switched off.

Back on Fisher Island, on this sunny Christmas Eve, her greeting was frosty. 'You can forget about our Christmas together. I don't trust you. I'm scared of you,' she said.

'Hang on a minute. I've come back from Germany specially. This kidnapping thing is pure invention. They just want to play us off against each other,' I replied. 'But if it's of any help to you, we'll call the police and celebrate Christmas with a few of them around.'

I picked up the phone, and she gave in. We had Christmas together. Barbara and I hardly spoke a word, but for the children it seemed to be the same as always. Their eyes shone, and Noah gently placed his hand on my knee. 'Nice that you're here, Daddy.' I spent New Year's Eve in Germany with my lawyer, Stock. The Christmas truce was over.

BECKER VERSUS BECKER

IT COULD HAVE BEEN THE BECKER COMPANY OUTING: babysitter, cook, bodyguards, my mother – about a dozen people sitting late one afternoon in the bar of the Marriott Hotel in South Beach. Happy hour had just finished, and from our brown leather stools we could see the beach in front of the hotel begin to empty. It was unusually chilly that evening. The next day, 4 January 2001, was the hearing to decide whether *Becker* v. *Becker* in Miami would have to be public or could take place in private.

My American lawyers had requested that the case be heard behind closed doors to protect our children and our privacy. In Florida, the public have a clearly enshrined legal right to inform themselves about state-run business. The so-called Sunshine Law gives everyone access to documents; it's even possible to video-record meetings of government representatives. In Germany, not even the father-in-law is allowed to attend family court hearings, let alone strangers or the media.

'Corona beer all round.' I tried to calm everyone's nerves. The actual court hearing on the issue of whether *Becker* v. *Becker* could be dealt with in Miami was scheduled for Monday 8 January. Only my appearance was planned for the next day. 'We'll be out of there in thirty minutes,' my two US lawyers, Robert Kohlman and Donald Hayden, had promised me at our meeting that afternoon. Nevertheless, the mood was tense. Everyone was mentally preparing to be called as a witness. The idea was to refute Barbara's claim that the Beckers had lived on Fisher Island for five years, by calling the cook, the bodyguards and other members of staff to the witness box – which was why I'd had them all flown in. But they all seemed scared of Barbara. She really must have had some power over them.

The hearing was to take place at ten-thirty on the twenty-second floor of Miami's family court, the twenty-eight-storey building on First Avenue, near Interstate 95. I'd never been in court in my life (my tax hearing in Germany was still a thing of the future), either as defendant or witness. In this case I was the claimant, not the defendant, but I was nervous all the same. I drove up in my black Mercedes M-class wearing a dark suit and tie (not my usual style). The waiting mob of press people didn't help my nerves. Around a hundred reporters were besieging the entrance. The twenty-four journalists admitted by Judge Maynard Gross, known to his friends as Skip, were already waiting, among them a cameraman and a photographer. The images they captured would be accessible to everyone.

I stood there with my right hand raised and my left hand, wearing my wedding ring, out of sight, and swore to tell the truth and nothing but the truth.

'What is your name?' It was translated into German for me.

'Boris Franz Becker,' I replied. Yes, my middle name is Franz, after my father's father, as tradition in our family demands. My sons also bear their grandfather's name.

The judge in his green chair played lazily with his ballpoint pen. A gold chain dangled from his wrist. He'd seen it all a thousand times before, but for me the experience was raw and painful.

'What is your profession?'

'I was a professional tennis player for fifteen years.'

'Where do you live?'

'In Munich, Germany.'

'Do you have children?'

'Yes, two boys.'

I'd asked my lawyer Mr Kohlman for my questions to be translated into German. I replied in German, and this was translated into English. I speak English quite well, but I preferred under these circumstances to answer in my mother tongue, and the translating also bought me a little thinking time. Kohlman, who'd been brought in by Baker & McKenzie as a family lawyer, explained that my children had to be guarded constantly because of threats we'd received. He also explained that all my advertising contracts included confidentiality clauses and therefore couldn't be made public.

Enter Sam. 'Samuel Burstyn is a well-built man who waves his papers around as he strides up and down. His hair is as uncontrollable as the man himself. From the outset, Burstyn tries to destroy the picture of "Franz" Becker, the former professional tennis player from Munich with the two little boys. But the Beckers are Germans, they married in Germany, their children were born in Germany, they speak German. There can be no grounds for a discussion of their divorce in Miami of all places,' writes *Spiegel* correspondent Alexander Osang, who recorded our exchange.

'Mr Becker, isn't it the case that you speak perfect English?' asks Burstyn.

'Only as far as "forehand", "service" and "backhand slice" go,' Becker replies.

'Why aren't you allowed to discuss your contracts?' asks Burstyn.

'Contracts may not be discussed in public. This is different from the way it is in America,' says Becker.

'But we are in America,' says Burstyn, and laughs. It was a good comment. 'Isn't it the case that you do not want to talk about your financial affairs because you are under criminal investigation by the German tax authorities?'

'I've been in a legal tug-of-war with the Bavarian tax authorities for four years,' says Becker.

Burstyn stalks through the courtroom like a cockerel, waves papers under Becker's nose, tosses dates into the air and shrieks when Becker has apparently understood an English question before it's been translated. He jabs his glasses at his foe.[1]

This guy cornered me and grilled me. Never mind my lawyer's thirty minutes – 'Four hours' torture,'[2] more like. *Spiegel* wrote: 'At the end of the hearing Becker looks more like Herr Becker from southern Germany than the former world number one tennis player. More Franz than Boris.'[3]

Skip rejects our motion. Most of the German papers cheer. First set to Barbara! The hearing scheduled for 8 January should, except for a few sensitive issues, be public. Today's hearing alone had been a novelty for Germany – the news channel N24 had broadcast all four hours of it live. 'It was all very exciting,' *Spiegel* reported Jörg Howe, chief editor of SAT.1, as saying.[4] Howe went on to promise that, for the hearing on 8 January, 'As long as the judge admits the public, we're broadcasting it.' His colleague Hans Mahr from RTL also planned a special broadcast, as though it was the most normal thing in the world to do. '*Not* broadcasting it would be problematic. If the judge makes it public, we certainly mustn't ignore it.'[5]

No one could have known at that point that the whole thing was part of my match plan. I would have liked a somewhat smoother ride, of course, but the strategy was to display Boris in this relatively unimportant hearing as the victim who was being hung out to dry. Two reasons. First, there was Barbara's lawyer, Sam. By coincidence, I'd met Mr Burstyn before. An acquaintance of Barbara's and mine, one Daniel Deubelbeiss, had invited us to a home match of the Miami heats a few weeks before our break-up. I was introduced that night to Mr Burstyn. During our conversation I got the impression that he didn't like Germany or the Germans at all. So it seemed to me important that he got the chance to vent his feelings and take it all out on the blond, blue-eyed German tennis hero. If allowed to do this in public, he'd be more amenable to an out-of-court settlement.

Much more important, however, was my humiliation in front of Barbara. She had threatened to finish me off, but after those 107 minutes of questioning, she got cold feet. If someone like Boris Becker, who'd played tennis in front of millions of people and given interviews in front of thousands of cameras, could be driven to the edge by one lawyer, what would happen to her when she was being grilled by my lawyers? And Kohlman and Hayden would have built up a real head of steam after having been made to look like losers in this public hearing.

'Boris, we have to meet at once.' I couldn't believe my ears. I'd only been out of the courtroom for a couple of hours when Barbara called me on my mobile. 'Please come to the island.'

I was in turmoil. The grilling had unsettled me, and my people looked as if they'd collectively reached the end of the world. But I went, on my own.

I entered our home carefully, like a husband coming in after a night out on the tiles with his mates, expecting his wife to be behind the door brandishing a rolling pin. What was going to happen? Bodily attacks, or some other provocation? But Barbara was sweet and gentle, like she'd been when I first fell in love with her. She was open, understanding, even loving, and she gave me the impression that she was sorry for what had happened to me. 'We have to find a solution,' she said in a firm voice.

I was defensive. 'It was tough today. But my lawyers will follow this example and interview you in the same way about your claim to have been resident in Miami for the past five years and so on.'

Her eyes showed real fear. 'Let's come to an arrangement, let's find a compromise,' she pleaded.

'What kind of compromise do you have in mind?' I asked her coolly.

'Please call Sam,' she said.

At six I called Sam, the very same man who four hours earlier had been trampling all over me. 'Hi, Sam. It's Boris.'

I'd rediscovered my English. I made a date with Sam for the next day, which was the Friday when Barbara should have been facing my lawyers, starting at nine in the morning . . .

We met for lunch in the elegant Bankers Club: Barbara, Sam, me and Stock. We sat there over steak and salad like four business partners. Sam was being matey. He understood, he said, how I'd made a contribution to race relations by marrying a black woman. He praised me for my courage and explained how he was really on my side. Then he advised me, 'Follow your instincts.' But that was the last thing you should do in court. Stock and I got hard-nosed.

'Let's talk about maintenance. But we'll do this only if we get the divorce – right now, that is,' said Stock. What lay behind this was that if she'd settled for maintenance without divorce, Barbara would have gained the right for an American divorce after six months.

'No, we don't want to divorce. We're so good together.' It was as if Barbara had suddenly realized what she'd set in motion. 'No, no, no,' she said, and talked for ten minutes about us as a couple as if nothing had happened. 'Well then, I'll become a singer,' she then announced, and started to sing in a low voice.

Sam stepped in. 'Barbara, it's too late now. This is about facts and figures, not feelings. Your husband is suggesting a fair deal.'

We finally shook hands and agreed to reach a watertight deal over the weekend so that the court hearing on Monday would no longer be necessary.

That evening I took my people to Joia, South Beach's 'in' restaurant, which used to be part-owned by Madonna. The place was right opposite our hotel. It had become a sort of officers' mess, where those involved in the battle by day got together at night. Dozens of journalists gathered there and exchanged what little information they had. They besieged us, but we managed to shield ourselves from them, and in their desperation they invented a new journalistic form: they interviewed each other. The man from RTL interviewed the man from *Bild* about his impressions, and vice versa. Even Sam came to Joia that night, and he bought me a drink. But I briefed my people to remain prepared for battle. Before I could trust an out-of-court settlement I needed to see a signed document.

Daniel Deubelbeiss, who with his girth and his ponytail looked a bit like Meat Loaf, had become something like Barbara's battle adviser in this divorce. It was he who'd brought Burstyn on to the field. Together we worked out how much money Barbara would need for herself and the children. Barbara agreed to our proposal and I thanked Daniel for his punctiliousness. The maintenance we agreed on was astronomical, but that money was for my children. Barbara's share was in line with our pre-nuptial agreement. In addition, she got the apartment on Fisher Island, in exchange for which, however, she had to give me her share in the finca on Majorca. The lawyers at Baker & McKenzie transformed the figures into a contractual agreement and the next day the German lawyers of both parties agreed on the German wording. Everything went well.

On Sunday night we went to dinner on Fisher Island. Some German friends who'd been passing by were there too. At half past nine Barbara's phone rang. Daniel was on the line. 'Sam's got a problem. Your lawyers haven't given their approval yet.' Barbara called Sam, and when she put down the phone she

was upset. 'Sam doesn't believe you. He says you're a cheat.'
Sam Burstyn had threatened that he'd only continue to
negotiate if his lawsuit was accepted and my claims, based on
the Hague Convention, were withdrawn.

'You see, Barbara, now we're back at square one. You have
to trust me, otherwise it'll be your turn tomorrow. The
lawyers want their showdown, but I want this to be over. I'm
not messing around with you. I'll say it again: I will keep my
promise. My lawyers will agree to it tomorrow.'

The hearing was scheduled for nine on Monday morning.
Barbara and I were waiting with some of our lawyers in a
conference room at Evan Marks's, Barbara's American family
lawyer. From here you had a wonderful view of the sea, but
on this particular morning none of us cared for it. An hour
before the hearing, Marks was still insisting the suit be
accepted. My lawyers refused and demanded the hearing.
Burstyn, who was supposed to be on his way to the court,
came on the telephone and asked for an adjournment. That
was fine by me. After all, I'd made that very suggestion the
day before – but Burstyn hadn't wanted to listen then. We
spent just seven minutes in court and the hearing was
adjourned to 18 January. Burstyn, who had brought his small
son to the court for the second part of the show, declared to
the judge that the wording of the contract was 90 per cent
settled.

Barbara shed tears of relief. She knew that she no longer
had to make a statement in court and that I had kept my
word. Thirty minutes later we were to meet at Burstyn's to do
the fine-tuning. Thirty minutes turned to sixty, one o'clock
came, five o'clock came, and finally at seven o'clock Barbara
and Evan Marks produced a counter-proposal which was no

longer anything to do with what had been agreed. The new demands were roughly fifteen million Euros higher than what had been discussed between Daniel and me. I was furious. Did the whole show have to start all over again? I rejected it and set Wednesday as the deadline by which they had to return to the old agreement. The media described it as an ultimatum. At the same time the news broke in Germany about the paternity case that had been brought against me in London. And the Munich tax authorities were also making hay while the sun shone by demanding a payment of ten million marks.

If you want to win a tournament you have think match by match, set by set, point by point. London, Munich – at that moment they didn't interest me. I had to get Miami done; then I could deal with the next problem. One step at a time. Another reconciliation talk with Daniel, another million on top. On Thursday 12 January, around nine p.m. it was finally done. Barbara – who looked wonderful that night in her black leather trousers – was the first to sign the German and English versions of the two agreements: one about the consequences of the divorce and the other about the division of the assets. Then me. Barbara jumped up, cheered and shouted, 'I don't have to go to court!'

Burstyn said, 'Now that the hay's in, let's go celebrate.'

I looked at him, aghast. 'Guys, today is the saddest day of my life. I've just got divorced. I don't feel like celebrating.'

Barbara went with her people to a steak house; I went with a few friends to Joia again. Campari and soda, a few beers, a seafood risotto. I felt empty.

*

My return flight is scheduled for Sunday afternoon. The divorce hearing at Munich's family court is set for Monday at ten. At last, I get to sleep in, no more agonizing thoughts, no more discussions with lawyers. Then Barbara calls me. 'Why don't you come over one last time?'

It is a wonderful Saturday morning. There's no wind; the waves roll gently on to the white beach. The children laugh. Barbara's happy. We swim in the sea, eat at the beach bar, play with the boys. It's like the old days, as if nothing has happened. Noah pleads with me, 'Daddy, stay another day.' I stay overnight at the hotel on the island. The next day it's the same: pure happiness and harmony like in a trashy romance. At midday I say goodbye. 'Noah, I'll be back in time for your birthday.' Noah beams.

Barbara says, 'You don't have to go now. Let's postpone the divorce proceedings. Why don't you stay?' She walks me to the ferry and wraps both arms around me.

'Barbara, this is like a dream. We mustn't forget the last four weeks. A lot has happened. I've made mistakes and you've made mistakes. I'm flying back to Munich now and I'm going to get the divorce over and done with. If we're still on good terms afterwards – who knows? Thanks to the children we'll always be together. And if the old flame is rekindled, I actually wouldn't mind. I still have feelings for you.'

By ten twenty-four on Monday morning it's all over. I almost missed my own divorce. The plane was delayed and I had to change in the car, getting into my dark-blue suit and putting that tie on again. The judge was already waiting impatiently in room 616 on the sixth floor – my lucky number is seven. It took twenty-five minutes. Barbara had made a declaration and was represented by her lawyer Heinz Stolzki.

We leave the building together and walk the six minutes to the office of my lawyer, Georg Stock, at Promenadeplatz. 'Becker's walk became a media event,' *Bild* would write.[6] Dozens of cameras follow us and I can't resist a smile. A glass of champagne in Stock's meeting room, one last press conference, and then the chapter of the Beckers' marriage is closed. Back in Miami, it takes another eleven days before Burstyn withdraws Barbara's lawsuit. Even he's finally got it: the show's over.

PIGEON-HOLING

WEST GERMANY'S YOUTH, WROTE THE *INTERNATIONAL Herald Tribune* in 1986, 'have returned to conservative values ... Their emblem is Boris Becker – the money-making, apolitical, 18-year-old tennis star – and not Petra Kelly, the 38-year-old founder of the Green party.'[1] I had been 'manipulated into a spectacular figurehead in the West German republic, without raising a single objection',[2] according to the East German author Klaus Ullrich in his book *Der weiße Dschungel* (*The White Jungle*), published by an East German house.

From New York to East Berlin it was clear: Boris Becker was rich, right-wing and reactionary. After all, my dad was a dyed-in-the-wool conservative; in Leimen we went to mass, and Becker the altar boy ran around the parish with the holy water. My mother ironed my father's shirts, and they sat down together to watch the German equivalent of *Crimewatch* on the television. Good old conservative provincial world.

This, however, had little to do with my real position in society. I have never presented myself at a party political meeting – unlike John McEnroe, for example, who appeared in November 1999 at an address of the former basketball star Bill Bradley, who wanted to become president. I never allowed myself to be courted by the left or the right. And my encounters with the great and the good left me with ambivalent impressions. After Wimbledon 1985, I chatted with President Richard von Weizsäcker, a decent man and a Christian Democrat, on the sports programme *Aktuelle Sportstudio*. Gerhard Schröder of the SPD invited me to a private discussion at his official residence and addressed me with the informal 'du' to 'help the relationship along'. During the time of his predecessor, CDU Chancellor Helmut Kohl, however, I wasn't offered so much as a cup of coffee. In his sixteen years in power, Kohl exchanged no more than half a dozen words with me. Perhaps he was annoyed that I was at least as popular as he was! He certainly didn't like my going to the Hafenstraße in Hamburg to find out how the squatters lived. In those days a few houses had been taken over by squatters and sprayed with colourful graffiti. My sponsors Müllermilch saw me pictured manning the barricades and were annoyed. 'If you support anarchism or any other illegal movement then we can no longer sponsor you. That is self-evident,'[3] *Bild* quoted the dairy producers as saying. 'Have you gone mad?' a well-known voice demanded. It was not my Christian Democrat father, but Ion Tiriac.

What I found remarkable was the public response to the squats. Many people were confused and didn't know how to react. After all, it could have been their sons and daughters throwing stones then getting off their heads with marijuana.

I never doubted that some of those guys found pleasure in violence, but most of the squatters were simply disillusioned young people unable to accept the alternatives the political system had on offer.

I never came to terms with Germany's stereotypical thinking, where everything belongs in predetermined little boxes. My mother had often warned me, 'Son, preach whatever left-leaning theories you like, they'll never accept it, because you'll always be numbered among the rich and therefore among the right.' Well, let them. I stuck to my views, even though they didn't always fit into the left–right scheme of things. Even my father couldn't cure me of this. I'd wind him up with my own ideas or ones that came from the Greens or the Reds. We often clashed, so much so that when Karen wrote her letter of condolence to my mother, she said that she still remembered those lively political discussions we used to have in Leimen.

Outside home, thinking came in pre-packaged portions: Becker advertises for Deutsche Bank, therefore he's a right-wing supporter of the consumer society. Becker shows sympathy for the squatters, therefore he's on the left. One day I was a capitalist, the next day a communist. 'In those days, whenever the federal president, or a columnist, or anyone interested in creating a better Germany mentioned the young Boris B., they were always lecturing from an assumed position on the moral high ground, from where they wanted to demonstrate to young people across Germany and all over the world what kind of lessons they had to learn from his situation,' said the journalist Herbert Riehl-Heyse. 'Look – was the message – at what you can achieve if you make a commitment, work hard and have enough willpower, and furthermore have two nice middle-class parents, one of whom is a part-time councillor for the CDU and a guest of honour at Wimbledon. Around 1985 and 1986 Becker was clearly en route, with the help of an alliance of Weizsäcker and *Bild* and everything in between, to be the idol of the young people of Germany . . . No wonder, then, that German youth, who used to nickname him Bobbele, began to be annoyed with him.'[4]

I never wanted to be a role model; I was co-opted by the nation. At the Davis Cup, people shouted 'Deutschland' and waved the black, red and gold flag, while I was reading books about student rebellions, Red Army Faction terrorism and the German identity. I read everything I could lay my hands on, sometimes several books at the same time, from Eckermann's *Conversations with Goethe* to *The Baader-Meinhof Group* by Stefan Aust. No one had recommended this book to me. I just wanted to know what was happening in Germany. 'It was not a time of contemplation,' wrote Aust. 'Every day the papers ratcheted up the fear people had of the Baader-Meinhof group. They stirred up the public's emotions and gave the members of the group, who studied their actions' reflection in the media, a feeling of their own importance.'[5]

In May 1968, while students worldwide were rebelling, little Boris had just started crawling. I was named after Boris Pasternak, the author of *Dr Zhivago*, which my mother had read before I was born. What if I'd been born earlier, in one of the poor quarters of Latin America or a half-ruined house in the Bronx? Which side of the barricades would I have stood on in 1968 then? The inequalities of the world have not passed me by, nor have I been willing to accept them. My own wealth hasn't prevented me from having my disputes with champagne society, people who at the big tennis matches in Germany were mostly interested in getting themselves into the limelight. In 1989, at the Davis Cup final against Sweden in Stuttgart, I felt particularly disgusted by the whole VIP thing. All this feasting and wheeling and dealing by people who in all honesty were acting against the interests of the true fans. Long before the start of the tournament they'd sold thousands of tickets to anonymous sponsors. I understand those who feel that tennis was spoiled by things like that.

One Christmas Day in the early 1990s, I bumped into Peter Ustinov at the Hotel Oriental in Bangkok. I didn't really know who he was. He introduced himself and we started talking. He'd been following my career for years, he told me. Would I like to have dinner with him? When people meet me for the first time, they are often astonished that I can count to ten and string more than one sentence together, and about things other than tennis. There were no such problems with Ustinov. He's a fascinating man, and very good company. But he too couldn't resist analysing me afterwards. 'A very German mixture,' he declared. 'Sometimes this brutal, incomparable presence, then a sensitive, poetic pessimist. Now a thundering serve, then that very German, rather self-destructive melancholy gnawing away at him.'[6]

The things I sometimes did and said annoyed Tiriac, in particular, who saw his advertising strategy jeopardized. 'You're young, you've got millions,' he said to me. 'You've got scores of women knocking at your door. What more do you want?' And when I replied, 'Substance, Ion. Meaning. Some sense to it all,' he looked at me in pity and said no more. He had other priorities. The way he saw it, he'd been deprived when he was growing up, whereas in our house the fridge was always loaded. I wasn't in love with money. When I was sixteen I dreamt of having a hi-fi, but that was it. But I didn't know then how important those piles of money would one day be in securing my freedom.

At the beginning of my career, I found it hard to act naturally. I stuttered and hesitated. Those smart reporters made fun of me, especially the ones who disliked Becker anyway. I was eighteen, nineteen, and I knew that every word I said could be torn apart. It made me uncertain; I kept analysing what I wanted to say, knowing that any word I uttered could be misinterpreted. In private I was relaxed and easygoing; in public I talked excitedly in short sentences. At some point I realized that some people would always envy me, and from then on it didn't matter any more.

'In the short period of transition from teenager to twenty-something, from adolescent to voter,' wrote Hans-Josef Justen in the paper *Westdeutschen Allgemeinen Zeitung*, 'he's had more experiences than whole generations of hundred-year-olds.'[7] It's funny how when people talked about me there were often hints about a political career. After my 6–3, 6–7, 6–7, 7–6, 4–6 defeat by Sampras at the ATP final in Hanover in 1996, the Austrian newspaper *Standard* announced that Becker had begun to present himself as a superhuman phenomenon who might even become president of Germany one day. I'd only just turned twenty-nine. President? Why not Pope, or at least chancellor? I had turned into Hercules, who had power over the masses and therefore political potential. But what on earth could I achieve in politics that I couldn't achieve from the outside? I know a few influential people, I'm not a card-carrying member of any political party, I've got a few Euros in the bank and I'm independent. And I'm no pushover. If someone steps on my toes too often, I react. As a party member I'd have to hold myself back, be disciplined. That's out of the question for me; it always has been.

In 1993 I happened to meet Günter Grass at one of the wooden tables at Schumann's. After some small talk he started telling me the story of Sisyphus in Greek mythology, who repeatedly rolls a rock up a hill. Just before he reaches the top each time, the rock rolls back into the valley. Sisyphus, undaunted, begins his labour all over again. Grass, who is now a Nobel Laureate, thought he saw certain similarities with my life. 'Every tournament you start from zero again. How do you cope with that?' Grass has always been politically active, especially during the era of Billy Brandt, but he still maintained his freedom to say and write exactly what he felt and thought. Like him, or any other citizen, I'd also like to assert my right to comment on controversial issues, such as racism, which affects me personally. I'm responsible for the future of two children and a woman of dark skin. That's why I didn't hold back in December 1998 in Leipzig, on the German singer Marius Müller-Westernhagen's fiftieth birthday, when the issue of xenophobia, racism and Nazi graffiti came up.

I'd met Marius a few years earlier at the Hyatt Hotel in Cologne. Right from the start it was clear that we had lots in common, not least our wives: black and beautiful. (I'd always been a great fan of Marius's songs and gigs; his song 'Wieder Hier' – 'Back Here Again' – in particular, moved me greatly.) The entertainer Thomas Gottschalk was also at the birthday party. His viewing figures, which can reach twenty million for his *Wetten, dass . . .? (Let's bet that . . .)* programme, tell you all you need to know about how popular he is. He lives in Malibu, California: a stranger in America. His sons go to high school and nobody takes any interest in who their dad is. 'Let's do something about the resistance to the reform of the citizenship and nationality law,' Marius suggested that evening. 'With this chancellor, surely it should be possible.' And that was that. Thomas put in a call to Gerhard Schröder.

At the end of January, an advertisement financed by the German press and information office appeared in five national newspapers. Under the huge headline 'We' and our three portraits, came the text: '... want to be proud of a modern, open, federal republic of Germany. Part of this has to be an up-to-date citizenship and nationality law. A passport means home. Those who are born here should also belong here, with all the rights and obligations this brings. Those who live according to the laws of our country should have the right to become citizens of our country. In many countries in the world, naturalization is a matter of course. People can adopt a second home without having to relinquish their first. That's why we support the federal government in its reform of the citizenship and nationality law.'

The reaction was typically German, and the pigeon-holing began again: the right claimed that this campaign was a waste of taxpayers' money and they ignored the sense and the necessity behind our commitment to it. The left celebrated us as 'the three angels for Schily'[8] (Schily is the Interior Minister), and *Spiegel* announced in its column 'Zeitgeist': '*Lindenstraße's* Victory', *Lindenstraße* being the German equivalent of *Coronation Street*. Pop meets politics – that was, at least in Germany, relatively new. 'Never before in the history of the Federal Republic [of Germany] have three superstars, two of whom represent the social mainstream, taken such a strong stance over such a controversial political issue,' said *Spiegel*, 'and that in an official advertising campaign financed by a Red–Green federal government, which just a few years ago had been the political nightmare of the majority of voters.'[9]

Naturally the racists were outraged, and the grey hair of some of the older Gottschalk fans might have turned a little greyer still when their Tommy decided to support foreigners. One thing is for sure. We'd hit a chord. The younger generation is no longer inhibited by feelings of guilt because of the crimes of the Second World War. Trips abroad and contact with other cultures and with people of different skin colour have long been part of normal life here. Regrettably, there will always be attacks on strangers in our country, but that is also true of other countries. Multiculturalism is a reality in Germany, even if many don't want to accept it yet.

If there has ever been a miracle in the world, and something that has really given me hope, then it has been South Africa and Nelson Mandela. This man's story has affected me deeply and motivated me: Mandela, a freedom fighter who battled for equal rights and against oppression, apartheid and hatred, and risked his own life. Mandela was my hero even before I met Barbara Feltus, with whom I personally experienced the racism in this world.

We once visited Mandela in Cape Town on the occasion of a charity tournament for the Nelson Mandela Children's Fund. He was even more impressive than I had imagined – his charm indescribable, his charisma extraordinary. Having chatted with us before dinner, he changed the seating plan. He wanted to sit next to us and find out how Germans treated their black fellow countrymen, and what the reaction of the whites had been to Barbara's wedding to one of their national heroes. Mandela talked to us about his solitary confinement, which he had to endure for eighteen out of a total of twenty-seven years in prison. He never gave up hope because he knew, as he put it, 'My body is behind bars but my spirit is free.' He spoke without hatred, the very personification of reconciliation. Next to us the white tennis player Amanda Coetzer sat and cried. The words of her president brought tears not only to her eyes but to others' too – the US black professional tennis player MaliVai Washington, who played in the Wimbledon final in 1996, and French player Yannick Noah, who came originally from Cameroon.

Mandela reminded us that not far from where our marquee now was, members of the black resistance had once been executed by their white oppressors. His words made me shiver, and I said nothing. Andre Agassi, however, who was also among the guests, made an attempt to ease the emotional tension. 'Which, Mr President, are the best restaurants in town?' And Brooke Shields was similarly carefree: 'Where are the best streets for shopping?'

Mandela pretended not to hear them and told us how he used to fish on Robben Island and supply himself with fish and mussels. Day in, day out, year after year, mealie porridge and fish, mussels and mealie porridge. 'And fate would have it that at my first state dinner I was served mussels.' Only then did he get back to Andre's question: 'I know nothing about restaurants.'

The white South African Johnny Clegg started to sing 'Free Nelson Mandela'. Yannick Noah gave a speech in which he reminded us of slavery, and we were all deeply touched. Barbara said she'd never seen me so worked up, and she was right. The crystal goblet I was meant to present to Mandela slipped out of my hands. Barbara said afterwards that this was like falling on your nose or splitting your trousers when curtseying before the Queen. But Mandela remained calm. 'Here broken glass means good luck,' he said.

In January 1999 we bumped into each other again, at the ceremony in Baden-Baden to present the Deutscher Medienpreis (the award given by the German media to outstanding personalities). Nelson Mandela was receiving the award. He saw us and insisted we joined him at his table. Other guests, however, were already sitting there: Oskar Lafontaine and the chancellor. Lafontaine vacated his seat; I don't know if Schröder was relieved. I was embarrassed. We moved closer together and I was able to speak to my hero one more time. 'You've come a long way, Boris,' Mandela said.

STIFFER THAN A STARCHED COLLAR

'PARIS IS A MOVABLE FEAST,' WROTE HEMINGWAY ABOUT THE French capital city. But for me Paris was always a problem. I won the indoor tournament at Bercy three times, but I never won the Grand Slam on clay at Roland Garros. I reached the semi-final three times, playing on a surface on which my main opponent was always myself.

My game plan has always been to attack; that's in my nature. On clay, however, the aim is to make fewer mistakes than your opponent. Paris is won by those who minimize risks and who hang on in there for four or more hours. Once I was very close to victory – against Edberg in 1989 – but it didn't happen. I lost the fifth set 2–6.

For me, Paris was always the hardest tournament of the season, not least because the French don't make life easy for foreigners. You have to take your life in your hands just to get a breather outside the stadium. Drivers see the black and white stripes of the pedestrian crossing as some kind of courage test-zone, along the lines of: 'Let's see if that pedestrian dares get in my way.' Tournaments usually have chauffeur services with brand-new cars and pleasant drivers. When I had to take a Paris cab, however, I was likely to be greeted by the taxi driver's partner – a poodle or even a Great Dane sitting on the front passenger seat, which would bark loudly before returning its attention to the traffic. Regrettably, I never had much of a chance to sample the Parisian way of life, the *savoir vivre*, the French ease. The capital might have been the height of charm and chic at the time of Yves Montand or Edith Piaf, Coco Chanel or Jean Gabin, but now Parisians fight over a parking space or even over a table in a café. They're always rushing past you to some place some-where else. It's not unlike Manhattan, where everyone's also running. Composure and tolerance are words that seem to be missing from the Parisians' vocabulary. A lot has been said about how rude the staff are in the capital's hotels and cafés, but I don't really want to add my own comments. Only this: it's true. Germany, which allegedly exports its most capable hotel managers across the world, is not exactly spoilt in this respect either. Not a hint of friendliness – unless a VIP, such as Herr Becker and his entourage, has got a reservation. The gentlemen behind the Louis XV reception desks of Paris hotels are stiffer than their starched collars. Compared to these *messieurs*, the *dames de pipi*, the lavatory attendants in the traditional restaurants, are extremely cordial.

Paris is undoubtedly a jewel, glittering with history. But it's also marked out by the rudeness of many of its inhabitants towards foreigners, particularly those of colour. Without this the city would be almost unbearably beautiful. Barbara loves the shops and the luxury. She would plunge into the turmoil, filled with enthusiasm, and each time she would come back disillusioned. She thought she could feel rejection and latent racism. As Voltaire wrote in *Candide*: 'Oh yes, I know Paris. You will find all sorts there. It's chaos, a mob of people all out for pleasure, and scarcely a soul who finds it.'[1]

As a tennis player you don't get much chance to make contact with local people. I couldn't get a feel for the Parisian way of life, and you probably have to live there to comprehend it. The aggression doesn't bother me – I can be aggressive myself. What irritated me in Paris was more the combination of superficiality and arrogance. I say this as one of the privileged among the many visitors. My French? *Ça va*. I can afford to reside at the Hôtel de Crillon at the Place de la Concorde; in my early days I used to stay at the Royal Monceau at the Avenue Hoche. I've spent so much money at the Ritz that I had to win at Bercy just to cover my expenses.

In 1995 I played the French Open, France's international championship, once more. Another attempt to win this tournament on clay at Roland Garros. I'd have given an arm and a leg for it – almost. In the third round I encountered Adrian Voinea from Romania, number 128 in the world rankings. If it had gone the way the journalists wanted it, I'd have beaten Voinea, followed this up with victory over Stich or Michael Chang, then I'd have faced Spanish clay specialist Sergi Brugera. Instead I was up against a rainstorm. The match got under way all the same. At 3–6 I asked for the game to be brought to a halt, without success. I lost the second set too, 4–6, and the match was stopped at last. I was two sets down against a nobody. It was as if I'd wandered on to the wrong film set, and all the while the Romanian was turning into his country's hero.

There was a glimmer of hope the next morning. The third set went to me, 6–3. Then in the fourth I was out, 5–7. I looked at the sky and wailed, 'Someone up there doesn't want me to win on clay!' Over the next few years I had to cancel Paris again and again due to injury. The thought of having to battle my way across the capital never put me off playing there, but victory was always to elude me.

I'd like to avoid misunderstandings. I've criticized Paris and the French but really I do value France: the countryside, the castles in the Bordeaux area, Deauville, Normandy, Aix-en-Provence, oyster beds, vineyards, *pâté de foie gras*, champagne – it is a blessed country. I've made friends with many French people, among them Guy Forget, Henri Leconte and Yannick Noah. Yannick suffered under the burden of his fame and the expectations that came with it as much as I did in Germany. One night he was so depressed he wandered through Paris and seriously thought about jumping from a bridge into the Seine.

Yannick sought refuge and anonymity in New York. His first wife and two of his children still live in Manhattan today, while he now lives in London, though not in the centre. He plays tennis with the seniors of the ATP tour, he's a successful musician, and he supports the children's charity Enfants de la Terre, which is managed by his mother.

When the French Davis Cup team played its final against Australia in Nice in December 1999, Yannick stayed in London. His reason was that he didn't want to attract attention or disrupt Guy Forget, his successor as team leader. The French team lost, despite the thousands of fans who'd painted their faces blue, white and red and sang the 'Marseillaise' before the match began. The atmosphere in the hall, the organization, everything was fabulous – as you'd expect from France. And I was welcomed as a guest at the final with choruses of French voices. *Merci la France.*

LOVE AT FIRST STEP

WINDSOR CASTLE 1998 – PROBABLY THE LONGEST TABLE IN the world. How many people were sitting at this table? Maybe two hundred. I could barely make out my wife at a distant corner about a hundred metres away. The German ambassador had invited us on the occasion of the state visit of the then German president, Roman Herzog. I was very nervous. I got there too early – most unlike me.

While we were still waiting outside the Green Room to be received by the royal family, I kissed Barbara. One of the German president's officials told me off. 'You can't do that here.' I kissed Barbara again. I'd already enjoyed my whisky in the Blue Room and the Red Room. This place was growing on me. The suits of armour, the panelled walls, the evening dress, uniforms and medals – it was an impressive sight. When it was our turn, I bowed and Barbara curtseyed, as protocol demanded. Prince Charles, Princess Anne, Prince Andrew, Prince Edward and the Queen were charming and interested.

'Will we see you at Wimbledon next year?'

'How's the capital Berlin developing?'

'Have you ever been to Nürnberg?'

'What's the name again of those little speciality cakes? *Lebkuchen*?'

Princess Anne mispronounced it slightly so that it came out sounding like 'little love chicks' ('Liebküken'). Her brother Andrew talked about golf. He has a handicap of seven and could practise daily on their own nine-hole course in the grounds of Windsor Castle. The German head of state was standing somewhere nearby and didn't have a word for us, not even a nod. Roman Herzog wasn't a great fan of mine – in contrast to Richard von Weizsäcker, who in 1987 had introduced me to the Queen in Berlin. I liked Weizsäcker, and he liked me. At the Olympic Games in Barcelona he'd even asked me to be his 'tour guide' through the Olympic village.

Prince Edward was relaxed and chatty. 'As children we used to play *jeu de paume*, the predecessor of modern tennis, here in this hall. Sometimes the balls ended up in the chandeliers.' A splendid setting for our sport, I thought to myself. What must the royal servants have said? Shattered mirrors, scratched marble, a strike on the painted face of a venerable ancestor? Barbara whispered in my ear, 'It's like *A Thousand and One Nights*. So beautiful. Look at the Queen Mother – ninety-eight and so dignified.'

Unbroken traditions, protocol and a splendour that mirrors England's history. You could see here how the nation saw itself, a nation that had been forced to give up its hegemony over the world but continued to be civilized in its dealings with others. London, with its millions of inhabitants, still had that village feeling. People queuing patiently at the bus stop.

Waiting outside the Royal Opera House in the rain and fog. Waiting outside Wimbledon with tea in a Thermos flask, a woollen hat over the ears and plenty of consideration for others. It's fun to be among these people.

Before the invitation to Windsor, Barbara and I had been looking at houses in Wimbledon with a view of the scoreboard. For several months I'd been thinking about buying property in London. If Wimbledon's my living room, as I have been known to say, then London is part of my soul. I enjoy myself here. I regard the British highly: their sense of democracy, fair play and their multi-ethnic society. I can also understand, though, that Britons who have lived through the war have their problems with Germany and the Germans. In 1940, five German bombs hit the Wimbledon grounds. One of them damaged the roof of Centre Court. War, and bombs over England – you couldn't fail to understand the resentment. I just wish the English would be reasonable enough to accept that my generation doesn't feel directly responsible for it.

We've learned from the misery of the Nazi dictatorship and we're alarmed whenever a few idiots decorate themselves with swastikas. But we can't change history. We can only show that we think, feel and believe differently. Supposedly 'typically Teutonic', I was married to a black woman. My mother had to flee the Russians and she knows the fear and guilt our nation has had to cope with. In my first years at Wimbledon, I was surprised how few British journalists were prepared to let go of their wartime clichés, even if they were only talking about tennis. They called me a Panzer, or they announced over the radio that the Becker serves hit the ground like 'the missiles of the Wehrmacht'. There was talk of 'Blitzkrieg', and in 1992 the *Evening Standard* remembered my first Wimbledon triumph with these words: 'As the seventeen-year-old raised a triumphant arm in a victory salute, the image seemed hauntingly familiar. It was almost as if a Josef Goebbels' Hitler Youth poster had come to life. There was something about those penetrating blue eyes, that shock of fair hair, the sheer physical power, that seal of self-belief. Forty years earlier such a figure would surely have been captured on film by Leni Riefenstahl in her portrayal of the German people as a race descended from Nordic Gods.'[1] This is just silly.

I had a number of arguments with my father about the Nazi past. It seemed to me sometimes that he was almost in denial of it, in the same way that millions of Germans tried to forget about the National Socialist tragedy. My father, who was born in 1935 and was a child during the Third Reich, looked for explanations for the disaster, and these occasionally came across as excuses. After one heated discussion I pushed my chair back from the dinner table, stood up and shouted, 'Heil Hitler.' A stupid thing to do, especially since my father never tried to avoid the debate. He wasn't someone who'd stick to a position no matter what, and back then I wasn't politically active anyway; I was just a tennis player. The discussions with my father were a good training ground for me. They prepared me for the reactions that I would face abroad as I got older.

I've never been directly attacked for being German. But being a German abroad means always facing up to the past, even though it was more than half a century ago, even though it happened before you were born. It means understanding history, dealing with sensitivities and correcting distortions.

What the foreign press writes about Germany is often incomprehensible, so I try to tell the sceptics that a new Germany exists now, more democratic and freer than before.

We've still got our problems, of course. Neo-Nazis, xenophobia, party-funding scandals. But don't these problems exist in Britain too? Or in France, the USA, Russia? Before he left office in October 1999, Gebhardt von Moltke, the German ambassador to the UK, accused the British of 'deep ignorance' of the German reality, and in an interview tried to explain that Germans are neither Huns nor Krauts who eat sausages all day long.[2] He also had to give reassurances that those Germans who claim the sun-loungers at the hotel pool by draping them with their towels at five a.m. are in the minority.

'Admit it,' one British paper wrote, 'we're all agreed: we hate them.' They were writing, of course, about the Germans – all of them, including Boris Becker. But I never felt that I was hated, not at Wimbledon, nor during my encounters with the royal family. The British fans have always been, in the purest sense of the phrase, 'without frontiers'. Boris Becker was primarily a player, and Wimbledon was the stage on which he performed. And I honestly never gave up on a single ball, even risking injury when I did my dive volleys.

I often whinged and complained on court, but I never gave up. I suffered after defeat, and I was so angry I felt hatred, but it was hatred of Becker and nobody else. There was a certain amount of friction between the British commentators and me, but perhaps at some level they understood that my passion for Wimbledon was also a passion for their island. 'The kid was the Kaiser of Wimbledon,' announced the *Daily Mail* in 1986, '. . . with the smile of a child, the charm of a prince, the eye of an assassin.'[3]

British society is, as far as I can judge, full of in-consistencies. Even the language divides upper and working class, Oxford and the East End, aristocrats and Cockneys, the Derby at Ascot and football at Arsenal, rowing at Henley and racism in Wolverhampton. Why should it be any different at Wimbledon? The two-tier system exists here too: the seeded players and the rest. The royals and the commoners. The stars play on Centre Court or Court One; the others, like me in 1984 against Blaine Willenborg, on Court Fourteen – a mini disaster. Being on Centre Court is like being in church: silence and devotion. On the other courts the disruption is continuous.

The old players' lounge was much too small: 128 men, 128 women, with partners, friends, coaches and physiotherapists. Five or six hundred people. Where could they all go if it rained? During the second week, the seeded player needs some peace and quiet in the changing rooms, but there's little chance of that. The seniors arrive, as relaxed as if they're at an old school reunion. They're noisy, tell jokes and talk about the good old days. But Sampras, Agassi and Becker are still in the tournament and they need to focus, however much they might respect the older players. Things have improved now. There are new changing rooms, a great players' restaurant and better medical facilities. Wimbledon does move with the times, but slowly.

The sixteen seeded players are allowed to practise for one hour a day on the Wimbledon lawn – with another seeded player. The 112 unseeded players get thirty minutes per week, sometimes four of them at once, in a small space at the training ground in Aorangi Park, ten minutes' walk away. Even there the two-tier system is at work. The top players practise on the courts at the front; the others at the back.

I always got round these problems, which were particularly bad after rain stopped play, by hiring three lawn courts for the duration of the tournament. Two were used for tennis practice, a third for playing football. They belong to Mohamed Al Fayed now. He bought them for his football club in Fulham. We also rented two or three houses in Wimbledon, close to the courts; one for me and my family, the others for my physio Waldemar Kliesing, racket-stringer Uli Kühnel and coach Mike de Palmer.

In the house I could be on my own, to read or stare at the garden for hours on end. Even Noah was a good boy then, the very picture of quiet. 'Papi has to work' – he accepted that. We distracted ourselves with good films on video. I'd read from five until seven-thirty in the evening, say, then have dinner with Barbara. After dinner another video, perhaps, then sleep. When it rained during matches, I'd go 'home' and wait in front of the television for play to resume. This was a significant advantage over those who sometimes had to wait in the crowded players' lounge for five or six hours.

The changing rooms at Wimbledon had no windows, no skylights. You got one towel for the showers – a dry one in exchange for a wet one. The three tables in the massage room were so close together that the players lying on them could hold hands.

Class differences are not the sole preserve of Wimbledon. Once you've played the big tournaments for a few years and you're high up in the rankings, the tournament director may drop hints about which court you will play on and roughly when. This allows the top players to prepare themselves in good time for the match. It was a great honour for me when in 1999 I was allowed to play several times on the Centre Court at Wimbledon. I hadn't expected this. It wasn't a bad decision. For one last time, I was the main attraction.

My love for Wimbledon also has something to do with the playing surface. In 1983, I played my first youth tournament in England on grass. My timing was already good during the practice session, and I found that despite my weight and height I was able to move better on grass than on any other surface. I made it straight into the semis. It was something like love at first step. Sadly, few tournaments are played on grass now. There used to be Forest Hills and Melbourne, but there's still Halle in Germany, Rosmalen in the Netherlands and Queens in London.

Which other tournament could offer so much history that the organizers are able to open their own museum? At Wimbledon an honorary librarian, Alan Little, was commissioned to cover every last detail in the *Wimbledon Compendium*, which has been published annually since 1990. 1911: the first double-handed backhand. 1972: a South African lady player dared for the first time to play without socks, 'shocking'. A Frenchwoman was the first player to wear spectacles, in 1931. Jimmy Connors and John McEnroe battled it out for 256 minutes in 1982's final. I was the youngest champion in history. When the Briton Arthur Gore won in 1909, he was already 41 years and 182 days old. The Filipino Felicismo H. Ampon was, at 1.5 metres, the shortest player. The Czech Milan Srejber and the Belgian D. Norman were the tallest at 2.03 metres, until they were topped by Ivo Karlovic in 2003 at 2.1 metres. Miss M. H. de Amorin, a Brazilian, lost in 1957 after seventeen double faults in a row. I'd have had to be sent to a mental-health institution after an experience like that. So would John McEnroe, I imagine. I hold another Wimbledon record, though it's a negative one: on the way to my triumph in 1985 I equalled American Ted Schroeder's 1949 record for lost sets. He also went on to win.[4]

Wimbledon is a reflection of an older world, and I treasure it. It's an understated classic. There's hardly any advertising, apart from Diet Coke, Slazenger and Rolex, whose pale-green lettering almost disappears. The dress code for the players between 1963 and 1995 called for 'predominantly white'. Today, it's 'almost entirely white'. There are bottles without labels for your own drink mixtures. The bowing and curtseying to the royal box, which unfortunately stopped in 2003, was as much a part of Wimbledon as the presence of the Kents. Prince George was made club president in 1929, and this honourable office has been passed down the family line ever since. When it rains, spectators sit in their seats for hours, patiently waiting for the next ray of sunshine.

Wimbledon has given me freedom and independence. 'The young man who as the seventeen-year-old from Leimen believed he had conquered Wimbledon for all time has in subsequent years got to know every aspect of the lady,' wrote sports journalist Ulrich Kaiser about my relationship with Wimbledon. 'She's taught him that she can't be won for eternity. She has torn his ligaments, and taken him to her heart. She threw him out when he thought he had rights over her, and she took him back once he'd worked his way up through the rounds again to the foot of her throne. She gave reassurances when there were only two candidates left, then unexpectedly decided in favour of the other. She led him to believe the whole world was his, and she heard him think aloud that the time had come to retire. The lady had him see-saw between heaven and hell.'[5]

Of course I wanted to win Wimbledon, but I also wanted to be number one in the world rankings. Wimbledon was just one of the bricks I wanted to build my house with. Some journalists became almost sentimental when they realized that even I was getting older. It was only in the last two or three years of my professional career, when the prospect of becoming number one once more had receded for good, that I really focused on winning Wimbledon again. It was, as Ulrich Kaiser observed, as if I 'focused only on Christmas and forgot about the other 360 days'.[6] Christmas in June and July – why not?

At Wimbledon in 1999 I saw it clearly: that I would be bound to the grass of Centre Court, the Queen, the island and the reporters known as 'hacks' until the last serve of my life. Today I return to my 'living room' as a BBC commentator and *Times* columnist – an observer now, with another angle on the court. This is an adventure, seeing my old love in a new and different way.

SERVE: GERMANY

ADOLF HITLER WANTED VICTORY OVER THE ENEMY. IN JULY 1937 the battalions got into position at Wimbledon: USA against Germany, Davis Cup on Centre Court. The battle was to be decided in the final match: Gottfried von Cramm against Donald Budge. Ted Tinling, responsible for Wimbledon protocol, was to accompany the players on to the court.

The phone rang in the changing room. Ellis, the steward, called von Cramm: 'Sir, long-distance call!' The German aristocrat took the receiver and stood to attention. He didn't say a single sentence, but only repeated 'Ja, mein Führer' a total of eleven times. After he'd hung up, he apologized for the delay. 'Hitler was on the phone. He wished me luck.' Tinling noted in his memoirs that the German minister for sport was sitting in the honorary box.[1] Neither he nor the moral support from Berlin could save von Cramm from defeat, however (8–6, 7–5, 4–6, 2–6, 6–8). Von Cramm, who'd refused to join the NSDAP (the Nazi party), was later excluded from the Davis Cup team and for a short time arrested by the Gestapo.

It wasn't until I got called into the Davis Cup team that it became clear to me what von Cramm had meant to German tennis. He was a three-time Wimbledon singles finalist, and he'd won the mixed doubles. In the first match played by a German team after the Second World War – in 1951 against Yugoslavia – he won again for Germany. Twenty-five years later, he died in a car crash in Egypt. Von Cramm played 102 times for Germany in the Davis Cup; he won eighty-two times, but he never won the trophy.

In August 1970, German players reached the Davis Cup final for the first time. Wilhelm Bungert and Christian Kuhnke lost to the USA 0–5. As a young boy I'd dreamt of being asked to join the Davis Cup team. Whatever your world ranking, being asked to play in the national team is a confirmation that you belong to the elite of your country's players. It was March 1985, against Spain, when I looked for the first time on the black, red and gold banner from the perspective of a Davis Cup player. I was moved by the sound of our national anthem, and my father was similarly affected – the national anthem and the national team was a combination he loved. In my first match, I won against Juan Aguilera 6–3, 6–4, 6–4; in the second I was defeated by Sergio Casal 4–6, 6–1, 5–7. Only a handful of reporters showed up at the press conference afterwards. My team-mates Michael Westphal and Andreas Maurer and I were able to cross the hotel lobby without being asked for an autograph by a single fan.

All this changed dramatically after my Wimbledon win in July. We played against the USA in Hamburg from 2 to 4

August. I hadn't realized the extent of national euphoria over my victory in London until this encounter in Hamburg. The press conferences consisted almost entirely of questions directed at me. Whether I wanted it or not, I was pushed into playing the leading role in the team, and I admit it – the Davis Cup was becoming my passion. I played sixty-five matches, and won fifty-three of them. I felt comfortable in the group, where it was easier to cope with pressure. Instead of Serve: Becker, it was Serve: Germany.

I won my first singles match in Hamburg against Eliot Teltscher in straight sets: 6–2, 6–2, 6–3. Hans-Jörg Schwaier beat Aaron Krickstein in five sets. So in the doubles match with Andreas Maurer, against the world-champion team of Kenneth Flach and Robert Seguso, we only needed to get one more point. We reached match point. I served for the match, but somehow the idea of winning against the USA, the tennis superpower, was impossible to entertain. We lost. A disaster. Teltscher beat Schwaier, the score in the quarter-finals was 2–2, and then came the decisive match: seventeen-year-old Wimbledon-winner Becker against Krickstein, on clay. I finished him off in ninety minutes – 6–2, 6–2, 6–1. This is where the Becker legend was born: victory at Wimbledon and victory against the USA, all within the space of four weeks back in the summer of 1985.

In the semi-final in October we played against the Czechs in Frankfurt. In the first match I beat Miloslav Necir in three sets: 6–3, 7–5, 6–4. My partner Michael Westphal, the blond-haired Sunshine Boy and teenyboppers' hero, battled for five hours and twenty-nine minutes against Tomas Smid. He lost the first two sets, then won the next three: 7–5, 11–9, 17–15. The Westphal star was shining brighter than ever.

There'd been some friction between Michael and me because of my greater popularity, but on this occasion the team was holding together like never before. We were riding high on a wave of support from the spectators in Frankfurt, the sort of enthusiasm normally shown only for football.

The final in Munich against Sweden was now even bigger than premier-league football. Tennis was *in*. Edberg and Wilander, among the top five in the world, against Becker, number six, and Westphal, somewhere around number fifty, and the Maurer–Becker doubles pair without much of a track record. Michael lost to Wilander in three sets. I had to beat Edberg, my eternal rival. First set: 6–3. Some sobering up after losing the second set 3–6, then it got dangerous. The spectators went wild. In an atmosphere like that of a bull-ring, with the spectators cheering me on, I won in four sets – 6–3, 3–6, 7–5, 8–6.

The television reporter Dieter Kürten came running towards me. I had to give a live interview. I was dazed, unable to take it all in. Back at the hotel, we were like the Brazilian football team after winning the World Cup. What a sight – and the score was only 1–1. The following day, I played doubles with Andreas Maurer. We lost 6–4, 6–2, 6–1. The first jeers. I began to be afraid of the coming matches. Expectations had got way out of hand.

I had a bad feeling in my stomach before my match against Mats Wilander. I was tense and played two difficult first sets – 6–3, 2–6. In the middle of the third set, however, things started to fall into place. I won – 6–3, 2–6, 6–3, 6–3. The audience drummed their feet. Michael Westphal struggled at the limit of his abilities against Edberg. He won the first set, led the second 4–2, but Edberg made it. Sweden won the cup.

Nevertheless, we celebrated with our opponents into the early hours of the morning at the Munich club P1 – a great bunch, those Swedes. The most decent guys in the Davis Cup. We'd put up a great fight in the face of huge pressure. What was the worst thing that could happen to me after that?

The answer came in March 1986, in the next Davis Cup round in Mexico City, 2,240 metres above sea level. The hatred of thousands was focused on us. I managed to win 6–3, 6–2, 6–4 against the Mexican Leonardo Lavalle, who later hired Bosch as his coach. I took down Francisco Maciel, too – 6–3, 6–3, 6–1. Then, on the final day, it was down to Michael Westphal to win the critical point against Lavalle. We were almost hoping to lose because of the aggressive mood on the terraces, but Michael began to achieve the impossible – he led 10–8, 6–3. Policemen with machine-guns showed up and the first warning shots were fired. The next three sets went 3–6, 4–6, 3–6. We lost to Mexico in extra time on Monday, but at least we were still alive.

In March 1987, I suffered a bitter defeat in the Davis Cup against Spain. Sergio Casal gave me no chance – I lost 2–6, 6–0, 2–6, 3–6. The feeling of being invincible in the Davis Cup was history. At Wimbledon I lost in the second round. Bosch was no longer my coach. Doubts started to surface and the media prophesied my end. I wasn't even twenty. But now my friends Patrik Kühnen, Charly Steeb and Eric Jelen moved into the Davis Cup team and we became a watertight group. In July 1987 in Hartford, USA, before our group play-off against the US, we'd go every day into a park, sit down on the grass and play poker for hours on end. Even Niki Pilic, our usually strict boss, was seduced by the good team feeling. The journalists, however, had already got their knives out, predicting relegation for Germany, and the end for Becker.

We practised in the same hall as the Americans – but they looked down their noses at us. Stuart Bale, an English professional, left-hander and about number 200 in the world rankings, was there to help prepare us for the left-hander McEnroe. I saw Stuart again recently – he's now a cab driver in London. He's a great guy, still as full of positive energy as he was back then. Eric Jelen, who's cool when it matters (typical of people from Trier!), might have felt a little nervous before the first match, but he fought Tim Mayotte down in five sets, 6–8, 6–2, 1–6, 6–3, 6–2 – a big shock for the Americans. My opponent was McEnroe, one of the most successful Davis Cup players of all time and a real superstar. 'If Eric can do it, I can,' I told myself.

I lost my first serve and the first set. McEnroe tried to wind me up – 'motherfucker', 'arsehole', he kept calling me when we changed sides – but I decided to take that for the way people in New York spoke. McEnroe talked to everyone: the spectators, the line umpires, me. I didn't react. The battle began in the second set, which lasted two hours and thirty-five minutes – the longest of my career. When I double-faulted, the audience applauded, or the US players got up and waved the Stars and Stripes. I just went for it. John seemed tired and flat, and after six hours and thirty-eight minutes he finally gave up the ghost. I'd won 4–6, 15–13, 8–10, 6–2, 6–2. He slumped on to his bench and didn't say another word. I had to pull out of my doubles match with Eric Jelen, scheduled for the following day, because I was exhausted. Jelen played with Ricki Osterthun instead. They fought bravely, but lost.

By Sunday, however, McEnroe's motivation had returned.

Jelen lost to him, and I had to chase the final point in a match against Mayotte. The losing team would be relegated to another group. I played the first two sets well: 6–2, 6–3. The spectators in the hall appeared to be resigned to Mayotte's defeat. In the third set, however, I began to fall apart. Exhaustion crept over me and I lost my focus. McEnroe, self-appointed crowd leader, began to fire up the sixteen thousand spectators, who earlier had appeared to have dropped off to sleep. After four hours, Mayotte equalized: 5–7, 4–6. I was toppling over. Five break points against me. If he got the break, I was done for. But luck was on my side. Mayotte started to get nervous. Double fault. I took his serve, and eventually took the decisive fifth set 6–2. I ran over to Ion Tiriac's son, Ion-Ion, who'd bravely waved the German flag, took the black, red and gold banner out of his hands and ran five laps of honour. Got you, John McEnroe! We're staying in the world group, and the USA are getting relegated. This victory laid the foundations for our triumphs in 1988 and 1989.

I remember certain Davis Cup matches particularly well, such as the match against McEnroe in Hartford in 1987, my 6–2, 6–0, 6–2 win over Wilander in the final in Stuttgart in 1989 – and the match in the Munich Olympiahalle in 1989 against Agassi. The first two sets in the semi-final go to Agassi – 7–6, 7–6, and in the third set he's serving at 6–5. It's 30–15 – to this day we still have these points off by heart. I play a stop and go to the net. He runs up and lobs a return over my head. I play a winner from behind and instead of 40–15 we stand at 30 all. Agassi is stunned. He loses his serve, the tie-break and the next set. By now it's midnight. According to Davis Cup rules, both players have to agree if they are to carry on playing.

Agassi doesn't want to play on. The next day I have to play doubles, as of course he knows. Two sets each.

We play our fifth set the next day at eleven o'clock. I've had five hours' fitful sleep and everything hurts. After the decision against Agassi in the fifth set, which I take 6–4, I have a 45-minute break before my next match – with Jelen against Flach and Seguso. They'd already won two Grand Slams that year, but we beat them in four sets.

This encounter with the United States, great as it was, showed me just how fickle an audience can be. After my match against Agassi, after his surprising 4–6, 6–4, 6–4, 6–2 defeat by Charly Steeb, after our doubles victory, I didn't need to play another match – we had it in the bag. Relief washed over me: I was running on empty. Patrik Kühnen took my place for the match against Brad Gilbert – and what happened? The spectators booed, the press blew its top. Becker had dared not to play. That hurt. The state of my health clearly meant nothing to them. After all, we'd won against the USA! Patrik lost 4–6, 6–1, 4–6, but he'd really fought. The public jeered at him, but in reality they were jeering at me. The Swiss-German newspaper *Neue Zürcher Zeitung* realized: 'Even at times of triumph Becker is often treated harshly by his countrymen, mocked as an Armani-communist or a Rolex-socialist ... Such statements do no justice to the character of this sportsman, who, incidentally, enabled hundreds of others to leap on to the bandwagon and profit personally from his successes.'[2]

For more than six years I'd been working my butt off winning for Germany, and when after eight hours of high performance in just two days – the equivalent of five football matches in a row – I couldn't go on any more, the buckets of manure got tipped up over my head. The story the press got worked up over wasn't the victory but Becker's tiredness. Such ingratitude, especially towards Patrik.

Five months later, it was champagne and caviar once more, this time in Stuttgart at our victory over Sweden – 3–2. Suddenly I was a genius again. I wanted and needed to get out of this stifling national embrace and concentrate on other goals, such as getting to the top of the world rankings. So in February 1990 I decided to take time out in the first round of the next Davis Cup encounter, against the Netherlands. I was promptly, and heavily, criticized. The officials increased their pressure on me. Both sponsors and television demanded that Becker be in the team for the sake of the viewing figures. Tiriac fumed. 'You should be kissing his feet and praying that he'll carry on at all,' he said.

In 1990 I played twenty tournaments. By January 1991 I'd achieved my goal: I was, for the first time, number one in the world. After that I longed to play once more in the team, which in 1990 had been further strengthened by the addition of Michael Stich. The remuneration for Davis Cup matches had also improved greatly, based on each player's position in the world rankings. I was due to be paid 10 per cent of the net intake of all home matches, and I insisted, much to Tiriac's dismay, on sharing this money equally between my team-mates, as well as the fees paid by Davis Cup sponsors. 'You're mad,' said Tiriac, 'but since you apparently tend towards socialism I can't help you.'

Even before our first final against Sweden, in Gothenburg in December 1988, cracks had started to appear in the relationship between the officials and the professionals. The viewing figures on television increased dramatically. The

DTB, the German tennis association, raked it in, and we were paid off with a few thousand marks, plus victory bonuses. We demanded a doubling of our payments, and threatened to pack up and go home. The DTB paid up, with bad grace.

When I dropped out of the Davis Cup in 1990, the papers printed stories like 'Boris lets his team down' or 'Becker – the nation's bogeyman'. They attacked me so mercilessly that the then president of the DTB, Claus Stauder, stood up for me and said to the press, 'I'd like to declare myself a staunch defender of Boris, his totally committed supporter. I don't know any other player in the world who has done so much for his country. And in doing so he has earned the right to decide for himself the priorities in his career.'[3]

Stauder knew the figures; he knew how much money I'd earned the DTB. Ion Tiriac had made the point several years before: 'At the moment Boris is the locomotive that's pulling the entire railway station.'[4]

The top officials of the DTB, who'd risen through the ranks of the association, had been living in their own dull world until a boy called Becker arrived, stirring up within a matter of months the clauses and regulations that had accumulated over decades. The tennis craze caught them completely off guard and knocked them right off their feet. Representatives from the professional world turned up un-ceremoniously on their doorstep and started haggling over court-perimeter advertising and viewing rights. Tiriac stood at their side, offering advice and suggesting what to do, as always in potential money-making circumstances. The officials of 1985 are, in some cases, still in office today, repre-senting the eighteen regional associations in the federal committee, and it must have slipped their minds what we, the players, have done for the benefit of their associations. They'd also have liked to forget that we didn't just play for honour and glory in the Davis Cup, but wanted to get our fair share of the income too.

The regional associations simply couldn't stomach the fact that they couldn't control players like me, that they had to accept my conditions instead of imposing their own. The DTB had entered into a 125-million-mark contract with the German film company UFA for the television rights for the Davis Cup and Federation Cup, as well as the international championships in Hamburg for the men and in Berlin for the women. This kind of money would never have been paid had Steffi, Michael and I not played our part. And why shouldn't I get my fair share? I've earned plenty of money – no doubt about that. But I'd like just to ask the question once more: what happened to the rest of it?

A good deal of it went to the regional associations, and in Hamburg, site of the DTB HQ, a stadium was built at the cost of 25 million Euros. The DTB undertook this enterprise because the Germans were in direct competition with other international tournament venues and didn't want to lose out. The project didn't succeed. In the post-Graf/Becker era, the bar had been raised too high. It was inevitable that after our retirement things were going to get harder. But the enthusiasm for Steffi and me was just as out of proportion then as the lack of interest that tennis faces today. Many nations envy us our players like Haas or Schüttler. They have a chance to play at the very top. Perhaps they will become more popular as the memory of us fades.

My resignation from the position of Davis Cup leader at the end of 1999 came as no surprise to those who knew me well.

The decision had been made over the course of months. The quarrels with the DTB officials had become increasingly unbearable, and the discussions about Nicolas Kiefer had become absurd. I'd taken up the job with a rather romantic view of what it would entail. I'd wanted to give something back to German tennis. I wanted to bring my experience to bear in an effort to help the country become a tennis power once again.

I had no ambition to gain this post. The DTB approached me when my professional career was drawing to a close. I'd wanted Charly Steeb to share the position with me, not least because in October 1997 I was still actively playing as well as pursuing a number of other career interests. Niki Pilic, who'd won the Davis Cup three times with his team, was still under contract with the DTB and demanded a pay-off, but the DTB, the tennis association with the highest membership in the world, declared themselves unable to do this. In the interests of the team, and to allow for a harmonious changeover, I was prepared to help the DTB with their payment to Pilic. Of course this gesture was misinterpreted – deliberately.

Part of an initiative of mine for fostering new talent, the Mercedes juniors team, didn't take off in the way I'd imagined, thanks to opposition from the DTB bigwigs. They'd never admit to it, but I've heard it from those who were directly affected. Officials made it clear to the young talents that anyone who went for an interview with Becker would be banned. We had to watch and talk to the youngsters covertly. I took the best of those I was able to see, but they weren't the best we had in Germany.

I tried to build bridges between the Mercedes talents and the official association, but the officials weren't prepared to relinquish the power they'd accumulated over the years. In the end, the differences were too great to reconcile. After my last Davis Cup doubles match against Russia (2–3) in Frankfurt in April 1999, and then five months later at a relegation match against Romania (4–1) in Bucharest, I could no longer envisage a constructive working relationship. I often talked into the early hours with Charly (Steeb) about the problems in our associations and in the Davis Cup team. I never understood why we had so many conflicts. Other teams, such as Sweden and France, worked together in harmony, but we never achieved that, no matter who we had as team leader. Other teams' players earn far less than ours, but they are keen to play the Davis Cup for their country. Is our success story the reason young German players seem to start off their relationship with the nation, and the national team, on the wrong foot? Do our Davis Cup victories cast too long a shadow over them?

And yet, in spite of all these disputes, I remain committed to German tennis. This is why I, together with the new people of the DTB and my own team, have developed a new marketing and events concept for the Masters Series tournament at the Hamburg Rothenbaum, and have taken on the role of chairman. A 20 per cent increase in spectator numbers in 2003 – it's not a bad start. And even though the Davis Cup team is facing its first relegation in twenty years, German tennis no longer seems to be on a downward spiral.

BLOOD UNDER THE TOENAIL

A SMALL FRONT GARDEN, A BRASS PLAQUE AT THE ENTRANCE: a doctor's surgery in Munich Bogenhausen, a short distance from the river Isar and the pathways through the meadows. Birds are singing, dogs are fighting over a stick as if it were the last one on earth and toddlers are taking their first tentative steps on grass. Idyllic.

Me? I'm lying here on a white blanket, staring at the ceiling. Every now and again I take a look at the cannula in my lower arm, through which blood is pulsing from my veins into a separator. A few days after my very last match, my body, according to the expert diagnosis of Ulrich Kübler, is in a state of total collapse. The defence mechanisms of my immune system are drastically reduced, as a result of which I'm suffering from bronchitis, a complete lack of energy and a slightly raised temperature. Kübler explains that the infection cannot be beaten by antibiotics. Instead he wants to support the immune system by reintroducing lymphocytes into my body via the bloodstream. Conservative medics are sceptical of this procedure, but they couldn't offer me any effective alternative. I'd been to countless doctors and in the end was no better, nor any the wiser. One said black, another said white. Boris and his ailments – you could write a book about them.

The slightest draught could give me a cold. Some top athletes get ill just from flying, thanks to the constant changes in time zone and climate as well as the nature of cabin air itself. Because of the constant strain I'd been under and the short periods I'd had for recovery, Kübler told me, my blood showed a shocking deficit of essential amino acids. Most people think athletes are paragons of health: their lungs have greater capacity, their hearts are strong, their muscles are firm. In reality we're more like overbred racing machines. Tennis players are endurance athletes. We can cover twice the distance of a marathon runner, who runs forty-two kilo-metres. We have to play almost every week, whereas marathon athletes run about half a dozen races in a year. Even a double espresso had a much stronger effect on me than on an untrained body. My system was highly tuned.

At the Australian Open in Melbourne in January 1997, I faced Carlos Moya in the first round, after Steffi Graf and Michael Stich, whose matches were scheduled immediately before mine. I was practising with de Palmer on Court Fourteen, far away from Centre Court. When I'd finished and showered I would – as usual – eat, drink a few litres of water and play a few games of cards to unwind with Waldemar and Uli. This routine was part of my match preparation. The losers at cards would have to bow low to the winner. While players like Pete Sampras were being massaged on one of the neighbouring tables, we'd be slamming Jacks and Aces on to the padding of ours, yelling childishly. Our fellow players must have thought we were nuts.

But on this day in Melbourne things went differently. Steffi won in just twenty minutes. Her opponent simply gave up. Stich then wiped out his opponent at lightning speed. Over on Court Fourteen we had no inkling of this. All of a sudden, I was on. 'Uli, come on, get the pasta!' 'Waldemar, tape my ankles!' We played two quick rounds of cards. My preparation had gone completely to pot. Serve. The temperature on the court was 50°C and the spaghetti lay heavily in my stomach. The temperature on the ground was an ovenlike 64°C. I pulled ahead in the first set, lost the second to a tie-break, won the third, and in the fourth set dreamt of victory and escape from the relentless sun. Then I felt my energy drain away. 1–6 in the fourth set, then 4–6 in the fifth – over. Finished. I was out of the tournament.

I was in shock, as exhausted as someone who'd been wandering for days through the desert. Waldemar covered me in cool, damp towels which he kept changing. I felt as if I was still boiling inside. Out in the first round! I couldn't even speak. That night I showered over and over again: cold, hot, cold, hot. Then I switched on the television, and promptly switched it off again. I called Waldemar and booked flights to here, to there, to an island, to the jungle, to New York. My body had been destroyed – my soul even more so. Back at home the papers indulged themselves in writing about the worn-out Becker, the player they'd never allowed to grant himself a regenerating break every now and then just to enable him to stay the course.

The journalists put pressure on because they have to fill

their columns, and the sponsors because they want to make money. Sometimes I had to put my foot down and say, 'This far and no further, and if I need it, I'm going to take a break.' The managers aren't much better. 'Are you mad? It's just two hours and you can pocket fifty thousand dollars. And to-morrow it's eighty thousand for this event at the department store. It hurts? Knock back a pill. You'll survive.' At tourna-ments, top players get extra money for advertising, but you have to be careful not to overdo it. Taking the dollar bait too often really can make you ill.

Wimbledon 1996 was a horror story. In the third round I was to meet Neville Godwin, number 223 in the world rank-ings – manageable, I thought. The South African had come through the qualifying rounds into the main field. The night before the match I lay on the sofa, unable to sleep between fits of shivering and sweating copiously – flu, of all things, at this critical juncture. Waldemar called Dr Müller-Wohlfahrt and physiotherapist Hans-Jürgen Montag (who sadly is no longer with us), both of whom were in London looking after the German football team, which was playing in the European Championship. The football doctors gave me help and advice. Meanwhile, rain clouds appeared over Wimbledon and we began to hope that the match would be postponed, or at least interrupted.

The match goes ahead. I enter the court stuffed with anti-biotics and painkillers. My coordination suffers, my reflexes are poor, my head is full of cotton wool and I don't feel at home in my own body. Then: a very ordinary serve, just as I'd done a million times before. At the last moment I try to swing the ball around with my forehand. The serve is about 200 kilometres an hour, but I hit the ball too late, and that's when it happens: part of the extensor muscle in my right wrist tears. The pain is dreadful at first, quickly followed by no feeling at all. Godwin goes on to the next round, but he doesn't celebrate; he seems rather flat. 'I'd rather have played the match to the end and won – fair and square,' he says later at the press conference.

I was X-rayed at the Wimbledon hospital and then went to the hotel where the German football team was staying. I wanted to get the opinion of the German doctors, whom I knew, but their diagnosis was no different from that of their British counterparts. At the hotel, the footballers' physiotherapist Klaus Eder put a plaster cast on me. It had been the turn before me of Steffen Freund, the midfield player, who'd torn a ligament – that meant a six-month break for him, a major blow. He'd really wanted to play in the semi-final against the Czech Republic. Compared to him, I was lucky. We had a beer together. I couldn't lift my arm; he couldn't move his leg.

I was told I'd have to take a break for three or four months. I was relaxed about it. This is something sports professionals have to live with. It could just as easily have gone the other way, after all. If the match had been interrupted by rain, I might have had the chance to get over the flu and win Wimbledon one more time. Most athletes know the score. You fight for world-ranking points, and if you don't play, someone else snaps up the trophy and the prize money.

For years now I'd been playing with non-elastic tape around both ankle joints. At a final in Stockholm I won in spite of a torn ligament in my left ankle, which had already been operated on once. After the legendary Davis Cup marathon against McEnroe, my feet were so swollen I had to keep them in ice buckets for hours afterwards. Waldemar Kliesing was already my physiotherapist then. At that time he was working for the German tennis association. I trust him. 'A darling,' says my mother of Waldemar – but she doesn't know what he was like when he pressed his elbows into my thighs or forced a cannula under my toenail because I had a haematoma there. Nothing can prevent this kind of injury, not even the tailor-made shoes and inserts I always wear. During a match, feet sweat copiously. They slide and push up against the toe of the shoe. Sometimes after a Grand Slam tournament all ten toenails would have these pockets of clotted blood under them. I'd almost go through the roof when Waldemar started drilling into them.

While I lay on the massage table – sometimes for up to three hours, until well after midnight, while my rock-hard post-match muscles gradually eased up – we talked very little. 'I'm not a hairdresser,' Waldemar would say. He had trained in intensive care and occasionally had to apply the skills he'd learned there to me. The list of my injuries reads like the annual medical report of a football club for its entire team, including reserves: double torn ligaments in the left ankle, severe ligament strain, pulled muscle in the right thigh, inflamed tendons in the middle finger of the right hand, muscle spasm in the right thigh, inflammation of the left knee, inflammation in both feet, a torn capsule in the left ankle joint, a dislocated vertebra, a torn muscle in the left thigh, a septic toe, a pulled stomach muscle, back injury, a torn tendon in the wrist, an operation on the ligaments in my right foot. In addition I often had bronchitis, angina, sinusitis, and viral and intestinal infections.

As long as I could walk, I went on to the court, even with

pulled muscles. So long as the doctor told me that nothing would tear, I'd swallow a painkiller and off I'd go. I'd often wear my body out; I'd be weak, under stress and in pain. In the autumn of 1986 I played in Hong Kong, Sydney, Tokyo and Paris all within the space of four weeks – and won. After that I was burned out. My doctors forced me to take a holiday from time to time. Players themselves rarely have a real choice. They are required to play and can only cancel if they declare injury. A sick note is easy to get, however. I could go to a doctor today and show him at least eight points on my body that would earn me a sick note.

In Wimbledon 1994, in the third round, I felt a vertebra move in my upper back. I could no longer pull through fully. Waldemar sat at the edge of Court One. 'Go to the changing rooms at once – I have to sort that out for you.' I requested a toilet break from the umpire, and as usual an official accompanied me. I lay down on a wooden bench. Waldemar immediately found the right vertebra, and I was able to play on. My shadow, however, reported the treatment to the umpire. It was an offence against the Grand Slam Code Section III Q – 'Mr Becker received medical attention during a toilet break.' The penalty: a thousand-dollar fine. It resulted in a huge scandal. Should I be disqualified? Even the other players joined in. This was like the behaviour of a pack of wolves – as soon as the leader shows the slightest sign of weakness, he falls victim to the rest.

I had to run the risk of the code violation because I wanted to win. After my second Wimbledon success, I was financially secure for the rest of my life so I could have quit then. But there was more to it than money, and this is something that lies deep in my nature. I can understand what makes Michael

Schumacher climb back into the racing car after a fracture of the fibula and shin, before the bones have knitted fully together again. He wanted to become world champion at any cost, and then if at all possible for a second and third time as well. Either you enter the competition and mean it, or you don't enter it at all. That means going right to the limit and then beyond it. My ego drove me on. That's why I carried on in the face of pain.

Dr Müller-Wohlfahrt, who is also the team doctor for FC Bayern-Munich, travelled to most of my tournaments, for my own peace of mind. That was an expensive exercise for me, but I had to do it. 'Mull', as his friends call him, deserves my greatest thanks. Several of my cups are dedicated to him. So too did my sports physiotherapist Josef Schardhauser, whose experience in track and field athletics and football was of enormous benefit to me. And of course Dr Thomas von Mendelsohn, the practitioner and chiropractor with the golden hands. Not to mention Klaus Eder, who was always there when I needed him. After three matches I'd often be so tensed up that I was in danger of injury. When my wrist injury hadn't got better after three or four months, I explored every possible healing method. I came across the name of Muhamed Khalifa, who works near Salzburg in Austria. Steffi Graf is also one of his patients. He works solely with his hands, using no injections or other intervention. It's a sort of acupressure with hands, but at very high pressure. It hurt a lot, but it worked. The condition improved, though the symptoms remained.

Top sports players are obsessed, driven by the desire for perfection. Schumacher has to drive at full speed, or quit. When his competitor slides off the track, he doesn't feel for him. I've never called on an opponent to ask whether he was all right after, say, a knee injury. Don't have any illusions. In the streets of Rio de Janeiro or Nairobi, people get killed for a few hundred dollars. In my field the price is a few hundred thousand dollars, or a few million, but it's just as brutal, up to the limits imposed by the rules. In every match I reached a point where I faced the wall, and managed to jump over it – concentration and willpower made it possible. Beyond this point is where injuries lurk.

My body is worn out, but not ruined. When I enter into a show match today with one of my former opponents, it takes hours of treatment and preparation to get me match-fit. My body paid a high price, but I'm still here.

DOPED UP YET?

SURE, I'VE BEEN OFFERED DRUGS. BUT UNLIKE FORMER US president Bill Clinton, who claimed to have smoked marijuana but not inhaled, I can in all honesty declare this: I did neither. I'm clean. But what about the others? At the end of 1999, a total of 1,580 players were listed in the ATP's rankings computer. It would be hypocrisy to say that none of these players, all in their twenties, has ever touched cocaine or lit a joint. In 1995 at the US Open, Wilander and his doubles partner Karel Novak tested positive for cocaine and were banned.

It's known that drug abuse is a global social problem. The USA has millions of addicts: on Wall Street, in the Hollywood studios, at the high schools. According to a study published in 1999, forty-five per cent of American parents expect that at some point their children will give in to the temptation. Walking through Munich, I'd often see junkies injecting in doorways. The police don't react. Passers-by step over the exposed, blue-punctured legs. In 1999, my last year as a tennis pro, the number of drug-related deaths in Germany rose to 1,723 – that's 1,723 individual tragedies.

Of course, tennis players aren't exempt. They often have a lot of money in their pockets at an early age. Tennis writer Richard Evans wrote that at the end of the 1980s a number of professional players were using drugs. 'Cocaine flowed freely at virtually every party they went to in New York and Los Angeles and it would have been a miracle if a bunch of young men in their twenties with ready cash to burn had not got hooked up in the glitzy habits of the super-rich.'[1]

For me, the issue of drugs is nothing to do with morality or immorality, or addiction and atonement. I didn't want cannabis or cocaine to jeopardize my career. It doesn't take much imagination to picture the devastating effect on the public had Boris Becker tested positive for drugs. Diego Maradona was made ill by cocaine. The football officials could probably have halted his decline if they'd tried hard enough, but he was the football god and no one would touch him. *Il magnifico* – he was just there to score goals.

The Canadian 100-metre sprinter Ben Johnson, who was stripped of his 1988 Seoul gold medal because he'd had illegal help in achieving it, became the symbol of demise and immorality in sport. As it happens, he was Canadian, not US American, not white but black, not eloquent but self-conscious, a poor fellow like the boxer Mike Tyson, the poorest of the lot. He's got the whole world lined up against him.

People need, and cherish, sporting heroes. They are vital to a nation's self-esteem. The sportswear companies tie their fees in to rankings and their marketing strategies in to gold. Many athletes have fallen victim to this pressure. They are at the end of the so-called value chain. The peculiar physical development of some of the top athletics stars in the USA has invited speculation over the years, but rarely led to sanctions. And how else should they keep up when their competitors swallow, inject, de-tox their blood or tank up on oxygen, and then collect the prize money? Would I have stayed whiter than white if I thought my competitors were boosting themselves with chemicals, or if pills would have helped me to win Wimbledon more easily? I have my doubts.

Doping is part of the Tour de France; that's nothing new. The cyclists who take banned substances are grown-ups. Apparently they need the stuff in order to climb the murderous mountain stages. Sure, they cheat, but because so many of them seem to do it, they're cheating each other. Why the hypocrisy? Some years ago a top German cyclist was already being described in the press as a 'pharmacy on wheels'. The question to ask is which athletes start clean in the first place. I say: the tennis players, at least the vast majority of them. Of course, one or other might be tempted to enhance their staying power with medication just to get through a five-hour match. Of all the top-ranking players, however, only one has so far been prosecuted for doping: the Czech, Petr Korda. At the Wimbledon quarter-finals in 1998 he allegedly had the anabolic steroid Nandrolone in his system. Korda maintained his innocence, despite the fact that the test results didn't leave much room for doubt. How did Nandrolone get into his bloodstream? Korda said that he'd been given it in connection with a foot injury.

Despite Korda, I'd like to assert that our sport is clean. Coordination, a feel for the ball, sensitivity and timing cannot be achieved with the help of pills or injections. The 100-metre sprinter knows he has to run seventy or eighty steps in a straight line and for each step he needs a certain amount of energy and a certain reach. In our case it's not so predictable. A match can be interrupted by rain or darkness. In the first four days of Wimbledon 1991, only fifty-two of the scheduled 240 matches went ahead. How could you calculate the right dose when a match could last sixty minutes or, with interruptions, three days? In tennis, stimulants are – in my opinion – almost completely useless.

My gut feeling is that everyone should be able to do what they want with their own body. My head, however, tells me that the world of sport can set an example, especially for our children. Children don't know what they are doing, and we need to show them – the family as well as the state. But I have no illusions. The more forcefully you prosecute, the more refined the methods of the prosecuted become. They know their product, and they know when to stop taking it. So I'm in favour of tighter controls, including blood tests. The sports players will be outraged; they see these kinds of test as a physical attack on them. But drivers suspected of being over the limit have to accept a blood test. So why the resistance?

Blood tests are the only way to make sport, including the Olympics, credible again. If these tests really become the norm, however, there'll be a great awakening. I have no real evidence, but I've been in close contact with professionals for more than a decade. Athletes do let themselves be seduced, because the sums of money they are fighting for are so immense. Just one or two pills more, and you can be rich . . .

OLD LIONS STILL BITE

SO IT WAS THAT IN JULY 1998 I SAT WITH THE ARCHDUKE OF
Austria, the Duchess of Westminster and the Kents in the
royal box, looking down on what had once been my stage. For
me the curtain had come down one year before in the final
against Pete Sampras. I told my opponent at the net, 'That's it.
No more Wimbledon.'

That would have been a worthy end! Pete was the greatest,
an exceptional champion. But what I saw in the 1998 final,
when he played against Goran Ivanisevic, convinced me I
might still be in with a chance. I wanted to play on Centre
Court at Wimbledon one more time. I'd no sooner made my
decision than the doubts appeared. Did I really want to
torture myself? Letting myself in for all that hard training
and touring again? Enduring the physical pain along with the
pain caused by hurtful headlines?

At that point I was bobbing up and down on the tennis
scene like a piece of flotsam at sea. I'd defeated Carlos Moya

in the second round at Stuttgart. Just two weeks earlier he'd won the French Open in Paris, a tournament I never managed to win myself. My father was in the grandstand, next to Ion Tiriac. At this point he wasn't far from death, but at Ion's encouragement he had postponed a chemo appointment to be there. Karl-Heinz Becker, this ordinary man from Leimen, next to streetwise Ion Tiriac – my guardian angels. What an odd couple. The sight moved me. I told myself then that this would be a good day to retire. I'd come full circle. These two men had shaped my life, and now they were sitting there happily talking about the past, about Ion's first visit to Leimen. He hadn't shown up in a Rolls-Royce but in a Bentley, though only those in the know could have told the difference. Whenever he came to our house he was always received – as is common in German families – with cake, then more cake, then a hearty meal with extra helpings for the guest. Whenever my parents visited him in Monte Carlo, they'd always present him with several kilos of sausages and cold meats too.

But in Stuttgart I realized I wasn't quite ready to give up my career, after all. I knew that playing around in minor tournaments wasn't my cup of tea. The fans were fed up with me, and I was fed up with myself. I just wasn't bringing in the results any more. And Barbara was pregnant again. It was clear that with two children things would have to change. One evening in December 1998 I asked Barbara, 'What do you think? Shall I draw the line, or have another go? I'm unhappy with the way things are. If I really wanted it, I could make it to the top again. But do I really want it?' Barbara never urged me to retire; on the contrary, she made several arguments against my retiring. Tennis was our lifeline. It meant stability as well as adventure. She wanted to see me as a tennis pro for a little longer. The exit from the tennis circuit she'd become so used to led only to insecurity, as far as she could see. Would I turn into a marginalized has-been, with no resort but nagging? She only knew the superstar: the famous man by her side who could earn a hundred thousand dollars in one day, and she also knew what I was like when I lost – unbearable.

We talked for a long time that particular night. 'I've only got one choice,' I said. 'For the whole of my life I've gone in by the front door, and now I have to leave by the front door too. I can't just steal away out the back. And my front door is Wimbledon. I've got to play one more time, however well or badly. It's all or nothing.'

It was 27 June 1985 that I played on Centre Court for the first time, against American Hank Pfister. In 1999 I set out to play there one more time. At the beginning of January we flew to Florida, where I started my preparation. I knew I could cope with the routine and the torture mentally, but what about physically? Would the ligaments tear, would the discs hold – how would my knees fare? In early April 1999, at the doubles in the Davis Cup against Russia, my ankle joint mutinied. It had been torn and twisted so many times that it wouldn't heal any more. After two or three hours of playing it seized up and I could no longer put my weight on it. It really needed to be operated on but there wasn't any time. Somehow I had to get myself through these weeks ahead of my appearance on grass. There, I hoped, I'd be able to get by. In my very first practice session, with Sampras, I had to give up after half an hour. I made a decision then that was unique for me, and for the first time in my career had injections of Cortisone.

On the Friday before Wimbledon, I said to Barbara, 'It's 99 per cent certain that I won't play. But I'm hoping for a miracle.' And in my first match, against the Scot Miles MacLagan, number 298 in the world rankings, I lost the first two sets. Other people would pack their bags at this point. I, however, can't give up. I just can't do it. I'd been two sets down before at many Grand Slam tournaments – at the US Open in '87, '89 and '93, in Paris in '91 and in Australia in '96. And every time I managed to win against the odds, I felt like a lion. It generates a certain respect from your fellow players, too.

These 'thrillers' were typical of my tennis life. Against Andre Agassi in the Davis Cup in the Munich Olympiahalle, for example: the first two sets went 7–6, 7–6 to him, but I still won. In Rio de Janeiro, against Luiz Mattar in the first round of the Davis Cup at the end of January 1992, I played one of my best matches ever. There we were on the court in temperatures of 40°C in the shade, surrounded by five-thousand-people's worth of Brazilian chaos, with ice cubes and little balls being chucked at me. I won the first set 6–4, then I lost the second 5–7 and the third 1–6. In the fourth set he led 5–2. All the same, I won the tie-break, even though the Brazilian had seven match points against me. I won the fifth set 6–0. Mattar couldn't believe it. After the match I was half-dead and hardly able to walk. The following week I played in Brussels: a final against Jim Courier, which was to become another drama. I lost the first two sets, but still managed to turn the match around: 6–7, 2–6, 7–6, 7–6, 7–5. Five match points and three tie-breaks. During this tournament I played three doubles with McEnroe, which we won, and John couldn't quite take it all in. He always made fun of me and my comebacks. 'Admit it! You go to church every morning, cross yourself three times and worship the Virgin Mary.' It did my self-confidence good to play a match like that every other month or so, but it cost me a lot in energy and I'd be mentally exhausted for weeks afterwards.

Against Miles MacLagan, during my last appearance at Wimbledon, my ankle stopped hurting in the third set. The injections had worked. And I won, in spite of having lagged behind at the start. The efforts of the previous six months had been worth it for this match alone. I'd held out, and I felt good about myself. But there was another excitement to come: Becker against Kiefer. The experts predicted that the young player would drive the old, toothless lion out of his territory because he'd become lazy and sluggish. Tennis reporter Simon Barnes wrote that 'Kiefer was just about the last person against whom Becker would have chosen to make his sentimental farewell to Wimbledon.'[1] And so it was. Wimbledon isn't Africa. Here even the old lions bite.

And for me the question was not whether I would beat Kiefer, or Australia's rising star Lleyton Hewitt. For me it was about an honourable exit for a tennis professional. I didn't care about my opponents. Only Becker mattered to me. Kiefer took it personally when I was cool with him both before and after the match, but that's how I approached a duel.

After victory over Kiefer, my fellow players kept their distance. No more small talk, no more jokes. The alpha male was back again. As Hewitt put it after his defeat by me in the third round: 'Boris walks around like he owns the court.'[2] Nevertheless, my exit came in the next round, when Hewitt's fellow countryman Patrick Rafter showed me the end of the line.

Wimbledon is more important to me than any individual opponent. Whoever I faced there, I was always playing out my own history. At this, my last appearance, the great Manitou nodded and said, 'I'll help you one more time. At least on the court . . .'

MY DEAR FELLOW PLAYERS

FRIDAY, ONE O'CLOCK, ROYAL ALBERT HALL, LONDON: instead of a concert, a tennis match. On show, the ATP Senior Tour, in which Jimmy Connors, John McEnroe, Yannick Noah and Björn Borg will demonstrate once more what made them so great. Men in dinner jackets sit on chairs covered in red velvet. For their firms, the sponsors, this tennis event is a festive occasion. Champagne corks pop.

Stefan Edberg has come with his wife. I twice lost Wimbledon to Edberg. He's wearing a dark suit and a colourful tie. For ten years he lived in a flat not far from the Albert Hall, but now he lives in Sweden, far away from big cities. He tells me that most of the time he drinks water; champagne isn't his thing. His youngest child is into ballet and gymnastics – her father's sport holds no interest for her. He plays tennis twice a week, and after having recently played two matches against me in Arhus and London (I won both!), he's now considering playing a few senior events.

Welcome to the past.

Connors and McEnroe haven't played together on English soil since 1984's Wimbledon final. Back then McEnroe destroyed the Connors legend 6–1, 6–1, 6–2. Today's is a revenge match, for which the British papers have dispatched their tennis journalists to the Albert Hall. Patty Smythe, John's second wife and mother of two of his six children, is sitting next to me and Barbara in the box. It's 1998.

Patty keeps going out into the corridor to try to calm her nerves with a cigarette. She only met John after the peak of his career. Today he's one of the most highly regarded television tennis commentators in the USA, an expert for the BBC, a successful author (*Serious*), one of the best on the Senior Tour (at forty-four!) and an art collector. In his gallery on Greene Street in SoHo he shows the work of the young avant-garde, among others.

Patty smokes for two minutes, then comes back in. John has won the first set 6–0. There are whistles and catcalls. Mrs McEnroe was a successful rock singer. She is well balanced, thoughtful, a striking contrast to John's first wife Tatum O'Neal, who must have inherited her excitable temperament from her Hollywood parents. John wins the second set 6–1. He raises his arms, and his people celebrate. The champagne corks pop again. Pure nostalgia. Patty's happy: 'Now we can go shopping!' Had he lost to his arch-rival, John would most likely have retreated to his hotel to lick his wounds. Instead, the men in dinner jackets stand up and cheer him, their Mac.

In the evening we meet up for dinner in my favourite London restaurant, San Lorenzo. Mara, the Italian owner, is godmother to our son Noah. She hugs John and kisses him on both cheeks. 'Is that for starters?' he jokes. We drink Chianti, either in spite of or because Mac has reached the final. The other people in the restaurant glance our way but nobody bothers us. John's hair's got greyer. He wears a small earring in his left ear. One day, he hopes, I will also play with the seniors. I reject the idea emphatically. 'Out of the question. I put on a show for long enough.' Four years later, I beat Mac in Graz and win my first senior tournament. Am I a U-turning pushover? Yes, I am! Once you've had a taste of top-class tennis, once you've taken part in this sport at the highest level, you're hooked. You have to have the atmosphere of the full stadium, with an audience that is rooting for you. You have to pour your sweat on to the court, and you have to have that clash of man against man: the match.

It's very companionable, this dinner at San Lorenzo, and it's an exception. What remains of the friendships from the upper ranks of the global tennis circus, where I played for so long? Almost nothing. On the other hand, there never was much there. Dealings between individuals in this thin, high-altitude air are sometimes whiny, often unpleasant and always distant. I was no better than anyone else. I've known Stefan Edberg for two decades and our encounters are friendly but superficial. Do I call Pete Sampras up when I visit Miami Beach? No. I practised with Björn Borg in Monte Carlo during his comeback attempt. He was still very strong, despite the wooden rackets he continued to play with, and undeterred. He's got charisma. Life's left its mark on him. But we only ever talked about the most banal things in the world. Have dinner together? Never. And even players I really liked don't stay in contact.

At the charity tournament in South Africa, Agassi and I arrived with our wives. We went on safari together. I'd never been so close to death before. The lion was right by our jeep and with one leap he could have sent us crashing into the headlines. Then an elephant, four times bigger than our vehicle. We edged towards it. Another twenty metres and I panicked. 'That's enough.' That night I didn't dare close my eyes. I thought about the lions, in comparison to which the snakes that were gliding in and out of the room seemed like pets. On the third day we watched a group of lions catching two zebras, but I'd have preferred to be back with my snakes. Sights as savage as this can set you thinking. What are you doing on this earth, and, more to the point, what are you doing in this wilderness with its own very different laws? The lions could have ripped us apart, just like they did the zebras. I comforted myself with the thought that two zebras a day was enough for the lions, so today they'd have no appetite for Beckers or Agassis.

I became fond of Agassi on this journey. We understood each other, and since we were no longer rivals we allowed ourselves some closeness. I was preparing myself for retirement, while he was rolling up his sleeves to start again at the bottom – he carried it off, too. Respect. Agassi is an incredibly good tennis player. He trained hard for his comeback. He'd lost and endured more than enough, but he was able to fan back into flames this unextinguishable ambition he has. Victory at the Australian Open in 2003, and once again the world's number one, at the age of thirty-three – the storyline of a Hollywood movie. Is this thanks to Steffi? His second wife must certainly be good motivation. What man wants to be reminded at the breakfast table that his wife has brought home many more trophies than he has?

Andre and I once went to the Oktoberfest, where we

knocked back a tidy amount and he revealed why he was so often the victor in our encounters (10–4 to Agassi). It was a trivial thing, but rather incredible too. At some point in the late 1980s, he'd noticed that during my serve I opened my mouth and stuck out my tongue in the direction in which I was going to send the ball. He spent four or five years just watching my mouth. My serve was rendered almost useless, while his return was his best shot. After that I kept my mouth shut.

In 1999 I played doubles with Pete Sampras in Queens, something he'd never done when I'd been a genuine rival. In one of the breaks he even gave me an insight into his feelings. He'd just broken up with his girlfriend. 'I feel terrible,' he said. 'I don't enjoy this any more.' Nevertheless he went on to win Wimbledon. Later he found a new love, started a family, won his fourteenth Grand Slam title with the US Open in Flushing Meadow in 2002 – and left the stage. The most perfect tennis player of all time had chosen the perfect exit. Hats off to you, Pete!

Tennis pros are individualists, egocentrics, solo entertainers. Of course, I had my friendships with Charly Steeb, Eric Jelen and Patrik Kühnen, which had begun in our childhood. After my father's death, Alex Corretja left a message of condolence on my answering machine. Slobodan ('Bobo') Zivojinovic even came to the funeral. But with most other players it was different. You had to reveal nothing, absolutely nothing, to your opponents. Anything you said would be exploited unscrupulously. If you were quite far ahead and wanted to win, you had to avoid at all costs showing your opponent who you were, or what strengths, weaknesses and feelings you had. Why should I have spent my evenings drinking beer with my opponents? No way.

Connors' and Lendl's approach to tennis was that it was like going to work; at the end of the day you had to be able to calculate what you'd earned. In 1987, Connors described himself in *Sports Illustrated* like this: 'In the early years of my career I was an animal foaming at the mouth . . . It was as if I had rabies. I've bitten a number of people on my way up, and that's how I wanted it. Now I don't have to bite anyone any more.'[1] Agassi and Courier, who, after all, trained together in Florida for many years, occasionally sat next to each other in first class during the interminable flights from Australia to the USA, and barely exchanged a word. 'Hi, have a good flight' – that was it.

At the beginning of my career, I played doubles with Lendl. I was one of the few players with whom the Czech-born player would talk at all; perhaps I had the advantage that my mother came from the same town as him, Ostrava. He spoke German quite well. We wouldn't talk about personal matters, though. Neither did we practise playing doubles. 'We'll meet in the changing rooms ten minutes before the match.' No more than that. Just like two workmates meeting at the start of their shift. He was no less likeable than the others; in fact, he was much the same as the rest. Lendl didn't care a bit for his fellow players. In the changing room he laughed at his opponents, made fun of their weaknesses, and would announce how much he intended to beat them by, along the lines of, 'Today, I'll give you three games.' During warm-up he often returned the balls unfairly, or hit them repeatedly into the corner. I don't believe he had much genuine self-confidence. He put a wall up around himself so that his opponents couldn't get near his sensitive side. The generation of the Noahs, McEnroes, Borgs and Lendls saw me as a newcomer, someone who'd intruded into their territory. I was excluded because I was so much younger. The beard I was growing then may have been the result of my sub-conscious desire to appear older and therefore to belong to the group.

In the autumn of 1985, at an event organized by Tiriac in Japan, I played my first exhibition match against Connors, in front of six and a half thousand spectators, and already there was trouble. I'd been six years old when Connors played his first Wimbledon final. I beat him in forty-two minutes, 6–1, 6–2. After the match, Connors stormed off the court and yelled at Tiriac, 'Can you tell your greenhorn that we're playing exhibition and we're supposed to offer the audience at least an hour of play!'

Tiriac apologized. 'He's seventeen and he doesn't know how it works yet. I'm sorry.'

Connors would have beaten me 6–0, 6–0 in twenty-five minutes if he'd had half a chance. I was intimidated by this scene, and against Vilas I played 7–5, 7–6 – deliberately tight. I could have beaten him straight, but I was frightened of doing something wrong. At any rate, I never lost to Connors, neither in exhibitions nor in tournaments. Since 1986 I've sat with him a few times in the players' lounge exchanging small talk. I also practised with him at several tournaments. When we played together, we didn't talk at all. We played at full throttle, strenuous but good. At each tournament he asked me, 'Practice tomorrow at ten?' It was like being knighted. I was part of the club and was being taken seriously.

There are players who constantly provoke others and are shocked when the tables are turned on them. This used to be the case with McEnroe, and Connors was even worse, playing to the crowd and abusing his opponent and the umpires. Compared to Connors or McEnroe, the players today are harmless little boys. Psychological warfare has always been part of the business. Even people I saw as my friends, like Yannick Noah, would use every trick in the book. During a tournament in Rome, Yannick and I played doubles together. He was my idol. I was happy, and we made it to the quarter-finals. Fifteen minutes before the match, he pulled out. His foot was badly injured and he couldn't play. It looked as if he wouldn't be playing in the semi-final the next day either, when I was due to play against him. I believed him. I was only seventeen. I had the prospect of reaching the final. This could have been my first breakthrough. But on the Saturday Noah suddenly ran like a gazelle, beat me in straight sets and won the tournament. Tiriac's comment? 'You see? Rule number one: never believe your opponent.' I learned something that day. Sometimes I even felt real hatred for my opponent, but hatred gives bad advice. In these cases I never played particularly well.

My strength was that I lost all fear as soon as I stepped out on to the court, even though beforehand I'd have been really nervous. Every player has his weakness. Everyone knew that Stich had only to be distracted two or three times and he'd lose control. He'd start arguing with the umpire and getting on everyone's nerves. Little things could distract him immensely and put him off his stroke. If you tried to provoke McEnroe you'd get the opposite effect – his play would improve.

Tactics are important. In every match there are one or two decisive moments when you realize your opponent is shaky and his resolve is crumbling, and that's when you have to shift up a gear. You notice it when his shoulders drop and his defence starts to weaken. I look out for gestures, body language, exclamations, tactics, how he plays certain balls, whether he suddenly risks everything or becomes super-careful. To do this, however, you have to know your opponent well, though certain basic rules apply to everyone. When the other player is behind and loses the first set, this is often the start of your success in the second set too. That's when you can tie it up. If a player suffers an early break, he starts risking everything. If you just hold out a little bit, it can be over in five minutes.

This clash of man against man without any support or any time out is one of the best things about tennis. But to keep this up over decades you have to be tough, just like Connors, who as long ago as 1974 defeated Australian Ken Rosewall to win Wimbledon. Or like his eternal rival McEnroe, who played twice against Connors in the Wimbledon final and who still can't let go of tennis and the Senior Tour. John is convinced: 'Tennis beats working.'

NEWS AT THE FIFTH HOLE

THE FOOTBALL BOOTS ARE LYING SOMEWHERE AT THE BACK of the cupboard. They are torn, twisted, and faded through lack of care. But I'd never throw them away: they represent childhood and youth. They're the souvenirs of a past that's even further away than the tennis life I've just left behind.

Who's never stood by a local pitch, watching people at a leisurely game of football, only to find the ball leaving the grass and coming to a halt by their feet? Shot! You see – you can still do it, even after twenty years. At fifteen I was playing at the Leimen sports club.

I think I would have made a good football player. As a child I was good at both tennis and football. I played midfield, and I supported FC Bayern from the start. Every Wednesday evening my parents watched European Cup matches; Bayern often won the Cup. As a child you want to be on the winning side, which is why I didn't go for local teams like Karlsruher

SC or Waldhof Mannheim. Today I'm even on FC Bayern's financial board.

The Bayern Munich Presidents Cup is being played at Gut Rieden in Leustetten, Lake Starnberg. Today I'm having a break from negotiations with business partners and counselling sessions in the living room with the midwife about the forthcoming birth – today is reserved for golf, my newest passion. I'm in the company of Franz Beckenbauer, Andy Brehme, Raimond Aumann – all ex-football pros who can't give up the ball, even if it's just a golf ball. My friend and adviser Robert Lübenoff, known as 'One Putt', as well as Klaus Eder, physiotherapist to the German national team, and Raimond all play together. One Putt and I always have fun. At every second or third tee there are refreshments on offer: ham sandwiches, *Leberkäs*, wheat beer and sausages – real Bavarian fare. Two hostesses in a golf cart purr away and return with schnapps.

I light a cigarillo. For golf purists, this is blasphemy. Smoking on the green? But, Herr Becker . . . Here, however, I'm in the company of friends and it's all very relaxed. The sun is warming us; the schnapps too. One Putt has found his rhythm, but I keep sending my balls into the rough. My bodyguard, discreet as ever, stands twenty metres away. His expression doesn't change, even when I mishit the ball. A mobile phone erupts into the scene. It's One Putt's. 'Steffi has retired.' So, Steffi as well. It's Friday 13 August 1999, six weeks after my Wimbledon farewell. Officially, she played 994 professional matches; I played 932. She won twenty-two Grand Slams; I won six. If the friendship between Steffi and me was turned into a book or a film, nobody would believe it. She was six and I was eight when we met for the first time.

I rode my bike to the sports centre in Leimen. She came with her mother. In those days I often had to play against girls, which felt like a kind of punishment, especially when the older boys – who later wouldn't have stood a chance against Steffi – used to say, 'Look at the redhead, fighting it out with the little girl!' It also got on my nerves when the coach, Boris Breskvar, ended the game just at the moment when I was set for victory. My mother comforted me: 'He really doesn't know how to handle children.'

Even as a child, Steffi was focused and introverted, and sometimes trained like a robot. Thanks to these supposedly typical German characteristics, it took quite a long time for her to become internationally popular, rather like Michael Schumacher in Formula 1, who always comes across as so brusque – as though all he's missing is the spiked helmet. Steffi was too determined for some people's liking – too correct, too cool, too 'Made in Germany'. Her star sign is Gemini. Perfection is in her nature. That's how she did her job. On the other hand, she's an extremely sensitive and compassionate person. This shows every now and then, but for a long time she didn't really live out her emotions. The most important thing for her was tennis success, and that's why she worked like a machine. It was much the same in my case, but from time to time other things mattered more to me. She probably told herself: To hell with my feelings, what I want now is to win Wimbledon for the eighth time.

The tax scandals concerning her father, the court case and his imprisonment took their toll on Steffi. I believe this also changed her way of dealing with her feelings. Steffi cried, and the people at home in front of the television cried with her. At last, something came from the heart, and the nation took her into its embrace.

We've been comrades in arms over the years. We didn't have to explain to each other about the pressure we were both under. We've always been in the same boat, from Brühl and Leimen to Wimbledon and back.

As a woman she fascinated me. It wasn't the infantile falling-in-love of a teenager that made me want to get to know Steffi better. It was a deep feeling of affection, an unexpressed understanding between like-minded people who shared the same fate. And, naturally, I was curious about her too: where did she get the power, the motivation, the inspiration that made her so successful? What had she got that I hadn't? And we all know that success is sexy – not to mention Steffi's legs! The Steffi I got to know was an exciting person, not in the least shallow, with a sombre side and a lively side. These weren't visible in the tennis player. Early on, she moved to Florida, and took an apartment in the heart of New York's SoHo. Black has always been her favourite colour, and she's always had a weakness for expensive clothes. According to media reports, she had a relationship with Mick Hucknall of Simply Red. His song 'Holding Back the Years' is one of my favourites. These things don't really fit the image of the Tennis Duchess ('Graf' means 'Duke'!) from Brühl, and Steffi was clever enough to keep this side of her life from the public. I didn't succeed in this endeavour, but then maybe I didn't want to.

I've always rated Steffi's incredible willpower, her ability to overcome her own resistance and to face the challenge over and over again. We saw each other mostly at the Grand Slam tournaments where both women and men played, such as

Wimbledon in 1987. I was the number-one seed, the Lawn-Tennis King. My opponent in the second round on 26 June 1987, Peter Doohan, was ranked seventy. After the tie-break in the first set I wasn't particularly worried. I'd been behind so many times before. By the fourth set, however, I felt that Doohan, who played for Australia in the Davis Cup, was in a kind of trance, being carried along by the audience, who wanted to witness a sensation – my defeat. Lendl, who was lying on the massage table in the changing rooms and had watched the fourth set on the television, claimed later, 'I saw it coming.'

Steffi, good soul, had watched parts of the first and second set before her match against Laura Gildemeister. She was sure I'd make it. She heard the noise that came from our court, across from hers and Laura's – the applause – and she was in no doubt: 'They're behind Boris. He's winning.' The victor, however, was Peter, not Boris. The players – such as Edberg, who'd followed my defeat on the television in the changing room – were 'shocked'. You can't expect sympathy in our business, however. The Becker obstacle had been cleared out of the way. Only Steffi had consoling words for me. To this day she has no idea how much she helped me.

After the next tee, One Putt has the report of the sports information service read out to him over his mobile. 'After weeks of inner turmoil, physical pain and conflicting state-ments, on Friday the thirteenth Steffi Graf has drawn the line under her unique career. "I'm announcing my retirement from tournament tennis, and I feel relieved that in the end it's been so simple for me to reach this decision. The weeks after Wimbledon haven't been easy because for the first time I wasn't finding tennis fun any more. This was a strange feeling, one I hadn't had before," declared the thirty-year-old former world number one in composed tones, from a press conference in her home town of Heidelberg.'[1]

The reporters were already waiting at the next hole. 'Boris, what do you have to say to this?' Boris? Why are they all calling me by my first name? I don't want to say anything. I don't have anything to say. Others can speak, like Franz Beckenbauer – he's always got something to say. I want to speak to Steffi herself first. The journalists won't let me off the hook. 'Boris, are you upset? Boris, is she the greatest? Boris, is she ill?'

'Herr Becker' – this is the man from the television – 'Herr Becker, our station will donate five hundred marks to the Beckenbauer Foundation if you give us a statement about Steffi.'

'I just want to finish my game here.'

And that's what I did, but it was no surprise that I lost to One Putt.

A little later I called Steffi. She was relaxed and happy. I congratulated her on her career and on making this decision at the right moment. We both knew what retiring felt like. I had no idea of her new love, Andre Agassi; she didn't mention him at all. But I wasn't surprised when I did learn of it. I knew that Agassi had had a crush on Steffi for some time, but first he had to get over the break-up with Brooke Shields, and Steffi had to get used to the end of her career. Now they are tennis's dream couple. Their son Jaden Gil is already seen by the British bookies as a potential Wimbledon winner (odds quoted at 100 to 1). Maybe he'll play Elias in the final one day.

ALI, OPEN YOUR EYES

THE FLASHING BLUE LIGHT OF THE POLICE CAR SHINES through the windscreen of our limousine. We're in a hurry. The flight had been severely delayed by bad weather. One of the police officers puts his arm out of his window and signals to the other drivers with his fluorescent red baton to make room for the cars coming up behind. The sirens howl and irritated drivers blow their horns. Snow and rain in Vienna.

We're on the way to the Staatsoper, to the World Sports Awards of the Century. Scores of sports legends have come: footballer Pelé, swimmer Mark Spitz, boxer Muhammad Ali, pole-vaulter Sergej Bubka. The driveway of the Hotel Imperial is blocked by parked cars. No problem for our escort – they go straight up on to the pavement, and we follow suit. We bump into Ion in the corridor of our floor. He's already dressed to the nines. Ali's close friend the photographer Howard Bingham, who's accompanied the legendary boxer for thirty-six years, is just coming out of his rooms. He, too, is in his tuxedo, but on his right foot he's wearing a patent-leather shoe and on the left a walking shoe. Bingham explains that back in Los Angeles he made a mistake when he was packing his things, but he plans to put it down to the latest, new-millennium Californian trend. I meet Carl Lewis, sprinter and long-jumper, in the lift. A little later he tells me that he's moved from Houston to Pacific Palisades in California, where he now lives in Arnold Schwarzenegger's neighbourhood. He's likely to keep his restaurant in Houston, but he'd now like to work on his film career and sprint along the beach in Santa Monica with his dogs. There's only one guy I don't see, and he's the one I'd particularly like to meet: Ali.

Outside the Staatsoper there's loud applause. The cold doesn't deter the waiting fans. Hundreds of photographers and television reporters wait around the staircases leading to the upper levels. How splendid this opera house is! We're in the front row, left-hand stalls. The voluptuous Brigitte Nielsen walks by; she made the headlines in Hollywood when she married Rambo: Sylvester Stallone. There's a crush all around her, and everywhere the typical Austrian greeting, 'Küss die Hand, gnä' Frau.' I turn around, and I'm gob-smacked. Sitting right behind me is Muhammad Ali! To me he's *the* global superstar: once a little 'nigger' forced to sit at the back of the public buses, today a man who's overcome every boundary of race and religion.

Cassius Marcellus Clay, the son of a sign-painter, challenged the American establishment and dared to condemn 'God's own country'. He followed radical Muslims and their illusion of building an Islamic nation on American soil. Ali was pure *black power*, and not just in the boxing ring. He campaigned against the Vietnam war: 'Keep asking me, no matter how long,/ On the war in Vietnam, I'll still sing this song:/ I ain't got no quarrel with no Viet Cong.' He was sentenced to five years in prison for refusing to do his military service. He didn't have to serve his time, however. America's conscience, including white America, and the world's outrage saved him from that. The conservatives held him in contempt; the FBI listened in on his conversations, but Ali continued to open his mouth. At his first world championship fight in 1964, he entered the ring in a white robe with the words 'The Lip' embroidered on the back. And he boxed like he talked. After the sixth round, his opponent Sonny Liston spat out his gumshield. 'That's it.' Ali was world champion at the age of twenty-two. This was his Wimbledon.

My hero stands up with difficulty, but won't accept any help. Barbara shakes his hand. 'I'm Boris Becker's wife.' Ali pulls her towards him, kisses her cheek and whispers, 'I know everything about you.' Dozens of photographers gather round us, and it's just like Sugar Ray Leonard once said: 'If you put Ali next to Castro and Gorbachev in a room full of people, everyone would gather around Ali.' He's turned beatings into poetry and marketed himself like no other megastar before or since. Norman Mailer, who wrote a best-selling book about Ali, *The Fight*, described him as America's greatest ego. In January 1974, when I was a seven-year-old boy, my father woke me up to watch Ali fight his 'Rumble in the Jungle' against George Foreman in Zaire. His legendary footwork, the Ali-Shuffle, even bewitched ballet choreographer George Balanchine. As Ali himself announced to the world, he could 'float like a butterfly and sting like a bee'.

Now he's closing his eyes and dropping back into his seat. Is it the spotlights, the jet lag, the illness that's getting to him?

Ali's trembling. It's Parkinson's. Cells in the central part of the brain deteriorate, resulting in loss of memory, shaking, paralysis. Up on stage Mark Spitz, nine-times gold-medal-winner, says his thanks for his award as best swimmer of all time. You could never know the agony you were going to experience on the way to success, says the American. It helped, 'the innocence of never having done it before'. In Ali's case there were consequences he surely couldn't have foreseen.

In the best-seller *King of the World*, which I re-read after meeting Ali, David Remnick spells out Ali's significance: 'a symbol of faith, a symbol of conviction and defiance, a symbol of beauty and skill and courage, a symbol of racial pride, of wit and love.'[1] In 1965, Ali met up with the Beatles in a training camp in Miami for a commercial gig. Cassius Clay to John Lennon: 'You're not as stupid as you look.' The Beatle replied, 'No, I'm not. But you are.' Ali loved verbal sparring. He was never predictable. How much was fun, and how much was conviction? He could switch from comic to killer; he preached the word of Allah, but boasted of himself: 'I am the greatest.'

Howard Bingham gives Ali a gentle push. The presenters' announcements don't leave any doubt. Even in Vienna, Ali is the Man of the Century. The 2,400 people in the audience drum their feet and shout in chorus, 'Ali, Ali, Ali, Ali.' Ben Wett, the New York television producer, who knew Ali when he was still Cassius Clay, attempts to help his friend up from his seat, but Ali pushes his hand aside. He knows that the cameras are focused on him and he doesn't want to look like an invalid. After all, he'd been world champion for almost a decade: the most beautiful and the fastest. He slowly moves towards the steps. His whole body trembles. It's impossible not to think at this moment of the Olympic Games in Atlanta in 1996, when Muhammad Ali carried the torch to light the Olympic flame. He had to climb endless steps. Yet another step. Ten, six, five, four . . . Ali, you're nearly there! Don't give up, Ali. Go on. And then, with the last of his strength, the legend lit the flame in front of billions of television spectators.

The speech that he and his advisers have prepared for this moment stays in the pocket of his dinner jacket. His words – 'I won many fights. This one is the greatest' – are hardly audible, and surely exaggerated. But what the hell, he's a crowd-pleaser. They keep shouting his name, and he responds with a quick bout of shadow-boxing. The people in the Vienna opera house reach for their handkerchiefs.

Next to Barbara is another giant of sporting history: Rod Laver. He claps his hands as well as he can. Laver, the only tennis player to win four Grand Slam tournaments in a year – in 1962 and then again in 1967 – is, like Ali, marked by illness. He's had a stroke and is partially paralysed. Later, over dinner, the Australian, now living in the Californian desert, tells me that at the end of July 1998, during a television interview, he suddenly felt piercing pain and heat in his right arm, his shoulder and his head, which at first he put down to the spotlights. It became more and more difficult for him to talk, and the pain became unbearable. In the days that followed, he was unable to put sentences together. A few months later, when he finally managed to get some words in order, it sounded like 'some new kind of Latin'.

But Laver didn't give up. This idol of mine, as well as of so many other tennis professionals, held on to his sport. After many months of rehab, he, a left-hander, finally managed to throw the ball with his right, partially paralysed hand, for his serve. In golf he came back up to a handicap of ten. He used to have a handicap of four. I'd really hoped that this impressive though equally modest man would receive the award of Sports Legend of the Century. Instead, Michael Jordan gets the award, although he hasn't even made the trip to Vienna. Rod Laver applauds for him. Fair play, as always. At the dinner afterwards I look over at Ali. His table is under siege.

'Mr Ali, an autograph please.'

He puts down his fork and with his shaking hand draws a temperature curve on to a piece of paper.

'Apologies for disturbing you, but I'd like a photo of us together for my boys,' says a man in white uniform. Ali gets up and closes his eyes. The flash goes off without him noticing it. His body falls back on to the red-velvet chair. Another man appears, also in white uniform. Another photo request. Ali gets up again, sits back down, gets up again. How does he do it?

At two in the morning, I'm sitting in the bar of the Imperial with Mark Spitz and we're having champagne and cigarillos. Spitz is forty-nine, grey-haired, with a family. He hardly swims any more; his gold medals are in the safe. He's invested in stocks and shares and keeps an eye on developments via his computer. Buying and selling – a hobby that keeps him happy. A few hours later, in the VIP lounge at Vienna airport, I meet Spitz's fellow swimmer, Michael Groß, whom the papers nicknamed 'the Albatross' during the Olympics in Los Angeles. He won three gold medals.

'What do you do now?' I ask him.

He works in admin for a PR agency in Frankfurt. Two children, a new house, a decent income, hardly any holidays abroad.

'So, quite middle class,' I venture to say.

Groß nodded. 'You could say that.'

'Are you happy?'

'Depends on how you look at it.'

I can see it. That's how it goes. The exit into reality, into this other world where there's no applause. We take off for Frankfurt. I have to get to the German Indoor Tennis Championships; he has to get back to his desk.

When I arrive, I call my family, as usual. They're still in Vienna. Barbara's all excited. 'Guess where we've just been? With Ali! He had someone call us up. He wanted to see Boris, Barbara and the children.' Ali was in his suite, my wife tells me, sitting in an armchair in the centre of the large room, just like a king. The windows were high, the walls decorated with tapestries. Next to the television lay a pair of red boxing gloves. On the floor, in a white box, was the Sportsman of the Century crystal cup he'd been given the night before. Ali asked for a photo with Noah in boxing stance. But the little boy was too nervous to approach the sitting giant, not least because Ali opened his eyes wide (just like he did when Sonny Liston lay on the floor like a beetle on its back) and growled like a lion.

Noah only dared move when Bingham guided him in Ali's direction. Ali closed his eyes, shook, and mumbled something. Then he pulled my son towards him. Without saying a word, he made Noah's hands into fists and signalled Noah to put his fist under Ali's chin – George Foreman would have liked an invitation like that! Bingham, taking photos, said to his friend, 'Ali, open your eyes.' Ali did so.

Barbara was sitting on a chair near Ali and was still enjoying the scene when he suddenly tipped over towards her.

'He's fainted!' cried Bingham, clearly upset. Barbara caught the toppling Colossus in her arms. Then Ali opened his eyes. 'Thank you – the trick worked!'

The Champ had his victory, and for Noah this settled it. 'Mr Ali doesn't just hit people, you know!'

JOHN MCENROE: MAGICAL AND BEAUTIFUL

Former Spiegel *correspondent Helmut Sorge interviewed John McEnroe for this book.*[1]

How will tennis historians assess Boris Becker?

McEnroe: As one of the most charismatic players of all time. Not even one in a million but only one in a billion could be like him. I'd feel honoured if historians mentioned me in the same breath as Boris Becker, along with Jimmy Connors, Björn Borg, Andre Agassi and Pete Sampras – as far as the last twenty-five years of professional tennis go. What Boris has achieved for the sport is really impressive. Just think about how he flew around the court! I've always been astonished by how he did that, even on clay. It was magical and beautiful to watch those leaps on grass, just breathtaking. I never dared do that. I didn't want to break my bones and drop out of the game for months. Boris had the courage, and the instinct.

You wrote off his first win as 'luck'. Why?

McEnroe: Well, of course, there was a great deal of luck involved. I don't mean to belittle him. When you're good, you need some luck too, otherwise you can't win the Grand Slams. It surprised me when he won. Yes, you could say it was a shock. We'd played each other in Milan a few months before that. He whined, got fed up with the linesmen, and reminded me of someone I knew well: me. At that match I told him, 'Until you've won something, keep your big mouth shut. You have to work your way up the ranks first, then you can open your mouth.' I won 6–4, 6–3. Then he wins Wimbledon! That's what I got for opening my mouth. I just hadn't thought of him for that at all. But that's a bit like how it happened for me in 1977. I had to qualify for the main field in Wimbledon, and I got through to the semis. My opponent? Jimmy Connors. He beat me in four sets. I was amazed at my own result. The odds against me were 250 to 1. I told myself I'm either much better than I think I am, or the professionals are not nearly as good. The truth lay somewhere between. I'd assumed, as Boris must have done in 1985, that the gap between the juniors and the professionals was much bigger than it was. I hadn't noticed how quickly I'd come on. Mentally, though, I wasn't ready to win a tournament like that. I think that Boris, looking back, might have felt the same way about his first Wimbledon success. The victory took him by surprise and hit him hard. After Wimbledon I played tennis for another twelve weeks, then I enrolled at Stanford University in California in the hope that a handsome guy like me, twenty-one in the world rankings, would have girls at my feet. They took no notice of me whatsoever. Another reason to work harder and aim for the top. I wanted to show the girls just who they'd been ignoring. In 1985 Boris was relatively unknown: number twenty in the world, unseeded, seventeen years old. Being the new kid on the block can be an advantage. Players at the peak focus on their true competitors – the other top players – and mostly ignore the younger guys, who suddenly jump up in front them, risking a thick lip. 'Wait a minute,' I kept teasing Boris. 'Who are you anyway? Santa Claus?' Although I've reached five Wimbledon finals, I never played against Boris in Wimbledon. It just never happened. One or other of us would drop out early. There were two years when I didn't play at all because I was fed up with the tennis circuit. Of course, I would have loved to play against him at the peak of my career rather than at the end. That's why in ten official encounters I only defeated Boris twice. Jimmy Connors, by the way, never managed it. That's a small comfort.

In 1987, at the Davis Cup match between USA and Germany in Hartford, Connecticut, you launched several verbal tirades at Boris Becker. Didn't you like him as a person?

McEnroe: I hold him in high esteem. Today. He's one of the most interesting and impressive men of his generation. A real personality. Back then it was different. The Davis Cup is a tennis event where you can let yourself go and cheer un-inhibitedly for your own country. I won forty-one out of forty-nine singles for the USA and eighteen out of twenty doubles. I love the Davis Cup. In the normal professional way of things there's an unwritten law not to support one player over the others. My enthusiasm, my commitment, got

misinterpreted as psychological warfare. But you try everything within the rules that will get you to the next round. It
releases all kinds of patriotic feelings. We tried everything
against Germany, but still we lost. We should have won. I
gave my all but it wasn't enough. Six hours and thirty-eight
minutes. In my entire career I've only played for more than
five hours twice: against Boris and Mats Wilander. After the
first three sets against Boris, when we'd already played for
almost five hours, I said to my people: 'You've got to do something, massage me or something, because I've had it.' After
the massage I got up and my spirit followed me, but my body
just stayed right there on that table. I was finished. My arms
and legs couldn't do any more, though my head was still clear.
Everything hurt, and I couldn't move a thing.

*If Boris threw a fit, did it irritate you, or did you say to yourself:
There's my mirror image?*

McEnroe: Those crises of nerves must have been much more
problematic for him, because he's normally someone with
good self-control. Once Boris Becker had lost his nerve, things
would go badly for him. In my early days, if I was annoyed
with one of the spectators, I'd yell, 'Hey, jerk, keep still!'
The audience would go wild, the umpire would caution me,
and then I'd serve an ace. I'm used to yelling and throwing
insults. I didn't grow up in New York City for nothing!
You're always being pushed around and sworn at there. 'Get
out of the way, asshole.' All the time. That's daily life there.
And when I hear these kinds of insult on the court, it feels like
home. Let's not forget: New York isn't a little provincial town
in Germany. My parents have been married for over forty

years, and they still yell at each other. That's normal in New York. For them, and for me. I wanted to test Boris, and he wanted to test me. I'm stubborn; so's he. Let's put it this way: two strong characters. Irish; German. I never meant anything personally. In Stratton Mountain I tried to upset him and make him mad by whispering things to him when we changed sides. 'You're nothing.' Or: 'Who do you think you are, nutcase?' Boris was so self-confident, at least on the outside, that it bordered on arrogant. How he made his appearances, stalking around the place. I was nervous during that match. I hadn't played for six months and I wanted to show him who was boss. He won – 3–6, 7–5, 7–6 – and didn't say a word. This hit me much harder than if he'd been abusive. Boris must've said to himself: 'I won't let this screwball McEnroe get at me.' It was a kind of verbal tug-of-war between us. I wouldn't have stood a chance against him physically, anyway. He's more physically imposing. So I provoked him, sure, in every way I could think of. I remember an indoor tournament in Bercy in 1989. How many times did he interrupt me with his coughing? Strangely enough, he always coughed at break point. Before the match I decided that I'd cough every time he coughed, just to show how often he did it. It had already become a habit of his, and he didn't want to give it up, precisely because it irritated his opponent. So the coughing got under way. Becker: cough. McEnroe: cough. He coughed. I coughed. Finally, Boris reacted. 'John, don't fool around. I've got a cold.'

'You've had a cold for four years now.'

More coughing. Then I stopped. I could've won that match, because he wasn't in good shape. But he won it all the same – 7–6, 3–6, 6–3. Afterwards I got into trouble with Tatum, my wife back then, because of the coughing. 'How can you do this to Boris?'

'Why? You're asking me why? Whose side are you on? It's a fight, and these things happen. There's no room for a love-and-peace party on the court.'

She begged me: 'Apologize to him, John. I really want you to apologize.'

'Have you gone nuts? Apologize? What for? I'm not apologizing. No way. Never.'

'Never' lasted until I met Boris in the hotel we were both staying in. 'Boris, what happened in the last match, I didn't mean it personally.'

He was relaxed, which is always easier when you're the winner. 'That's OK. It's all part of the game.'

I was off the hook (with my wife, too). But all that fuss wasn't really necessary. Boris and I liked each other. Anyhow, our relationship has developed in a good way. I'd like to see him more often. He even invited me to his wedding, an honour that was extended to only a few people. So our relationship couldn't have been that bad. After my divorce, however, I was so depressed, really down, that I wouldn't have made a happy wedding guest. Besides, I had to look after my children.

Have any of your fellow players become real friends?

McEnroe: That's difficult. I've always got on well with Björn Borg, but we weren't so close that we'd have discussed really private issues. Players don't want to expose their weaknesses to their opponents so they can be taken advantage of on the court. No, conversations about problems are avoided. We're always on good form, at least to the outside world. At first sight tennis might not look very problematic, but mentally there's a lot going on. On the court the player is alone with himself and his defeats. Only one player can win Wimbledon. The other 127 are losers. It isn't easy for losers to keep their self-confidence, particularly if they are defeated in the first round. Then it's hard to hold on to your self-esteem, especially if that depends on professional success. My most bitter defeat must have been in Paris, in the final against Lendl. I led by two sets to love and then I lost. That was tough, really tough. But defeats aren't always negative. In 1980 I played the Wimbledon final against Borg and lost the match 1–6, 7–5, 6–3, 6–7, 8–6. The tie-break in the fourth went to 18–16. Unbelievable. Dramatic. I gained stature with this match, I earned respect, which was what I was playing for. So you lose a final in Paris, in Rome, at Wimbledon. Yes, but how many players make it into a final? Of course, I could've won a few more tournaments, but it wasn't to be. When I was sixteen, I never expected to win Wimbledon three times and the US Open four times.

You've played against Jimmy Connors for more than two decades, and still there's some hatred between you. How come?

McEnroe: Hatred is the wrong word. There have been times when we didn't speak a word to each other because Connors seemed to need to feel contempt as some kind of motivation. How many times did he get mad with me, then call me the next day and say, 'Let's practise!' I used to ask myself what his agenda was. Maybe we were going to play together in the final and he just wanted to check out what kind of shape I was in.

I did practise with him, because I knew we both meant business. After hitting the ball back and forth a few times, Connors would say, 'Let's play a set, OK?'

'OK.'

One set, maybe two, then goodbye, and later on insults, hits below the belt, aggression. I hate losing. And his pride doesn't allow it either. Our personalities just aren't compatible. If we meet nowadays, we exchange a few words. After all, we're not in Wimbledon any more.

Boris Becker has lamented the loneliness of the tennis professional. Did you feel lonely too?

McEnroe: It did bother me at the end of my career. To be honest, in some tournaments I didn't feel like I was giving 100 per cent because I was thinking about my children, thinking about my family and asking myself the question: 'Is this really more important than spending time with them?' Of course, I could have travelled with my family, but that brought its own problems. So if I say to them that they can't come with me because I need to be able to concentrate, it looks really self-centred. Or say I travel with them. How does it look then? In Paris, for example, there were always photographers outside the hotel door. 'OK, guys, take your pictures and then leave us alone.' Promised. Then every time we just wanted to go for a quiet walk in the park on our own, those guys would follow us. Result: I didn't want to go out at all any more. But the kids didn't want to stay in. And my wife wanted to go shopping. So there'd be trouble. By the time I got to the tennis court, I'd already half lost. When I was single it was quite pleasant for about the first few years. But the better you get, the lonelier the hours. The contact between winner and loser is not without psychological problems. So it led to conflict, even with friends.

Do tennis players earn too much money today?

McEnroe: The recognition of our achievements through money is a positive development, of course. But it's bad if the players don't show the sort of commitment they should for this kind of remuneration. We, and I'm talking about Connors, Lendl, Borg, belong to a generation that understood how lucky they were. Borg was the first tennis professional who was rich enough to quit at the age of twenty-six. Other great players, like Rod Laver or Roy Emerson, who after all won the Wimbledon singles twice in the sixties, had to struggle in exhibitions, give training lessons, run tennis camps, in order to earn enough money. What we earned decades later must have seemed incredible. But that was just a fifth of what the professionals cash in today. On an all-time career earnings list, Borg would probably feature somewhere between number 100 and 200. Players you've hardly ever heard of earn more money today than Borg ever did. Some of these professionals don't achieve anything, because they're rich and not motivated enough. Let's look at the development in European football. Too many matches, injured players, weak performances. Just like tennis: too many tournaments, worn-out players, no drama. Charismatic people like Becker and Agassi are rare in this world. Connors, Vilas, Wilander, Noah – now playing on the Senior Tour. Who will pull in the crowds when Sampras and Agassi don't want to play any more or can't play any more? Boris could come back tomorrow and win against the majority of players. He's still among the top five or six best grass players in the world.

What influence did Boris Becker's style have on tennis development?

McEnroe: He's not built like a typical tennis player, more like an American football player, a linebacker. He'd stand there on the court with such self-confidence. 'Here I am,' his manner said, and you were in no doubt about that. For his age he was physically far ahead. He didn't win solely through power, though the modern rackets enhance the serve a great deal. Boris represents the change that took place in our game. I'd have preferred him, well, all of us, to continue playing with wooden rackets. Perhaps our 'finesse' wouldn't have been lost, and 'feeling for the ball' would still have been called for. Instead we developed the 'hit' men: serve – boom. Forty-six aces in one match. In his matches at Wimbledon in 1992, Ivanisevic scored a total of 206 aces, a record. The grounds have got faster, the balls lighter. The opposite would have been preferable. If I had to decide, I'd make a few technical adjustments. The serve has become too important, so I'd try to take out some of the power by shortening the serve line by a few centimetres. The players would have to think about precision once more. But I don't mean to criticize Boris's success. He had one of the best serves in the history of tennis.

Can you understand why he, at the age of merely thirty-one, has ended his career as a tennis professional?

McEnroe: I guess in his heart he no longer believed that he could win Wimbledon or any other Grand Slam tournament again. And the other tournaments don't mean anything to him any more.

Have you paid the price of fame, both psychologically and in your private life? Boris has found fame quite a heavy burden.

McEnroe: In a way, yes, but only to a certain extent. But it's nothing compared to what Boris had, and still has, to endure. In the history of tennis there's never been anyone who had to cope so much with the burden of fame as Boris. It's impressive, how he copes. He's a strange guy; I really mean that in a positive sense. Boris has had luck in his career, but above all he's had the power, and the self-belief, to come through it all. Many others would have been broken.

AN END AND A BEGINNING

IT WAS THE END OF JULY 1999. I STOOD ALONE ON THE terrace of my London hotel. The tennis professional Boris Becker had just retired for good. No more cheering crowds, no more Centre Court at Wimbledon, no more Davis Cup matches like the one in 1987 in Hartford against John McEnroe. Eighty-three times I'd entered the singles arena at Wimbledon; seventy-one times I'd exited victorious. No player apart from Connors won so many Wimbledon singles – not McEnroe, not Sampras, not Borg.

Like a diver returning from the depths and slowly re-adjusting his body to normal pressure, I had to readjust to normal life. Instead of an athlete, I was now going to be an entrepreneur.

From the terrace of the Conrad Hotel in London's Chelsea Harbour, I looked down into the darkness at the shapes of the yachts anchored below. The rigging tapped out a rhythm against the masts in the wind. From time to time you could see lights leisurely drifting along the Thames. It was a peaceful moment. A few hours earlier I'd bid my farewell to Centre Court at Wimbledon after my defeat in the quarter-finals by Pat Rafter, number two in the world ranking. Before that match I'd still been nurturing ambitious dreams of appearing in the final one last time. The perfect ending. Why not?

But then the rain had arrived – two days' worth. Typical Wimbledon. I lost my rhythm. On Tuesday I'd taken a deep breath and enjoyed the fact that I was still in the running in the second week. I'd been careless enough to read the Sunday papers – Becker striding about on Centre Court like its landlord, Becker who'd had such an enormous influence on the culture of professional tennis. Perhaps I had too much time to think – about the following day, for example, or the day my son was due to be born, or the continuing stressful confrontations with my wife.

The red rose Noah had given me on my return to the hotel was in the toothbrush mug. I wanted to be alone at this moment, out on the terrace. I cried tears of liberation, and tears of rage and despair. The tennis chapter was closed and my career was over. At first I was overcome with relief. I crossed myself three times, thinking: 'That was a miracle, the way it all turned out.' But later, in the hotel, I had another of those arguments with Barbara that had made our lives together so unbearable over the past few months. It was awful. The trigger had been harmless. What does someone do before going into retirement? He has a drink with his colleagues, says goodbye to them and centres his new life round his family. That's what I wanted to do. After the match I went straight to the Deutsche Haus for the last time. The last interviews, a few beers with the journalists. After all, these Wimbledon reporters had been part of my working life for a decade and a half. In the evening I wanted to take my team, Waldemar, Mike and Uli, out for a farewell dinner. They'd been my closest colleagues in the final years and had stuck with me through thick and thin. One last evening with my mates – then goodbye.

I must have underestimated the effect of a couple of little bottles of Beck's and the speed with which alcohol enters the bloodstream immediately after strenuous exercise. Otherwise I might have been more level-headed when Barbara started creating a scene on my return to the hotel. She couldn't understand why she wasn't the number-one priority. 'One last time with the boys, Barbara, just one last time to say goodbye. After that it'll be me and you.' It didn't help. We argued for two hours. Then she started going into labour; she was seven months pregnant with Elias. Were the contractions a response to stress, a cry for sympathy, or was Elias really going to be a premature baby?

Barbara decided to ask her friend Kim Steeb to take her to hospital. 'If it gets serious, call me. I'll come straight away,' I promised. I didn't get a call. I got a letter from my mother instead. While I was standing there on the terrace, she'd been watching me from a neighbouring balcony. She'd seen my sadness and my tears and felt my anger. She came over and tried to take me into her arms, but I was unreachable, even to her. 'Leave me alone, Mother, please.' She left. A few minutes later, a letter was pushed under my door. I remembered my team, picked up the phone and cancelled our dinner at Nobu, the Japanese restaurant in the Metropolitan Hotel. 'I can't make it. I'm having problems with Barbara.' Then I recognized the handwriting on the envelope.

'An exciting period of your life has come to an end,' she'd written on the hotel's letterhead, 'and now the wonderful times can begin, the times you'll share with your wife and children. Enjoy them, and always stay true to yourself. For now just take it easy, and sleep on it.' What drove me out into the night in spite of my mother's advice I don't know. Perhaps I wanted to end the day in the way I'd promised myself I would. At any rate, around eleven o'clock, after a few glasses of white wine, I was sitting at the bar of the Nobu after all. The kitchen had closed, so all I had was lemon sorbet in vodka. Cheers!

I'd noticed her two weeks before. I'd been to the Nobu with friends to mark the start of Wimbledon and she had looked at me for those exact two extra seconds that tell the experienced hunter she's up for it. And here she was again. She walked past the bar twice, giving me the same look. A little later she got up from her table and went off in the direction of the loos. I followed her. Five minutes of small talk, then into the nearest suitable corner for our business. Afterwards she returned to her girlfriends, and I drank another beer, paid up and took a cab back to the hotel. There was still no news from the hospital, so I went to bed around two o'clock.

The next morning I went to see Barbara. It had been a false alarm. We packed our twenty-eight tennis bags and suitcases and left England. I was no longer even thinking about the surprising encounter of the night before.

Next February, my secretary in Munich waved a fax under my nose. 'Dear Mr Becker, we met a little while ago at the Nobu in London. The result of our meeting is now in its eighth month,' was the gist of it, and a telephone number was given. At first I couldn't think what this was all about. I called the number. The female voice told me in English, in un-ambiguous terms, 'In a month's time your child will be born.'

That cut the ground from under my feet. Of course I still remembered that evening. I intend to refrain here from describing in detail what we did or, rather, what we didn't do. But dammit, this was impossible. This was absolutely impossible.

After that, we talked on the phone every week. No one in my circle knew about it. Eventually I flew to London to meet the lady in a hotel. Sure enough, a heavily pregnant woman appeared. The tone of our conversation was businesslike. If I wasn't prepared to take responsibility, the press would be informed, and I'd get the same treatment that other celebrities had got, like Mick Jagger, whose love-child with a Brazilian model had dominated the papers for weeks. There was no mistaking the threat.

On 22 March 2000, a girl called Anna was born at the Chelsea and Westminster Hospital and I decided to accept the child if it was proven to be mine. I'd had a bit on the side at an extraordinary moment in my life. This wasn't a crime, and in no way was I going to be blackmailed over it, even if it meant ten headlines in *Bild*.

Obviously it caused me a great deal of shame. How was I going to deal with it? How was I going to tell my wife, my mother, my son? Noah was already old enough to understand things like this. I wasn't afraid of the public, but I was very worried about what my own family would say. One Friday in September 2000, two months before we separated, I seized a moment when Barbara and I were alone at home in Bogenhausen. The children had gone to bed, and Barbara was working in the kitchen. So I took a deep breath and told her everything, every last detail of how and why it had happened. She was surprised, but she wasn't hysterical. She couldn't believe how it had happened. That it had happened like that.

'You have every right in the world: you can leave, or you can decide how we can carry on. But I still love you, and if it is at all possible for you, then let's stay together.'

Barbara thought about it for two days. 'I don't yet know how, but we'll manage.'

I was relieved.

My mother's reaction was typical.

'You've become a grandmother again,' I announced over the phone, before roughly outlining the circumstances.

'That's nice. Now we've got a girl,' she said. She didn't tell me off or criticize me. So, that was done.

I didn't confess to Noah until the following summer, during our holidays in Majorca. I'd dreaded this moment for months. Every morning I woke up with the terrible question hanging over me: How can I explain to my beloved son that I've betrayed and hurt his mother? And that there's now a little girl who's my daughter and his sister? We were on our own in the car. That's when I explained to my little one, in simple language, what he needed to know – the hardest confession of my life. He listened, and didn't say a word. He didn't ask any questions; he still hasn't. I was immensely relieved. But the time will come when he'll want to know everything.

After several months of negotiation over where, when and how the paternity test would be carried out, I went secretly to a London hospital to give a saliva sample. In February 2001, there was no longer any doubt. Anna is my biological daughter. To pile on the pressure, news of the Becker baby broke in London at exactly the same time as the separation and divorce struggle with Barbara in Miami reached its peak. 'Boris . . . now he faces a paternity suit' ran the headline in *Bild* on 10 January 2001.

This infidelity hastened the end of my marriage to Barbara. For months the tension between us got tighter and tighter. Although we really wanted to try again after I'd made my confession, it got more and more difficult, especially for me. Barbara was prepared to work around the situation and come to terms with it. But I had the tax inspectors on my back, among other problems, and I was on the defensive with Barbara, which went against the grain for me. She had me in the palm of her hand. She had the trump card for every argument: London. Eventually, with this and all my other problems, I couldn't bear it any longer.

The London judge who later determined the level of my maintenance payments said that I'd behaved 'generously'. The media talked of payments in their millions. Once again the story of 'poor Becker' did the rounds, the man who got fleeced again after his divorce. In England, however, these matters are covered clearly by the law and the amounts involved are far below those imagined by some members of the press.

Anna lives with her mother rent-free in a flat that I own. She receives a monthly maintenance payment that's far below what's usual in America and slightly higher than in Germany. Anna's future is financially secure, but to talk in terms of millions is completely wrong.

But what will become of the child? And what kind of person will she be? I didn't know her mother at all when we had our sole encounter. We didn't have much contact afterwards either, until shortly before Anna's second birthday, when I saw her for the first time. I hadn't seen Anna as my child before this moment; the doctors had done that. Would I develop fatherly feelings towards her?

'Look, there's Daddy.' That's how Anna's mother announced my arrival. I entered the flat with mixed feelings, but Anna was absolutely normal. She didn't jump for joy, but she seemed to trust me. We played alone together for over an hour. Of course I found myself examining her. Who does she look most like? How does she behave? Since then I've visited Anna every other month, and my relationship with her mother has also stabilized. We talk about Anna and her future. I've also talked with Angela Ermakova about her own problems, the curse of her popularity in the press, something she's brought on herself. She's well known in London today. But the media presented her as the one who took Becker for a ride. If she goes out with her girlfriends, they get labelled in the same way as her. If she goes out with men, they are only after one thing.

I was careless, stupid and irresponsible that night, but I've stopped feeling guilty about it. I've faced up to what I did and found a solution. We can all live with this, and in fact I'm already looking forward to Anna growing up, to a time when we can talk about our relationship and about life in general. I'm going to tell her that not everything goes according to plan, that life can take the strangest turns, and that things can happen that you wouldn't imagine in your wildest dreams. But first, however, I've got a task to do. I want to learn to love my daughter.

EPILOGUE

NOAH AND ELIAS HAVE CUDDLED UP EVEN CLOSER TO ME. Juey, the dog, has walked off. He probably found it too crowded on the bed. Hours must have gone by, but it's still dark outside. We all fell asleep over the children's Bible. Now they are lying quietly and contentedly in my arms, my two little lions. My entire happiness.

Noah takes after Barbara. He has her slenderness, her colour, her temperament, but his eyes have my expression. Of course, he was a much-wanted child. Every young father's dream: the first-born, a son! I was present at the birth of both children, and played an active part in Elias's arrival. Barbara didn't have any strength left and the doctor asked me to help. I literally pulled Elias into the world. He means as much to me as Noah, but the two are totally different, starting with their looks. Elias has lighter skin, blond curls and blue eyes, so he's more like his dad. He's only four – Noah is five years older – but Elias already has both feet planted firmly on the ground. He's the rock around which the waves surge. He's got his own mind, perhaps because we're more relaxed with him. By the second child, you've got a kind of routine. You don't panic every time a tooth comes through. Besides, Elias has spent a greater part of his life in Miami, away from public turmoil and the media spotlight. Right from the beginning he's been more grounded.

Noah was born right into the middle of the glamorous life of a tennis star: every week a new hotel, nannies, bodyguards, limousines and Lear jets. He was born with a silver spoon in his mouth. Deeply loved and cared for, but also very spoilt. All the same, he doesn't lack ambition at school, in sports or in life. He wants to know everything, and he wants to do everything better. He has to prove something, to himself, to me and to everyone else. When we play football or tennis, he gets upset if it doesn't go his way. He loses all control. I was just the same as a child. I took bites out of the net and hurled my racket to the floor. Losing was out of the question.

Elias is less emotional. He does his thing, and he's calmer, clearer and more straightforward about it. What he doesn't want to do, he doesn't do. The move to Miami was a stroke of luck for the boys. Noah, especially, had to learn to solve his own problems – at school, with his friends, and also with us, his parents. There are hardly any paid helpers. No hotel servant carries his toys around after him. Teachers aren't easy on him just because his father has won a tennis tournament or two. But he's holding his own. In Miami he's come out of his shell. A few years back, when we were going through crises, he instinctively took on the role of mediator. He'd praise Barbara in front of me: 'Mum's done this really well,' and reassure Barbara with, 'Daddy loves you.' He sensed that we were drifting apart and he tried to keep things together. Today he's rather smart. He can look after himself, and he knows how to use his charm. We might not see or speak to each other for weeks, but we're very close. We feel the same way about many things, and many people.

In spite of the divorce, Barbara and I have managed to keep going as a family. I'm very grateful to Barbara for this. She's doing a great job as a mother; I'm trying my best as a father. Our kids got a real taste of life at an early age. They don't have to turn eighteen before they discover how hard it can be out there. But they have a home that offers them lots of love, freedom and opportunities. Even though Barbara and I no longer live together as husband and wife, we still get along as father and mother.

Is it a miracle that it turned out like this? Yes. For some years I'd been confused, on the wrong path, pursuing the wrong goals. Fame and fortune had become my priorities. I was ruled from the outside and going the best way about losing myself. It was partly for that reason that I caused the break-up and destroyed the beautiful dream world. I have an excessive need to take things to the limits. In search of the way back to myself, I've crossed a few boundaries. I needed to feel alive again. Life, for me, means enduring pain and experiencing joy. Only then am I at one with myself.

The last two and a half years have been the toughest of my life, but they've also healed me. The fight for my life and my soul finally brought me back to a point where I have the courage to be honest with myself. Enough of the self-deception. Enough hypocrisy. I've made many mistakes, hoping they'd turn out all right. I'd hoped that the German state would recognize my success in sport and my role in the community as a service to the nation, and therefore not charge me as a tax evader. I hoped that separating from my wife would rescue our marriage and not destroy it. And I hoped that a thoughtless bit on the side during a tumultuous phase of my life wouldn't have any consequences. Reality, however, had no room for such vain hopes.

These experiences have taken away the last of my naivety. My love for Germany and its people has not changed, but the way in which institutions and society have treated me here has shaken my belief in the goodness of human beings. I'm well aware that you enter the world alone and that you die alone. I have my family, real friends, good partners and supporters, but in the end I was just as lonely in the dock as I had been on Centre Court. That's something I simply had to learn again.

So there's no contradiction when I say that the hurt and the pain of the past few years have done me good. They re-awakened that dormant instinct that once made me the best tennis player in the world: the killer instinct. Don't worry, I don't plan to murder anyone. I just want to aim for the top again with every means I have. I've already begun the fight for my happiness.

NOTES

Foreword
1   *Stuttgarter Zeitung*, 7.7.1986
2   Reported in *Neue Zürcher Zeitung*, 22.12.1985
3   Claus Jacobi, in *Welt am Sonntag*, 19.9.1999
4   *Neue Zürcher Zeitung*, 22.12.1985

The Man on the Moon
1   *Time*, 15.7.1985

What Is the Sense in it All?
1   Sir Edmund Hillary, *View from the Summit*, London 1999
2   *Daily Express*, 8.7.1985
3   *Washington Post*, 8.7.1985

The Weeks of Cold Silence
1   Doris Henkel, in *Boris B. 18 Autoren, 1 Phänomen*, ed. Herbert Riehl-Heyse, Heilsbronn 1992

Condemned to Freedom

1   Sport-Informations-Dienst report, 8.12.1996
2   *Abendzeitung München*, 23.10.2002
3   *Bild*, 25.10.2002

The Man Who Was My Mother

1   Editor's introduction to Johann Peter Eckermann's *Gespräche mit Goethe*, Kiel 1949
2   Statement by Günther Bosch, in *Süddeutsche Zeitung*, 22.1.1987
3   Ion Tiriac, quoted in *Süddeutsche Zeitung*, 23.1.1987
4   Ion Tiriac, quoted in *Die Welt*, 23.1.1987
5   *Welt am Sonntag*, 30.5.1993
6   *Welt am Sonntag*, 28.9.1997

The Burden of Fame

1   *Frankfurter Allgemeine Zeitung*, 9.7.1986
2   *Schweizer Weltwoche*, quoted in *Süddeutsche Zeitung*, 6.11.1986
3   *Sports*, 6/1993
4   Martin Walser, in *Boris B. 18 Autoren, 1 Phänomen*, ed. Herbert Riehl-Heyse, Heilsbronn 1992
5   *Frankfurter Allgemeine Zeitung*, 24.2.1985
6   *Frankfurter Rundschau*, 22.3.1986
7   Max Frisch, *Biographie. Ein Spiel*, Frankfurt am Main 1967
8   *Observer*, 14.12.1986
9   *L'Express*, 19.7.1985
10 Laotse, *Tao te king: Das Buch vom Sinn und Leben*, Munich 1998

And Everything Finally Dissolves Itself in Sleep . . .

1   Peter Harry/Pat H. Broeske, *Down at the End of Lonely Street*, New York 1997

In Monte Carlo with Two Romanians

1   Fyodor Dostoevsky, *The Gambler*, trans. Constance Garnett, Macmillan, New York 1917

Never Change a Winning Shirt

1   *Fortune*, 22.6.1998
2   Richard Evans, *Open Tennis. The First Twenty Years*, London 1998

Every Mother-in-Law's Dream

1   Niki Pilic, quoted in *Süddeutsche Zeitung*, 13.11.1991
2   *Frankfurter Allgemeine Zeitung*, 16.11.1991
3   *The Times*, quoted in *Abendzeitung*, 2.7.1999
4   Michael Stich, quoted in *Bild*, 23.9.1997

Greetings from the Beetle

1   Norman Mailer, *The Fight*, Boston 1975
2   Günther Bresnik, in *News*, quoted in *Die Welt*, 23.7.1993

Has Everyone Here Gone Mad?

1   John Steinbeck, quoted in B. Kim Taylor, *The Great New York City Trivia & Fact Book*, Nashville 1998

No Street Battles in Bed

1   *Playboy*, April 1988
2   *Bild*, 30.5.1990

Why?

1　Press report lübMEDIA, 5.12.2000
2　*Stern*, 14.12.2000
3　*Der Spiegel,* 11.12.2000
4　*Bunte*, 12.12.2000
5　*Bild*, 6.12.2000
6　*Sun*, 6.12.2000
7　*The Times*, 6.12.2000
8　Statistisches Bundesamt census 1989
9　Deutsche Presse Agentur 061123, December 2000
10　*Bild*, 11.12.2000
11　Miami-Dade Circuit Court Number 00-30252 FC 07
12　*Stern*, 28.12.2000

Becker versus *Becker*

1　*Der Spiegel*, 8.1.2001
2　*Focus*, 8.1.2001
3　*Der Spiegel*, 8.1.2001
4　*Der Spiegel*, 8.1.2001
5　*Der Spiegel*, 8.1.2001
6　*Bild*, 16.1.2001

Pigeon-holing

1　*International Herald Tribune*, 21.1.1986
2　Klaus Ullrich, *Der Weiße Dschungel*, Neues Leben, Berlin 1987
3　*Bild*, 30.1.1990
4　Herbert Riehl-Heyse, in *Boris B. 18 Autoren, 1 Phänomen*, Heilsbronn 1992
5　Stefan Aust, *Der Baader-Meinhof-Komplex*, Hamburg 1989

6 Peter Ustinov, in *Frankfurter Allgemeine Zeitung*, 27.3.1998

7 Hans-Josef Justen, in *Boris B. 18 Autoren, 1 Phänomen*, ed. Herbert Riehl-Heyse, Heilsbronn 1992

8 *Süddeutsche Zeitung*, 1.2.1999

9 *Der Spiegel*, 8.2.1999

Stiffer than a Starched Collar

1 Voltaire, *Candide*, London 1947

Love at First Step

1 London *Evening Standard*, 18.6.1992

2 Gebhardt von Moltke, in *Daily Telegraph*, 12.10.1999

3 *Daily Mail*, 7.7.1986

4 Alan Little, *Wimbledon Compendium 1999*, The All England Lawn Tennis and Croquet Club, London 1999

5 Ulrich Kaiser, in *Boris B. 18 Autoren, 1 Phänomen*, ed. Herbert Riehl-Heyse, Heilsbronn 1992

6 Ulrich Kaiser, in *Boris B. 18 Autoren, 1 Phänomen*, ed. Herbert Riehl-Heyse, Heilsbronn 1992

Serve: Germany

1 Ted Tinling, *Sixty Years in Tennis*, London 1983

2 *Neue Zürcher Zeitung*, 19.12.1989

3 *Die Welt*, 30.1.1990

4 *Stern*, 10.4.1986

Doped Up Yet?

1 Richard Evans, *Open Tennis. The First Twenty Years*, London 1988

Old Lions Still Bite
1   *The Times*, 25.6.1999
2   Lleyton Hewitt, quoted in the *Mail on Sunday*, 27.6.1999

My Dear Fellow Players
1   *Sports Illustrated*, 1987

News at the Fifth Hole
1   Sport-Informations-Dienst, 13.8.1999

Ali, Open Your Eyes
1   David Remnick, *King of the World*, New York 1998

John McEnroe: Magical and Beautiful
1   For John McEnroe's in-depth observations and com-
    ments, see his autobiography *Serious*, Little, Brown, 2002
    (published in the US as *You Cannot Be Serious*, Putnam,
    2002)

INDEX